THE ESCAPE OF
SIGMUND FREUD

DAVID COHEN

BOOKS

First published in Great Britain in 2009 by
JR Books, 10 Greenland Street, London NW1 0ND
www.jrbooks.com

A catalogue record for this book is available from the British Library.

ISBN 978-1-906779-23-8

1 3 5 7 9 10 8 6 4 2

Printed and bound in Great Britain by Clays Ltd, St Ives plc

This book is dedicated to Zoltan Gruber, my Austro-Hungarian uncle, who had to flee the Nazis. 'My boy, I always carry twenty thousand dollars in cash in my pockets in case the Gestapo come back,' he once said to me. He survived the war and went to live in Paris.

My uncle was no psychoanalyst but a very astute money smuggler. He was a survivor like Freud and would have understood many of the dilemmas the founder of psychoanalysis faced during the 1930s.

'States of conflict and turbulence alone can further our knowledge'
– Sigmund Freud, *An Outline of Psychoanalysis*, 1940

Contents

Acknowledgements

I owe much to Brian Farrell who taught me about Freud years ago at Oxford. Interviews with Viktor Frankl (who felt Freud ignored him) and Harald Leopold Löewenthal made me all the more interested. I have continued to be surprised by the way 'normal' psychiatrists (who believe in medication) keep on being interested in – and influenced by – Freud and 'the talking cure'. My good friends, the late Dr James MacKeith and the thankfully very alive, Dr Harvey Gordon, are among those. Both encouraged me in this project.

Many libraries and librarians have been helpful – the John Rylands University in Manchester, Manchester City Reference Library, the Institute of Psychoanalysis Library, Swiss Cottage Library in London, the Royal Society of Medicine Library, the Librarian of the Vienna city archives, the Austrian State archives, the National Library in Vienna as well as the usual suspects – the Library of Congress in Washington D.C., the Wellcome Library and the British Library. The Freud Museums in London and Vienna remain inspiring, as does the Jewish Museum in Manchester. The Vienna Criminal Museum which contains many exhibits relating to forgery is fun to visit if forgers and murderers are of interest.

I am grateful for very useful discussions on Freud with Dr Riccardo Steiner, with Dr Lesley Sohn who is still practising analysis at the age of 88 and with Michael Molnar, the Director of Research at the Freud Museum in London.

Professor R. Werner Soukup of the Technical University, Vienna explained to me what Sauerwald's chemical work was all about. Jonathan Edwards of the Royal Society of Chemistry was also most helpful with that.

My thanks to my friend and agent Sonia Land for believing in the book, to Jeremy Robson for very constructive criticism which made it better, to Lesley Wilson for seeing it through to reality, to Lesley Levene for very sharp copy editing, to Petra Coghlin, to Aileen La Tourette, to Dr Murray Hall in Vienna for sharing his information about Freud's publishing activities and Sauerwald, to Kurt at Vienna's engaging Lhotzky's Literaturbuffet for his help, to Brian Levene and to Martin Hay for comments, to Hantie, to Daniel Sisspela and Dr Gabriele Kohlbauer-Fritz of Vienna's Jewish Museum, to Julia Ross, to my cousin Anita Frank and to Meike Currie who helped me make sense of some the documents relating to the Sauerwald trials.

Author's Note

In 1925 Edward Bernays wanted his uncle, Sigmund Freud, to write an autobiography. He had had, he said, a good offer from an American publisher. 'What deprives all autobiographies of value is their tissue of lies,' Freud shot back. 'Let's just say parenthetically that your publisher shows American naivety in imagining that a man, honest until now, could stoop to so low for five thousand dollars. The temptation would begin at one hundred times that sum, but even then I would renounce it after half an hour.'

Eleven years later Freud's friend Arnold Zweig, the socialist writer, asked for his permission to write his biography. Freud was as fierce as before: 'Anyone who writes a biography is committed to lies, concealments, hypocrisy, flattering and even to hiding his own lack of understanding, for biographical truth does not exist and, if it did, we could not use it.' He added, with a reference to his beloved Hamlet, 'Was the prince not right when he asks who would escape whipping were he used after his desserts'?

I have chosen to ignore my subject's obvious distrust of biographies. My excuse is that I concentrate on how Freud managed, after many hesitations, to leave Vienna once the Nazis took over. Since I offer new information, especially about the Manchester branch of his family, this book has as many characters as one of the Dickens novels Freud so loved. I introduce new characters as they occur, but it also seems sensible to have a list of the most important 'players'. This forms Appendix 1.

Freud's discoveries did not stem just from analysing his own dreams or treating his patients; he was possibly the first great artist-scientist to grow up in a now very familiar institution, the extended stepfamily. Modern psychologists speak of the blended or reconstituted family, pushing foodie metaphors to the extreme. Freud was born into a stepfamily and lived much of his life in one. Those experiences helped shape his ideas to the end of his days.

Appendix 2 details the letters and other material that scholars still do not have access to 70 years after Freud died.

CHAPTER I

The Bureaucracy of Hate

Vienna, 25 July 1947

Anton Sauerwald looked very haggard for a man of 44. His doctor, Karl Szekely, had written many times to the court to explain that his patient was suffering from tuberculosis and the proceedings should be delayed. Sauerwald had spent a month in hospital. However, Judge Schachermayr would have no more delays. Marianne, the accused's wife, sat close to her husband. She had told the court that he had no secrets from her.

For most of the war Sauerwald had been an officer in the Luftwaffe, not a pilot but a technical expert. In March 1945 he was captured and sent to a prisoner of war camp at Bad Heilbrunn run by the Americans, but in June he was released and returned to Vienna. The Nazi defeat had shattered a long-treasured private dream. Throughout the war he had looked after 15 allotments belonging to a group of Nazis who planned to build a small estate for like-minded people. Their slogan had been '*Miteinander Füreinander*' ('Together, for each other'), but their dream was now over.

Sauerwald was an extremely well-educated man. When he was 24 years old, he published four learned papers in the *Monatshefte für Chemie* (*Chemical Monthly*), one of the leading journals in the world in the field of chemistry. He had a doctorate from the University of Vienna, where his professor was a distinguished organic chemist, Josef Herzig, who is still remembered for one particular reaction he discovered. Herzig was also a friend of Freud's and regularly visited him to play cards in the evening. Sauerwald always liked and respected 'Herr Professor Herzig'.

Once in Vienna, a city in ruins and a city of betrayals, Sauerwald could not find his wife. Three months before the war ended, she had abandoned her factory job and fled westwards, not wanting to be captured by the Russians. Sauerwald spent a night at the house of his mother-in-law, Anna Talg, but in the confusion that reigned at that time she did not know where her daughter was to be found. Sauerwald then went to his wife's grandmother's house in Kritzendorf, but Marianne was not there either.

While Sauerwald was searching for his wife, someone else was looking for him – and oddly enough this man also suffered from lung problems. Harry Freud, Sigmund's nephew, was an officer in the American army and he insisted that Sauerwald must be tracked down. Harry had excellent contacts: one of his cousins was Edward Bernays, who had worked for Woodrow Wilson, the American president who took the United States into the First World War. Harry believed that Sauerwald had robbed his family and destroyed the business, the Internationaler Psychoanalytischer Verlag or publishing house that his grandfather had helped start in 1919. He forced his way into the Sauerwalds' old flat to seek out documents that would prove the man's guilt. No one would stop an American officer.

A few days later, when Anna Talg was asked by the police to describe her son-in-law, she found it hard to say anything much about Anton Sauerwald. His nose was normal; his ears were normal; his mouth was normal. His eyes were blue-grey. He had absolutely no distinguishing characteristics apart from his blond hair.

At the end of October 1945, at Harry Freud's insistence, Sauerwald was arrested and the police started to investigate every aspect of his past. The archives of the city of Vienna make it possible to trace the complex legal proceedings that would lead to two court cases against Sauerwald.

This completely normal man was charged with war crimes. The police inquiries resulted in Sauerwald being imprisoned, first in Gefaengnis 1 and then in Gefaengnis 2. He lost the flat on Witterhauergasse, in Vienna's 18th district, where he and Marianne had lived since the mid-1930s. He had to go to the civil courts to be allowed even to set foot inside his old home. The city had given his flat to a new tenant, Frau Leidersdor, and Sauerwald claimed she had robbed him of the contents of a wardrobe and chemicals (including gold and some catalysts) worth 50,000 Reichsmarks.

Frau Leidersdor had a good grasp of publicity and told the press that she was being harassed by the man who had robbed Sigmund Freud. In 1946 the Vienna papers published two stories which would have done a modern tabloid proud, portraying Sauerwald as a vicious Nazi who was trying to boot a defenceless woman out of her home.

The *Neues Österreich* even managed to obtain a letter that Matthias Goering, the cousin of Hitler's deputy, Hermann Goering, had written to Sauerwald. It seems likely that Frau Leidersdor found the letter in the flat and 'leaked' it. Addressing Sauerwald as a fellow member of the Nazi Party, Matthias asked him to send a book by a non-Jewish psychoanalyst, August Aichhorn, but to remember to rip out the foreword by Freud as he didn't want anyone to think he was reading Jewish 'filth' (in a superb Freudian slip, Goering mistyped Freud's name as Frued). Then, as Sauerwald must have collected money from the sale of goods belonging to Freud, Matthias said he wanted at least 1,600 marks to help with some expenses. Finally, he signed off with a cheery 'Heil Hitler'.

The publication of this letter seemed damning. Sauerwald's lawyer, Franz Petracek, who had been his friend since their schooldays, told Sauerwald he would no longer represent him.

Sauerwald was sent to be tried in the new *Volksgericht*, or People's Court, which was set up as soon as Germany surrendered in June 1945. The records of the People's Court are now housed in Gasometer D, a once elegant Victorian brick building whose interior has been developed into a tacky shopping mall. The Vienna city archives are the source for all material relating to Sauerwald's trial. Sixteen per cent of the defendants in the People's Court were accused of financial fraud, as Sauerwald was. He was also charged with having been a member of the Nazi Party, which had been outlawed in Austria after civil disturbances in 1933 and 1934. The specific charge was of having been an 'illegal', meaning an 'illegal' Nazi.

The People's Court trials were not as high profile as those at Nuremberg, but the Allies were still keen on proper legal processes. They wanted to show that the Nazis had been defeated by civilised people who followed rules. As a result, everything took a great deal of time. In fact, Sauerwald's trial lasted longer than anyone's at Nuremberg.

The prosecution case against Sauerwald was simple. From the moment they took power in Germany in 1933, the Nazis passed decrees to limit the personal and financial freedom of Jews. All Jewish holdings of over 5,000 Reichsmarks had to be declared. The Nazi Party paper *Der Angriff* (The Attack) made it clear that 'all Jewish assets are assumed to have been improperly acquired'.

The Nazis appointed a trustee or *Treuehandler* to every Jewish business. The *Treuehandler* was supposed to ensure that these improperly acquired Jewish assets were used for the greater glory of Germany and the Nazi project. In Austria, after the Nazis annexed the country, there were at least 9,000 such trustees, who were also called *Kommissar*. Anton Sauerwald was better qualified than most, having studied medicine and law as well as chemistry.

As soon as he was appointed *Kommissar* to the Freud family, on 15 March 1938, Sauerwald controlled not only their assets but in effect their destiny. By this time the Internationaler Psychoanalytischer Verlag was being run by Freud's son Martin and had a stock of several thousand unsold books in Leipzig. Despite Sigmund Freud's international reputation, the publishing house was a financial disaster. But the Freud family had money and Sauerwald had abused his position to seize that as well as assets, including manuscripts, artworks, books and much else of value, the prosecution claimed.

When the proceedings started, the court had asked Sauerwald whether he pleaded guilty or not guilty. 'Not guilty,' Sauerwald had replied. Over the next 18 months, he protested his innocence in many statements provided for the court, insisting that it was incredible he should be so charged.

Sigmund Freud had died in London in September 1939, the court was told, but many other members of his family had also suffered at the hands of the accused. Harry Freud had excellent reasons to press for the arrest of Sauerwald. But Harry tended to be flamboyant. He managed to get hold of some of Adolf Hitler's personal notepaper, for example, and wrote a note on it to the Freuds' housekeeper, Paula Fichtl – not that he said anything of importance in it. Paula, who revered the Freuds, said that Harry was the only member of the family who was not really clever.

As the case proceeded, with many delays, the prosecution failed to draw attention to one crucial fact. In the autumn of 1945 Sauerwald was reunited with his wife, Marianne. Two years later in July 1947 Marianne wrote in desperation to Martha, Freud's widow, who was then in her late eighties and living in Hampstead. Marianne explained her husband's plight; she did not know who else to turn to. If the Freuds were honourable, she said, they would rescue Sauerwald from the terrible difficulties Harry Freud had created for him. Martha Freud did not reply herself but handed the letter to her daughter Anna.

Anna Freud did respond, but the copy of her letter in the files in the Vienna city archives is not signed by her, or indeed by anyone. It is hardly very original to suggest that if someone does not sign a letter it points to ambivalence on their part. Sauerwald had also asked for letters of support from Freud's lawyer, Dr Alfred Indra, from the well-known psychoanalyst Dr August Aichhorn (whose book Matthias Goering had wanted) and from Princess Marie Bonaparte of Greece, who was related to the British royal family (she was also an analyst; Freud had even treated her).

Anna Freud's letter was clear, if unsigned. She said it was wrong for Sauerwald to be charged with harming the Freud family. So did Dr Indra and Princess Marie Bonaparte. They all agreed that Sauerwald had actually helped the family in very difficult circumstances.

Anton Sauerwald was hardly the only German or Austrian to help Jews. The most celebrated 'helper' is, of course, Oskar Schindler, the subject of Thomas Keneally's *Schindler's Ark* and Steven Spielberg's film *Schindler's List*. At Yad Vashem, the Holocaust memorial in Jerusalem, there is a list of Gentiles who took large risks to help Jews. Schindler is remembered with honour, as is Albert Goering, Hermann Goering's brother.

Sauerwald's name is not inscribed at Yad Vashem as one of the Righteous Gentiles but, like Schindler and Albert Goering, he did help at least one Jewish family. In fact, without his help it is unlikely that Freud, his wife, his sister-in-law, his daughter and his son, a total of sixteen relatives, associates and 'servants', would have managed to escape. Four of Freud's five sisters stayed behind in Vienna; all of them died in concentration camps.

This book will explain why a Nazi – and Sauerwald was a sincere Nazi – had every reason to expect that Sigmund Freud's daughter and his friends would come to his rescue. For a variety of reasons, it is not a story that Freudians have tended to explore.

CHAPTER 2

Biographies and Restricted Archives

The Library of Congress houses 153 boxes of correspondence between Freud and his family, friends and patients, as well as clinical notes and other papers, but not all of these can be read. Twenty boxes cannot be opened until 2020, 2050 or 2057; eight are closed 'in perpetuity'.

It is natural that Freud should wish to protect the confidences of his patients, even for 50 years after they died. The restrictions go well beyond this, however, and it is far from clear that all the closed items deal with confidential medical matters. By contrast, Carl Rogers, the founder of humanist psychotherapy, gave the Library of Congress all his papers with no restrictions. I include a list of material in the Freud Archives which is restricted at the end of the book, but a few of these restrictions need to be highlighted from the start.

Not to be opened until 2050 or 2057 are the following folders:

- Until 2050, some correspondence between Freud and his nephew Harry Freud, the man who had Sauerwald arrested; only one letter from Freud is not restricted. No other correspondence with a nephew or niece is restricted.
- Until 2056, correspondence relating to the Bernays family, with whom Freud became doubly linked by marriage. He married Martha Bernays, while his sister Anna married Martha's brother, Eli. One of Martha's sisters, Minna, lived with the Freud family in Berggasse from 1892 after her fiancé died. Freud and Minna travelled together to Rome in 1913.

Some claim that Freud and Minna were lovers and that she had to have an abortion.

- Two containers of papers relating to Minna Bernays are restricted in perpetuity. If she and Freud had a sexual relationship, that would not be surprising.
- The papers relating to Anna Freud, Freud's daughter, are also restricted in perpetuity. Freud called her 'Anna Antigone', because of her devotion to him. Antigone was the daughter of Oedipus in Greek mythology. Her friends always denied Anna was a lesbian, though she had a 50-year-long intimate friendship with Dorothy Burlingham, whose grandfather, Charles Tiffany, founded the famous jewellery store Tiffany & Co.; Burlingham had a husband, too. Despite her close relationship with Anna, Burlingham was analysed by Freud. The situation was a web of entanglements. In his biography of Anna Freud, Robert Coles, a distinguished psychiatrist and historian, merely says the relationship between the two women was 'complex'.
- The papers relating to Edith Jackson are also never to be opened. She was a wealthy American who worked with Anna Freud and Dorothy Burlingham, setting up nurseries for poor children in Vienna and London. She knew a good deal about the relationship of her two close friends.
- Freud's own pocket books are also closed in perpetuity.

In 1952 an American psychoanalyst, Leslie Adams, was planning a biography of Freud. Adams wrote to the British Library, which passed his letter on to Manchester City Libraries. He wanted information about Freud's British relatives and had got nowhere by asking fellow analysts. Adams was challenging in his letter to the British Library:

> It will guide you somewhat that the Freud family are morbidly reticent about the family history and that any work which must be done in this direction must be in spite of their cooperation. This indicates that behind this history is some disillusioning truth.

Adams never published his biography. Curiously, some of his notes have ended up in the archives of Manchester City Libraries; they had not been consulted till I happened on them.

There have been bitter, sometimes melodramatic rows about access to the Freud Archives. In 1964 the Manuscript Division of the Library of Congress received a gift of the papers of Princess Marie Bonaparte on condition that no one read them until 2020. In 1982 a historian, Phyllis Grosskurth, was not just denied access to these papers, but not told she might be able to consult copies of them in Paris. When she found out, Grosskurth went on the attack in the *New York Review of Books*. The Librarian of Congress, Mr Wilkinson, America's senior librarian, felt he had to defend the reputation of his institution: 'Although some say that great secrets about Freud are being kept by these restrictions, I have examined most of the sealed material, for administrative reasons, and can say that no great horrors will be revealed by any of these documents.'

It's a lovely phrase, 'administrative reasons'. The use of the word 'horrors' is, of course, intriguing, but the Librarian of Congress did not specify exactly how he defined 'great horrors'.

Even more dramatic were the rows that centred on Jeffrey Masson, an archivist who claimed that Freud had suppressed facts about the seduction of children in order not to shock too much. Masson's aggressive *The Assault on Truth* charted this 'suppression' and how the Freud Archives sacked him. A good view of the Masson saga (which ended in court) can be found in Janet Malcolm's *In the Freud Archives*.

Given the extensive scholarship on Freud, it is surprising to come across some strange omissions. No one had tried to get access to the archives of the school Freud attended from the age of ten. The files matter in considering Freud's escape, because one of his friends at school was the Josef Herzig who taught Anton Sauerwald. Very few scholars have consulted the Sauerwald files in the Vienna and the Austrian state archives. The exception is Dr Murray Hall of the University of Vienna, who is a historian of publishing rather than a historian of psychoanalysis. I have also made use of Harry Freud's letters, records and unpublished autobiography, again a rather neglected resource; they form a separate collection in the Library of Congress.

Two books which have never been published in English are also relevant to Freud's last years. Freud's sister Anna wrote an article about her brother after he died and then expanded this into her memoirs *Eine Wienerin in New York*. It took 50 years for these to be published, even though Anna had left instructions that they should appear when she died. Her memoirs give an insight into what it was like to grow up as a child in the Freud family and this puts some of Freud's work in a subtly different light.

The second book comes from 'below stairs'. Paula Fichtl joined the Freud household at the end of the 1920s as a maid and then became their housekeeper. A book about her life, ghostwritten with her full cooperation, appeared in Germany in the 1980s. The author had first met her when he came to have tea with Anna Freud in London. He had the sense to realise that Paula provided a different view of the family.

After Paula had been with the household for two years, a patient told Freud how pleasantly surprised they were that his fees included refreshments. This was the first time Freud had heard that Paula often offered coffee and cakes to patients while they were waiting for their session. He was amazed – a doctor did not offer snacks. Paula had the courage to tell the 'Herr Professor' (to whom she was devoted) that as the patients were about to face a stressful session of analysis, she thought it only polite. Her memories provide many other details Freud scholarship has tended to skim over or suppress. These range from the fact that Freud ate a soft-boiled egg every day to how much he charged per analytic hour in the 1930s. He was expensive, incredibly so – the point will be discussed later.

Freud was an avid correspondent and there are two sets of revealing letters which have been drawn on very little. The first was written in 1938 by Freud to his sister-in-law, Minna, while he was trying to arrange to leave Vienna. These letters have only been published in German. I have also drawn on a neglected collection of 238 letters between Freud and his nephew Sam, who lived in Manchester. The correspondence lasted 25 years, up to 1939, and helps explain why Freud fled to London. It has never been published in English.

The first biography of Freud was written in 1924; a hack job, he hated it. The great writer Stefan Zweig then included 100 pages on Freud in his book *Mental Healers* (1931; published in English two years later), in which he also wrote about Mesmer and Mary Baker Eddy, the founder of Christian Science. Zweig offered a good outline of Freud's ideas, efficiently introducing readers to the books which had made Freud famous: *The Interpretation of Dreams*, which was based on his pioneering analysis of his own dreams (1899), *The Psychopathology of Everyday Life* (1901), *Jokes and Their Relation to the Unconscious* (1903), *Three Essays on the Theory of Sexuality* (1905), *Beyond the Pleasure Principle* (1920) and *The Ego and the Id* (1923).

There was no other biography in his lifetime because Freud disliked the idea. He understood the strange nature of the relationship between a biographer and his subject. Many biographers idealise their subjects and so 'forgo the opportunity of penetrating into the most fascinating secrets of human nature'. Freud appointed Ernest Jones as his biographer, though he knew Jones would find it hard to be objective. The snide would say that was precisely why Freud gave him the job, of course. Jones was inclined to hero-worship and wrote, for example, that by the time Freud was 45 years old, he 'had attained complete maturity, a consummation of development that few people really achieve'. Freud managed this guru-like marvel by triumphing over his neuroses when he analysed his own dreams.

Knowing that he could be criticised, Jones claimed his own 'hero-worshipping propensities had been worked through' before he met Freud. Jones was susceptible to flattery, however, and Freud had encouraged the Welshman from 1908 onwards. Freud was honest about his motives, though not to Jones's face. Jones was a Chapel boy from the Welsh valleys. Fearful that psychoanalysis would be seen as some kind of Jewish sect, Freud was glad to recruit a Christian doctor, even one who had a few skeletons in his cupboard – most of them female. Jones was incidentally an excellent figure skater – perhaps the only analyst of importance to shine at any sport.

Jones nearly always presented Freud as a crusader fighting the demons of ignorance, so he made little of events like those of 13 October 1902. That day, Freud had an audience with Franz Josef I to thank the Kaiser for conferring on him the rank of Professor Extraordinarius at the hardly ancient age of 46. Bizarrely, Freud had to wear military uniform for the occasion. He wrote to his friend Wilhelm Fliess, admittedly with a certain irony:

> Congratulations and bouquets keep pouring in as if the role of sexuality had been suddenly recognised by His Majesty, the interpretation of dreams confirmed by the Council of Ministers and the necessity of the psychoanalytic therapy of hysteria carried by a two thirds' majority in Parliament.

There were many other examples of ignoring the positive. Jones, for example, suggested one psychiatrist had refused to discuss some of Freud's shocking ideas, saying such notions were 'a matter for the police'. In fact, Wilhelm Weygandt had written a glowing review of Freud's *The Interpretation of Dreams*.

Jones was also at pains to point out that while Freud's theories might be cutting edge, even scandalous, his subject was almost a monk. Freud had lost interest in the 'passionate side of marriage after he turned forty'. In fact, Freud slept all his life in a double bed with his wife. The two seem, at least, to have been quite physically affectionate, according to Paula Fichtl.

Jones's biography was written when many people who knew Freud were still alive, so discretion was required. Further, Jones himself took part in many of the dramas he described. Such involvement made it even harder for him to be objective. Jones dealt with Freud's last years in the third volume of his biography and sometimes wrote as if he were rather tired of his subject. He listed a series of events that happened each year and drew few conclusions, even saying of the year 1935 that nothing much happened then.

The bibliography lists the other major biographies; there are at least 20 which are anything but hack jobs. Despite their different approaches, they all tend to concentrate on how Freud achieved his 'breakthroughs'. As a result, Freud's last years have been studied less than any other period of his life. Yet he was not inactive. He still had patients, he still wrote and he had, like all other Jews in Central Europe, to work out how to survive the Nazi threat. His work after 1934 is far more than a mere coda to his career. He wrote about important subjects – the nature of monotheism, Moses, whether psychoanalysis could be terminable or was bound to be 'interminable' and why the Treaty of Versailles had led to the rise of the Nazi Party in Germany.

Freud could still contemplate, and enjoy contemplating, causing trouble. Three of his last books – *The Future of an Illusion* (1927), which explained why people believed in God, *Woodrow Wilson* (with William Bullitt; 1967), which dissected the psychology of the American president, and *Moses and Monotheism* (published in Holland in 1938 and in Britain two years later) – were bound to shock. Freud fretted about that but also loved it. Jones said Freud was a seeker after truth, but he was also a seeker after trouble. He got bored otherwise. One of Marie Bonaparte's friends said that Freud had so many thoughts in his quick mind that he could not follow all of them.

Three of Freud's last four books had the power to shock because they offended a number of orthodoxies. If the American president Woodrow Wilson had understood his own obvious neuroses, he would never have allowed David Lloyd George and Georges Clemenceau to bully him, which made him agree to a punitive Treaty of Versailles. The treaty ruined Germany and led to hyperinflation and social unrest in the 1920s. If the treaty had been fairer, as Wilson wanted, Hitler would have remained a rabble-rouser at the margins of power. If only the President had had a good therapist.

In *The Future of an Illusion*, Freud argued that if our Stone Age ancestors had been able to lie on a Neanderthal couch, they would have soon realised there was no God. Our ancestors' unconscious had created God to cope with the fact that they were small insignificant creatures who could die at any minute. Insecurity made human beings need God or gods.

Moses and Monotheism provoked fierce hostility too. Both Orthodox Jews and many Christians felt the book was blasphemous, partly because Freud described God as a deity with something of an identity problem. Yahweh was sometimes a tribal god, ready to advance in His Ark on the tribe next door and beat them to a pulp if they didn't bend the knee and offer in sacrifice 'sweet-smelling spices pleasing to the Lord', and sometimes a truly higher being, an advanced God of peace.

To the end of his life, Freud had something of the daredevil in him and enjoyed provocation. It is almost tempting to say that he wrote these last books so that for one last time he could 'épater les bourgeois'.

Less controversially, in the 18 months before his death, he also wrote *An Outline of Psychoanalysis* (1940), which some commentators think gives the clearest summary of his ideas. One might have expected biographers to consider these works in detail, but for a number of reasons they have tended not to.

The somewhat sparse literature on Freud's last years includes *Freud in Exile*, a series of essays the title of which is misleading. Only one book covers his last years: *The Death of Sigmund Freud* is about Freud in the 1930s, but for much of it the author intercuts between Freud preparing to leave Vienna and Adolf Hitler annexing Austria. His aim is to draw parallels between the dictator and the analyst. Anton Sauerwald, the key figure in allowing Freud to escape Vienna, is mentioned in detail on only four pages. Jones too makes just one mention of Sauerwald, even though he met him.

Freud loved detective novels, including Agatha Christie's. Some of her mysteries take place around archaeological digs; Freud was also fascinated by archaeology. Freud and Christie were both diggers. In her novels and in his case histories, the past has to be excavated and explained. Only then can we know the truth and be at peace. Freud would not have been surprised that what he did not disclose arouses the 'detective instinct' in all of us. If papers have been kept secret, there will have been a reason for it, whether honourable, dishonourable, conspiracy, cock-up or the product of ambivalence.

Freud had an ambivalent attitude to total honesty, as he admitted in the preface to the first edition of *The Interpretation of Dreams*. If he laid bare every detail – and every interpretation – of his own dreams, he would have to 'reveal to the public gaze more of the intimacies of my mental life than I liked, or than is normally necessary for any writer who is a man of science and not a poet'.

The intimacies mattered. For readers to understand his theories properly, they had to know the personal details, palatable or unpalatable. That led to a 'painful but unavoidable necessity'. Freud arrived at a compromise that made sense, to him at least. On the one hand he was extremely frank, while on the other he held back some of the secrets of some of his dreams. He knew the compromise was flawed because he wrote:

Naturally however I have been unable to resist the temptation of taking the edge off some of my indiscretions by omissions and substitutions.

> But whenever this has happened the value of my instances has been very definitely diminished. I can only express a hope that readers…will put themselves in my position and treat me with indulgence.

Freud deserves our indulgence. It cannot have been easy to expose so much in public, especially at a time when so much was kept secret. In *The Interpretation of Dreams*, he revealed many shocking feelings and thoughts. In one dream, he pissed on a mound of faeces and flushed them away down the hill with a stream of urine. He called this 'the dream of the outside toilet' and interpreted it as follows. He felt, in his unconscious, that he had to wash away the cobwebs of the mind and soul so every man and every woman could face the world – I am tempted to write 'free of sin', but it would be more accurate to say with self-knowledge.

In the middle of his self-analysis, Freud wrote to Wilhelm Fliess, 'being entirely honest with oneself is a good exercise'. It was excellent advice which Freud knew was not easy to follow. Twenty-eight years later, when he was writing to his nephew in Manchester, Freud admitted he was willing to hide difficult truths. He told Sam how his mother, Amalie, had turned 90 but that her family had been less than frank with her, saying, 'We had made a secret of all the losses in the family.' He then outlined, in a distressingly long list, all the deaths she would never discover and be upset by: 'my daughter Sophie, her second son Heinz, Teddy in Berlin, Eli Bernays [Martha's uncle], and your parents. We had to use many precautions not to be discovered.'

The question of how many of Freud's relatives killed themselves and the effect it had on him has not been studied at all – and that is a worrying omission. There were too many of them. Freud was not ashamed of deceiving his mother; he wanted to protect her, even if she was in robust physical and psychological health, he said. In the light of this, it's interesting that he did not attend her funeral.

Anyone who writes a book about Freud has to guess how much readers will already know about his life and his ideas. Here I am concentrating on Freud's last six years, but he did not get to 76 years of age without history or baggage, as we say now. Freud would not have been very impressed by a biographer who tried to explain his final years without discussing some of his earlier life and would, I imagine, have 'put his head back and laughed like a child'. The celebrated American journalist Max Eastman, a friend of Charlie Chaplin's, wrote that Freud tended to do that; Eastman interviewed Freud in 1926 for a book called *Heroes I Have Known*.

Freud was always very modest – he had a good sense of historical perspective – but was also a little vain. The last years of his life reveal both his courage and his ambivalences. Freud was brave, provocative and a great pioneer, but he was human, with limits and secrets. Seventy years after he died, it is hardly improper to reveal the last of these secrets.

CHAPTER 3

The Making of a Psychoanalyst

Our experiences as children shape us, Freud argued. On 6 May 1856, he was born into a complicated family which had what would now be called 'stepfamily issues'. Jacob had two sons by his first marriage, Philipp and Emanuel. After the death of his first wife, Sylvia, Jacob remarried. Very little is known about his second wife, Rebecca, other than that the marriage lasted only two or three years. There do not appear to have been any children.

Then, in 1855, Jacob married Amalie Nathanson, who was 19 years younger than he was. Sigmund was their first child. Jacob had been brought up as an Orthodox Jew but his marriage took place in a Reform synagogue. He noted in his diary that Sigmund 'joined' the Jewish community on 13 May 1856, by which he meant that his son had been circumcised (the Torah commands that every Jewish boy should have his foreskin removed on the eighth day of his life).

The family moved to Vienna when Freud was four years old, after his father's business in Freiberg failed. They were very poor and took a modest apartment in a tenement block near Vienna's famous Carmelite Church. Jacob's eldest son, Philipp, also moved to Vienna and lived across the street. Philipp was not much older than Freud's mother and some authors, such as Marianne Krüll, have imagined Philipp and Amalie together as a 'couple', suggesting that they had an affair. But all Krüll offers in evidence are Freud's dreams 40 years later and the fact that Philipp and Amalie were close in age.

Soon after Sigmund was born, Amalie became pregnant again. She and Jacob called their second son Julius and adored him. At the age of two, Freud was too young to appreciate that the baby may have been named after the great Roman emperor; the child was sickly, however, and died when he was less than a year old. Freud 'discovered' during his self-analysis that he had been delighted when his little brother died. He did not want to compete with another male child. Jacob and Amalie then had five daughters. By the time their last son, Alexander, was born Freud was nine and his position in the family assured. He was admired for his evident intelligence. Anna, his sister, complained that her big brother was given a room of his own so he could study while the rest of the children were crammed into one room. Harry Freud was told that the youngest girls did not even have a bed but slept in the drawers of a big family chest. The family had already decided that Sigmund would be the successful one. Freud wrote that his mother's love always made him feel like a conquistador. It is a phrase which has been much repeated.

Clearly Jacob's children from his third marriage and his grandchildren played together. Emanuel's oldest son, John, who was a year older than Sigmund, was Freud's first friend. 'I have also long known the companion of my mis-deeds between the ages of one and two years; it is my nephew, a year older than me...The two of us seem occasionally to have behaved cruelly to my niece, who was a year younger,' Freud wrote to Wilhelm Fliess. 'Until the end of my third year we had been inseparable; we had loved each other and fought each other.' This close friendship influenced all his later relationships with people of his own age. He always had to have 'an intimate friend and a hated enemy' in his emotional life. Freud told Fliess that sometimes 'my childish ideal has been so closely approached that friend and enemy have coincided in the same person; but not simultaneously, of course, as was the case in my early childhood'. Freud repeated patterns of relationships, as we all do, but he could see it – sometimes at least.

The Freud family lived in an apartment on the Glockengasse in the heart of Vienna's Jewish district, Leopoldstadt. It was a working-class area, though some solid tenement-style houses survived the Second World War and are standing to this day. There were 50 synagogues within walking distance. The streets still have a slightly shabby feel compared to the splendours of the rest of the city. As well as its 50 synagogues, Leopoldstadt also had Jewish butchers, Jewish bakers, Jewish bookshops, Jewish shoemakers and Jewish second-hand shops which sold *Resten*, old and damaged goods. Pedlars hawked stuff on most street corners.

Leopoldstadt was not a ghetto by 1861, but its streets belonged to the world the Nobel Prize-winning author Isaac Bashevis Singer described in his stories. Many Jews had come from small villages like those in which the musical *Fiddler on the Roof* was set. One of its most haunting songs is 'Tradition', celebrating the customs that Jews lived by and which many chafed against. Some Jews stuck to the old ways, but many were confused at a time of huge cultural change.

Freud's sister Anna described their home as a place of some religious confusion. 'I did not know the difference between Jews and Christians,' she claimed. When she was eight years old, in her 'naivety', she did not know whether the Kaiser was Jewish, Catholic or Protestant. She assumed, since the Kaiser ruled over all of these faiths, that he was Catholic one month, Protestant the next and Jewish the next! There were odd prohibitions. Anna noted her father refused to let them give their teachers Christmas presents as other families did. Later in life, Freud refused to have a Christmas tree in his home but gave Christmas presents.

In her memoirs, Anna says that she never went to a synagogue as a child. Nevertheless, Freud was familiar with the stories in the Bible even before he learned to read and he was proud of the fact. He sprinkled his books with references to the prophets and to Jewish stories. Freud's third book, *Jokes and Their Relation to the Unconscious*, is full of Jewish jokes: of the 140 jokes he quotes and analyses, 46 are specifically Jewish. Freud was especially fond of jokes he found in his favourite poet, Heinrich Heine (who was also a Jew), ones about *schnorrers*, Jewish beggars, and matchmakers. Freud had a collection of Jewish jokes which, it is claimed, he burned. Why has never been explained.

The confusions in the family were not just religious. They reflected typical problems in stepfamilies, problems that have been researched in great depth now as governments worry that the death of the family brews social trouble. Few stepfamilies escape jealousy and insecurity.

According to Freud's would-be biographer Leslie Adams, just after he had finished his self-analysis, Freud said that he had 'meditated' (Adams's word) on 'How different would it have been if I had been the son of my brother rather than of my father?' It is hard to be sure if Adams's claim is accurate, but it is not totally implausible. Freud's father, Jacob, was rather weak. The young Freud may have felt Jacob was hardly the ideal father.

Until he was ten, Freud was educated at home. Then he went to school in the Sperlgasse, a street which houses Vienna's Criminal Museum. That is very appropriate, because while Freud was at school something happened which any family dreads. This tragedy would affect Freud deeply. Jones wrote just one sentence, and a vague one, about it.

Forgeries Leave Their Traces

Freud's uncle Josef and his half-brothers Philipp and Emanuel became involved in a major criminal conspiracy. Josef's brother Jacob, Sigmund's father, was not that impressed with him and described him as 'not a bad man but a simpleton'. By 1860, Philipp and Emanuel had emigrated to Manchester to make a living. Josef often travelled there from Vienna to deal in hardware and other things.

In June 1865 the *Neue Frei Presse*, then the newest paper in Vienna, reported that the police were on the track of counterfeiters of Russian roubles. This was something of an obsession with the Kaiser. Vienna's Criminal Museum is crammed not just with souvenirs and exhibits of popular grisly murders but with examples of forgeries, including a number of cabinets which have facsimiles of forged bank-notes. One forger called Silberberg became a celebrity because his banknotes were so convincing. Fake money was an outrage against capitalism, so the Kaiser ordered the police to make sure it did not happen in his capital.

The *Neue Frei Presse* provided its readers with lurid accounts of evil from New York to St Petersburg. Its attitudes were that of a top-class tabloid. On 26 June 1865, a few days after the first story, the paper reported that a Viennese man who had been passing forged 50-rouble notes had named a number of accomplices. One of those arrested in the subsequent inquiry was Josef Freud.

The case was heard by Judge von Schwartz in 1866. The facts as the prosecution outlined them were complex. Josef Freud often went to visit Philipp and Emanuel Freud in Manchester. When they searched his apartment, the Vienna police found two very suspicious letters sent by the two brothers. The first said, 'There is as much money as there is sand by the sea and that if we are wise fortune will not fail to smile on us.' The second letter asks if Josef can find a bank for the 'merchandise, where the turnover would be larger, faster and more profitable'.

At the trial the prosecution alleged that Josef Freud had met a certain Osias Weich in 1864. Weich told Josef that he had a good deal for him as he had bought some forged notes from a man in England. They had only cost him 25 per cent of their face value. Josef Freud rejected the deal but the two continued to meet. A few weeks later Weich made it clear he was in financial difficulties. The 'simpleton' Josef Freud lent him 300 florins. He claimed Weich then gave him as security an English envelope containing fake roubles. Josef had not been the one who started it, he swore. The supply of fake roubles came from London and from Manchester, now Philipp and Emanuel's place of business.

By 1864 Josef Freud was at the centre of the forgery, the prosecution claimed. He asked another accomplice, Simon Weiss, to help him find someone who would be interested in buying 400 50-rouble notes. Weiss promised Freud he could do this, but the two men fell out. Weiss then contacted the police.

On 20 June 1865, Weiss took Josef Freud to the Hotel Victoria in Vienna and introduced him to a 'client' who appeared to be willing to buy the rouble notes at 10 per cent of their face value. Josef Freud said he would go to fetch some more notes. He had no idea it was a set-up. While he was gone, Weiss and the police prepared the trap.

Josef Freud returned after an hour and began counting out 50-rouble notes. At this point, the police (some of whom had been disguised as waiters) put down their trays and arrested him. They took Freud's uncle to his apartment, where they found a further 259 rouble notes, as well as the letters from Philipp and Emanuel. Josef Freud had a total of 349 fake 50-rouble notes. Their total value was the very considerable sum of 17,450 roubles. Jacob's modest flat may also have been searched to see if there were fake roubles there.

The police sent the fakes to the Russian Imperial Bank in St Petersburg. Its directors commented that they were produced by copper engraving and lithographic print on ordinary paper. They were excellent forgeries.

Weiss was not prosecuted, presumably because he had helped the police. In court Josef Freud and Osias Weich gave different accounts of what had happened. Weich accused Josef Freud of having set him up. The prosecutor added that the motives behind this forgery were revolutionary, which seems more like official paranoia than fact. None of the plotters appear to have been politically involved. Simple greed was the motive. Political anxieties made the police conduct a very thorough investigation, however.

The judge found Josef Freud and Weich guilty of aiding and abetting the issue of counterfeit banknotes. Each man was sentenced to 10 years in prison. But the judge handed over Freud's case to the Supreme Court with a view to seeking leniency. It is not clear why he did that, especially given the Emperor's tirades against forgery. The Austrian Minister of Police, Richard Belcredi, even wrote an account of the case to the Austrian Foreign Minister, Count Mensdorff.

At the time of his uncle's arrest, Freud had just started going to the gymnasium or secondary school. His school friends must have known about the arrest, and known he was the nephew of the wanted man. Vienna was an anti-Semitic city. To be the nephew of a Jew accused of forgery cannot have been easy.

The Freud family was shamed. The young Freud read reports of his uncle's trial in the Viennese papers. Journalists asked embarrassing questions. Freud noted that his father's hair turned grey from grief – a recent paper in the *Journal of the Royal Society of Medicine* argues such changes of colour can occur as a result of trauma.

Freud was haunted by Uncle Josef for the rest of his life. He recorded nine dreams about him in *The Interpretation of Dreams*. He never commented on the fact that his uncle had the same name as Joseph, who in Genesis interprets the Pharaoh's dreams. Freud often had these 'uncle' dreams when he was under stress. One involved a telling pun, as it included the words '*für Onkel*' – for uncle. In English there is no hidden meaning but in German *furunkel* means a sore or carbuncle. Freud made much of the fact that his father's death freed him, but he failed to mention that his uncle Josef had died in 1897.

Freud was not very frank about the forgery or the trial, merely writing that his uncle had 'allowed himself to become involved in a transaction of a kind that is severely punished by law and he was in fact punished for it'.

The family feared that Freud's half-brothers would also go to jail, but the Manchester police did not bring charges because the fake roubles were not used in Britain and extradition procedures were then almost unknown. Freud was ten when his uncle was jailed.

The notes in Manchester City Libraries left by Leslie Adams include a copy of a letter about a conversation he had with Freud's son Oliver, who lived in Williamsburg near Boston and who died in 1969. Oliver told him, Adams claims, that Philipp was in financial difficulties when the family left Freiberg in 1860, which may have been why they went in for the forgery.

Adams argues that the 'disillusioning truth' the Freud family tried to hide was simple poverty. Freud's uncle and half-brothers had been pedlars who barely scraped a living selling '*alte Sachen*', any old rubbish. Given Freud's later fame, his early biographers said nothing about these impoverished antecedents.

Only one book, *Questions for Freud*, considers the impact the conviction of Uncle Josef had on Freud. The authors, Rand and Torok, suggest that it made him wary of outlining his theories in any detail because detail would allow them to be tested and, possibly, proved false or 'forgeries'. It was wiser to keep things a bit vague and muddled. This was not, of course, a conscious decision, the authors argue. Freud's unconscious fears made him imprecise.

Ernest Jones trumpeted that Freud was always a seeker after truth, but

Rand and Torok suggest that this was only 'as long as what he finds will obey his control'. They claim that Freud is 'the architect of a paradox' and that his 'flawed methods of investigations derive from the need to foresee his results'. Only that way could Freud be sure he would not be exposed as a pedlar of forgeries or false ideas.

Emanuel did not ever again become involved in crime. (It is harder to be sure about Philipp.) The brothers concentrated on their small textile business, though it was obviously precarious at first. According to Manchester City Council records, they set up at 26 Market Street in 1861. It was one of the best commercial streets in the city, so they could not afford to rent a shop but took one room on one of the upper floors. In 1863 they moved and the firm of Freud and Co. was described 'as importers of foreign fancy goods'. By 1865 they described themselves as importers of London, Birmingham and Sheffield goods. Three years later, they established themselves in the more glamorous trade of jewellers, which suggests they had more money than before.

By 1871 Emanuel was listed as doing business on his own and his home address was given as 12 Green Street in Ardwick. He was now a respectable citizen. Manchester City Sessions even record that Mary Callaghan, aged 35, was imprisoned for six months for stealing a quantity of twine and 'fents' – a word then used to mean remnants – belonging to him.

In 1875, when he was 19 years old, Freud visited his half-brothers in Manchester. The most dramatic news was that Philipp had got married to Matilda Bloomah, from Birmingham. They had one child when Freud came to see them. Pauline Mary (who would be called Poppy) was born on 23 October 1873 and in 1897 married Frederick Oswald Hartwig, who would run a successful company called Scientific Glass Blowing. His wife preserved the letters between Freud and Emanuel's son, Sam. Philipp's second child, Morris Herbert Walter, was born on 2 April 1876. He emigrated to South Africa as a young man.

Freud described his Manchester family in a letter to his school friend Eduard Silberstein, again not exactly truthfully: 'The unfavourable turn their business took caused them to move to England, which they have not left since 1859. I can say that they now hold a generally respected position, not because of their wealth, for they are not rich, but because of their personal character. They are shopkeepers, the elder selling cloth and the younger jewellery, in the sense that word seems to have in England.' The jewellery might be imperfect but his relatives were not.

Freud went on to describe his two sisters-in-law and reminded Silberstein that he had already met John, 'an Englishman in every respect, with a knowledge of languages and technical matters well beyond the usual business education'. There were also 'two charming nieces, Pauline, who is nineteen, and Bertha, who is seventeen, and a fifteen-year-old boy by the name of Samuel – which I believe has been fashionable in England ever since Pickwick – and who is generally considered to be a "sharp and deep" young fellow'. Sam was a character in Dickens's *Pickwick Papers*. Freud said nothing to his friend about his half-brothers' criminal history.

The fate of John Freud remains a total mystery. The only mention of him in any source I have been able to trace after this letter is when Frederick Hartwig (who married John's cousin Poppy) said that John had left his parents when he was quite young. Harry Freud claims in his auto-biographical notes that John was eighteen when he disappeared forever. John Freud is, like Jacob's second wife, Rebecca, one of the missing Freuds. Freud never referred to him again except in terms of his own history as a toddler.

Freud also stayed some days in London in 1875 and was to remember this visit fondly for decades. It has often been assumed that the two branches of the family stopped communicating, but there is a photo of the Freud clan in 1876. Emanuel Freud is in the back row, standing next to Sigmund but turned away from him. The twelve others in the picture are facing outwards but Emanuel is looking down and to the side. His right hand protects his midriff. He draws one's attention because he strikes a very odd pose for a Victorian family photograph where everyone usually faced the camera.

This complicated family had many sides to it. One story makes very clear that Freud's father was no patriarch but far weaker than one might expect the head of a Victorian family to be. In her memoirs, Freud's sister Anna tells a romantic teenage story. When she was 16 years old an uncle from Odessa on the Black Sea came to visit. (Amalie Nathanson, Freud's mother, had lived in Odessa for a few years; the city had a large Jewish population.) The uncle was smitten with Anna and took her to see *William Tell* at the opera. Amalie had to come as well, to act as chaperone. The uncle showered young Anna with chocolates and sweet talk. Then he proposed marriage. Her would-be husband can't really have been an uncle, as that would make the marriage incestuous, but he was clearly a close relative. Stepfamily issues again!

Anna spent a sleepless night dreaming of becoming a rich wife in Odessa. In the morning, she went to talk to her mother. Amalie was quite excited by the idea but insisted she discuss the proposal not with her husband but with her son, who had not yet turned 18. Jewish families were no different from other Victorian families in some ways. The form was for the suitor to ask the father if he could have his daughter's hand in marriage. Papa ruled. In the Freud household, however, the father was not so dominant.

'Sigmund was less than delighted,' Anna recalled, 'and explained to mother and me what was involved when a man of 59 [as this uncle was] wanted to marry a girl of 16.' Freud won the argument and the cradle-snatcher was sent back to Odessa in disgrace. Anna then became infatuated with one of Freud's friends, Eduard Silberstein. He was her first true love, but they were so innocent they never even kissed.

At the age of thirteen, Jewish boys are given a bar mitzvah. They read a portion of the law in synagogue and become full members of the congregation. One of the facts no biographer has pinpointed is whether or not Freud had a bar mitzvah, as would have been perfectly normal for a Jewish boy even if his family were not devout. Freud himself is silent on the subject. He once complained that 'my education was so un-Jewish' he could not even read Hebrew. Yet in a letter written to Eduard Silberstein just before he was to take an examination, Freud refers to an event which took place on 'erev' examination. In Hebrew erev means 'the eve of' – Jewish festivals commence in the evening, so Jews celebrate the eve of Rosh Hashana, the New Year, the eve of Yom Kippur, the Day of Atonement, the eve of Pesach or Passover. Freud, who knew no Hebrew, drops the Hebrew word casually, and correctly, into a letter.

Whether he had a bar mitzvah or not, Freud made it clear that he did not believe in God from his teens. Writing in the *American Mercury*, his sister Anna said of her brother: 'He grew up devoid of any belief in God or immortality. He had no need of it.'

Freud may have decided he could do without God but that did not mean that he did not learn, and absorb, a great deal about Judaism. His teacher of religion at school was Samuel Hamerschlag, who was a practising Jew. Freud wrote an obituary for him in which he said:

A spark from the same fire which animated the spirit of the great Jewish seers and prophets burned in him and was not extinguished until old age weakened his powers. But the passionate side of his nature was happily tempered by the ideal of humanism which governed him and his method of education was based on the foundation of the philological and classical studies to which he had devoted his own youth. Religious instruction served him as a way of educating towards love of the humanities and from the material of Jewish history he was able to find means of tapping the sources of enthusiasm hidden in the hearts of young people and making it flow out far beyond the limitations of nationalism or dogma.

One of Hamerschlag's other pupils at the Leopoldstädter Communal Gymnasium in Taborstrasse was Josef Herzig, who was three years older than Freud. The two young men were good friends – and nearly more. Freud asked Herzig for advice on some aspects of his first papers, which dealt with physiology and involved a little chemistry, Herzig's subject. In 1884, when Herzig was nearly 30, he started to court Freud's sister Rosa. Rosa and Herzig in fact went on holiday together for three weeks to Oberswaldorf, but the relationship did not blossom. Freud and Herzig stayed friends, however, and often played cards together. Herzig became a successful academic chemist and taught at the University of Vienna from the mid-1880s. Herzig was, of course, Jewish.

The young Freud may have rejected God, but he remained more involved with the Jewish community than he sometimes admitted. Herzig was the first of many Jews Freud worked with all his life.

As a young doctor, Freud struggled and failed to get a proper position at university. In 1885 he applied for a grant to study in Paris under Jean-Martin Charcot, the most dramatic 'mind doctor' of the time. Charcot used to present his patients to students almost as music-hall acts; there were star patients, like Augustine, who illustrated various forms of insanity. Charcot's son became an Antarctic explorer to get away from the madness.

After Paris Freud decided his future lay in studying hysteria. It was a sensible choice. Psychiatry was less closed to Jewish doctors than other areas of medicine because it was less respectable and more marginal. When Freud returned to Vienna in 1885, he worked closely with two Jews, Dr Josef Breuer and Dr Wilhelm Fliess. Both men were enormously important in his intellectual development. No non-Jew ever played such an influential a role. Working with Jews did not mean believing in Judaism. In 1891, when Freud turned 35, his father gave him a Bible and uttered the hope that his son would return to some kind of faith in Judaism.

The view that Freud played down his sense of Jewish identity comes partly from his authorised biographer, Ernest Jones, who shared much of the casual anti-Semitism of Britain's middle class in the 1920s. There was a more personal reason too. Jones sensed that Freud always felt closer to Jewish analysts and that made him a little jealous. Other commentators, like Sander Gilman, find it hard to accept Freud's loyalty to Jewishness. Freud suffered from 'internalised anti-Semitism', Gilman suggests, and looked down on the religious East European Jews as ignorant, superstitious peasants with long beards which were probably teeming with lice. There is no evidence that Freud looked down on religious Jews. It is true that he had his moments of ambivalence towards his father and that did sometimes lead to some ambivalence about his heritage. But Freud always felt Jewish.

The Marriage Question

Freud never seems to have considered marrying out of his faith, as many Victorian Jews did. He courted and, in 1886, married Martha Bernays, who came from a pious and well-connected Jewish family. The two families had already been linked in 1883, when Martha's brother Eli married Freud's sister, Anna. Freud and Martha were engaged for four years and wrote constantly to each other, as young Victorian people in love tended to do. Anyone who has read their letters will get a good sense of the young Freud: he is ambitious, passionate, driven but also anxious and insecure, often the charming, even humble lover, but also forceful. He shares his ideas with Martha and often discusses issues related to being Jewish. She knew about those.

Martha's grandfather had been a famous rabbi in Hamburg. Her uncle, Jacob Bernays, was one of the foremost classical and biblical scholars of the mid-19th century; Freud knew his work well. In one of his books, *Ein Lebensbild in Briefen* (roughly translated as *A Portrait of a Life in Letters*), Bernays described how he refused to convert to Christianity. One of his friends, Christian von Bunsen, the Prussian ambassador to London, wanted to help him get a professorship but he knew Bernays would never get a chair in Prussia because he was a Jew. Bernays should convert, von Bunsen suggested, but not merely to obtain a professorship. The ambassador was a subtle tempter.

Jews were consigned to the margins of history, von Bunsen told his friend. A great scholar like Bernays should convert and be 'in the mainstream'. In reply, Bernays quoted St Paul's letter to the Romans (11:25):

> For I do not want you, brethren, to be uninformed of this mystery, lest you be wise in your own estimation, that a partial hardening has happened to Israel until the fullness of the Gentiles has come in.

Paul said that the Jews have a right, even perhaps a duty, to remain Jews until all the heathens have converted to Christianity. As a scholar, Bernays could quote the New Testament to justify his refusal. But his 'inner core', he said, was Jewish. Freud's inner core was also Jewish. And he liked talking about it more than one might expect.

In a letter to his fiancée, Freud described meeting an old Jew, Nathan, who had no doubts about the romance of his religion. Freud seems to have approved, for he told Martha how Nathan had said, 'The Jew…is the finest flower of mankind. The Jew is made for joy and joy for the Jew.' Nathan then explained how his teacher, Martha's grandfather, the famous rabbi, used to explain how various holy days brought with them particular degrees of joy. The most joyous was Simchat Torah, when Jews celebrate the fact that God has given them the Torah and drink a good deal. (In biblical times it was wine, but once Jews lived in Eastern Europe, they toasted the Torah in vodka.) Then, Freud told his fiancée, a customer walked into the shop and Nathan dropped the elegiac tone and 'became a merchant again'.

Freud reassured Martha with surprising intensity: 'And as for us, this is what I believe; even if the form wherein Jews were happy no longer offers us any shelter, something of the core, of the essence of this meaningful and life affirming Judaism will not be absent from our home.'

After much opposition from her mother, Freud and Martha married. The wedding was not conducted in a synagogue. Martha's mother, Emmeline, did not want her daughter to marry Freud, because he was poor and came from a poor family. She had seen what poverty could do. In 1867, she and her husband, Berman, had had to come to Vienna because Berman was in desperate financial difficulties. He worked selling advertising, but he was an ambitious man and had gone into business on his own. He was financially chaotic, though, and in 1866 was put on trial for keeping false accounting records. He was made bankrupt and served a year in prison at exactly the same time as Uncle Josef did. The Bernays family was devastated.

So when Freud married Martha, they had both seen people they loved imprisoned. The nephew of the forger married the daughter of the embezzler. It's hardly surprising that Emmeline had wanted her daughter to marry someone who offered security. We owe the details of his great-grandfather's inglorious business career to Freud's grandson, Anton. Many of the Bernays letters in the Library of Congress are restricted, some in perpetuity. One reason, at least, is not hard to guess.

Freud and Martha's first son was born in 1887 and named Jean-Martin in honour of Charcot. The law required births to be registered according to religious faith. Today the old registers for Jewish families are still held in the offices of Vienna's main synagogue in a cobbled street near the city centre.

There's a kosher restaurant nearby. To see the register, you have to go through strict security, submitting to a search and passing through a metal detector. The Jews of Vienna still feel under threat. In most European countries it would be from terrorists these days, but Austria's neo-Nazis tend to get between 15 and 20 per cent of the votes in elections.

The Jewish archive is run by Dr Walter Eckstein. He smiled as he brought out the huge books and showed me the entries that record the birth of Jean-Martin Freud, mother Martha Freud and father Sigmund Freud. As I looked at the fine copperplate handwriting, I wondered whether Freud had his own sons circumcised, as Jews have done since Genesis. On this point, I can find no information and the two men who might have been able to help, his grandsons Clement and Lucian Freud, never responded to my inquiries.

The Hat in the Gutter

The Freud family tradition that has been much written about is far less intimate. Freud himself told the story of how, as a child, he saw a Gentile deliberately knock Jacob Freud's hat off his head. Jacob did not dare respond to the insult. He just bent down into the gutter and picked his hat up without saying a word. Vienna was an anti-Semitic city in the 1860s; a sensible Jew did not provoke a row with a Christian. But Freud felt his father should have stood up to the bully.

It did not make him admire his father any more when, in his teens, Freud found out that not all Jews were so timid and that some did stand up against bullies. Even before he went to see his half-brothers in Manchester, Freud would have heard of Moses Montefiore. Montefiore had made his fortune by the time he was 40 and devoted the rest of his life to improving the lot of Jews. He had some stirring successes. In 1840 in Damascus the 'mediaeval blood libel', that Jews used the blood of a Christian for making their Passover matzot, flared up again. Syrian Jews were persecuted. Sir Moses, as he was by then, got the support of the British Foreign Secretary Lord Palmerston and descended on the Khedive of Egypt. The Khedive was left in no doubt as to what his obligations were, or one of Palmerston's gunboats would start bombing. Camels raced across the desert to tell the Ottoman authorities to release the imprisoned Jews...or else.

Sir Moses then sailed to Istanbul and would not leave until he got a *firman*, a royal order, from the Sultan of Turkey, guaranteeing protection to all the Jews in his lands against similar false charges. The Gentile who dared touch Sir Moses's hat would have been quickly surrounded by British warships.

The position of the Jews in the Austro-Hungarian Empire was totally different, Freud knew. A Jew could never have become an important politician in the Habsburg Empire in the way that Benjamin Disraeli did in Britain. The Archduchess Maria Teresa, part of the ruling Habsburg family, even financed an anti-Semitic journal, the *Österreicher Volkspiel*. It had a field day in 1893 when a boy was murdered in Xanten in Silesia. The paper trotted out the blood libel again; Jews had to sup on Christian blood for the Passover 'sacrifice'. The 1890s also saw pogroms in Russia, with the result that thousands of Jews fled west. The new century didn't make for new attitudes. In 1913 a Jewish brickmaker, Mendel Beiliss, was tried in Kiev for the ritual murder of a 13-year-old boy.

There was no escaping the reality that Jews suffered, were hated and were the 'other'. In 1900 Vienna elected a rabid anti-Semite, Karl Lueger, as its mayor. Lueger's writings were to find a fan in the young Hitler, who said that Lueger's work taught him that anti-Semitism was the correct 'policy'. There is still a huge Karl Lueger Platz in the middle of Vienna.

Some of the most virulent anti-Semites were professional men, even fellow psychiatrists. Hans Blüher's *Secessio Judaica* argued that Jews should 'secede' from society whether they wanted to or not; another psychiatrist, Wilhelm Dolles, claimed that the Jew and the Christian were such different psychological types that they should not try to mix.

It seems to me that Freud was not ambivalent about being Jewish, let alone a self-hating Jew. He was firmly one of the tribe, but he did not believe in God. God was a man-made delusion and Judaism, like every other religion, was an illusion that neurotic Neanderthals had needed and that human beings now needed to evolve beyond.

Freud made his feelings about being a Jew clear in his preface to the Hebrew edition of *Totem and Taboo*. Again the intensity is evident:

No reader of the Hebrew version of this book will find it easy to put himself in the emotional position of an author who is ignorant of the language of holy writ, who is completely estranged from the religion of his fathers – as well as from every other religion – and who cannot take a share in nationalist ideals, but who has yet never repudiated his people, who feels that he is in his essential nature a Jew and who has no desire to alter that nature. If the question were put to him: 'Since you have abandoned all these common characteristics of your countrymen, what is left to you that is Jewish?' he would reply: 'A very great deal, and probably its very essence.' He could not express that essence in words, but some day, no doubt, it will become accessible to the scientific mind.

Freud tried to express what that 'essence' of Jewish culture was for him. Its roots are most obvious in the Talmud, with its commentaries about biblical texts as well as its commentaries about commentaries. The Talmud encourages the asking of questions. So did some books in the Bible like the Book of Job. Job cross examines God and God does not respond as if such questions were impertinent. Freud said:

> It was only to my Jewish nature that I owed the two qualities that have become indispensable to me throughout my difficult life. Because I was a Jew I found myself free of many prejudices which restrict others in the use of the intellect: as a Jew I was prepared to be in the opposition and to renounce agreement with the 'compact majority'.

In talking of his difficult life, incidentally, Freud was *kvetching*, to use a Yiddish expression: complaining, throwing up his hands to the heavens, demanding compensation from the Almighty in whom he did not believe. One might ask if, at the time Freud wrote this in 1925, he had much reason to *kvetch*. He had a devoted mother, a devoted wife, a devoted sister-in-law, devoted followers, devoted children, was about to be interviewed as a world celebrity by Max Eastman for his book on modern heroes; the only reason Freud didn't have a devoted rabbi was that he never went to synagogue. Freud was not a perfect man but in his *kvetching* he was perfectly a Jew.

Freud also wrote that, being Jewish, 'I found myself free of many prejudices which restrict others in the use of the intellect'. It was also a question of courage. He claimed he had the necessary 'degree of readiness to accept a situation of solitary opposition – a situation with which no one is more familiar than a Jew'.

One historian, Cora Díaz de Chumaceiro, has even suggested that Freud was so enraged by anti-Semitism that he ignored Richard Wagner's contribution to the study of dreams. The composer had developed his own dream theory half a century before Freud. Freud knew Wagner's writing on dreams when he wrote *The Interpretation of Dreams*, Díaz de Chumaceiro claims. *The Interpretation* discusses previous writers on dreams at great length, so not writing a word about Wagner seems an 'inexplicable case of omission'. Díaz de Chumaceiro insists that Freud, consciously or unconsciously, blotted out the influence that a hater of Jews had on him.

Freud, however, had the common sense to see that psychoanalysis would suffer if it seemed to be a Jewish monopoly, so he rejoiced when two Christians joined the 'cause' – as psychoanalysis was sometimes called – Ernest Jones and Carl Gustav Jung. Freud even asked one of his first followers, Karl Abraham, to forgive the fact that he had to pay so much attention to these *goyim* (the Yiddish term for Gentiles), who found it harder to accept the unconventional ideas of psychoanalysis. Gentiles were not so used to 'solitary opposition'.

A New Home and New Theories

In 1891, after five years of marriage, the Freuds moved to the mezzanine floor of 19 Berggasse. The street slopes upwards, which may be why it is called Mountain Street. Today, 19 Berggasse houses Vienna's Freud Museum. Two doors away from the entrance, there is a Café Freud, where someone has put up a number of portraits of Freud, including a pointilliste picture in which he appears covered in sequins. Freud belongs to us all now, even the sex industry. Across the road is a sex shop called Boudoir, in the window of which are a number of balloons with Freud's face on them, as well as copies of books by the Marquis de Sade. Few sex shops try so hard to achieve intellectual respectability.

When Freud and his wife moved to 19 Berggasse, he was not far away from the Jewish area. If he turned left out of his front door, he could amble down to the Donau Canal in five minutes. If he walked across the bridge, it would take 10 minutes to reach the end of Taborstrasse, one of the main streets of the Jewish quarter. Taborstrasse was the obvious route to take to the Prater, the park Freud had liked ever since he walked there as a small boy with his father. Anna's memoirs describe many days when they strolled through the Prater as a family and Jacob enjoyed a beer in its café. The great analyst never moved far from his Jewish roots.

Freud did not return to the faith of his fathers, as his own father had wished, but in one simple way he did what his father wanted: he lived for 47 years in an apartment block where nearly all the other residents were Jewish. The ground floor was occupied by a kosher butcher called Kornmehl.

Freud wrote towards the end of his life that he had been very happy in his marriage. In a traditional way, Martha and he had their separate spheres. She did not interfere with his work and he did not interfere with her house. Decades later, when their youngest daughter, Anna, wanted to change her bedroom, Freud said it was fine with him but that hardly counted as Martha ruled the domestic sphere. Anna was over 20 at the time. She complained that her mother was a stickler for punctuality and that they always had to have the main meal of the day at 1 p.m. But what did Martha serve?

Given their marriage 'contract', which stated that Martha should rule the home, it is possible that Freud hardly ever set foot in the kitchen, which would have allowed Martha to keep a partially kosher home at least. The appalling thought occurs that Freud's wife may have bought kosher meat from the kosher butcher downstairs without her husband ever knowing.

Rather usefully, Paula Fichtl included in her memoirs a number of the recipes that were the favourites in the Freud household from 1929. There was ox tongue, stewed carp, many kinds of soufflés but not one recipe for pork. Herr Professor's great treat was caviar at Christmas. One of his grateful patients brought him a huge pot once. For much of his career, Freud was too poor to afford such luxuries.

Martha's mother, Emmeline, wanted her daughter to marry a rich man. Given that her own husband had gone bankrupt and been put in jail, she must have been distraught when, before she died, her eldest son (who was called Eli) also faced financial disaster. Freud was too poor to help his brother-in-law much, though a whip-round in the family produced $500. Eli and Anna Bernays-Freud needed that to pay for their tickets, as they had to leave Vienna in a hurry to escape creditors. It is not hard to see why Freud opened secret bank accounts the moment he had any money to spare.

In 1896 Freud's father, Jacob, died. The old man had lived to 81 years of age, a number that would stick in Freud's mind for the rest of his life. He believed that his father's death freed him to pursue his radical ideas. For the next three to four years, Freud recorded his own dreams and tried to understand what they meant. 'Wise' men had, of course, been interpreting dreams since biblical times, but no one before had attempted a scientific analysis of their own dreams. They were the basic evidence for his theory which claimed how sexual children were.

Freud presented some of his early 'shocking' ideas to the Bnai Brith Jewish Society, a kind of discussion group. He felt he would get a more sympathetic hearing from his co-religionists, who knew something about what he called 'solitary opposition'.

The idea behind solitary opposition concerns seeing things from a new perspective. When they left their small and small-minded agricultural settlements where the rabbis ruled, many Jews stopped keeping the 613 commandments a good Jew is required to keep. They peered at the world and unpeeled their eyes; they blinked and their blinkers were lifted. They saw the world with the insight of the outsider. The outsider had no status in society to lose and so could take intellectual risks. It was not the meek who would inherit the earth but the risk takers. It is a splendid argument, grand, sweeping and very romantic.

There are problems with this theory, however. Charles Darwin (whom Freud greatly admired) developed the theory of evolution and in the process outraged the Church. The Bible was not the literal truth or the word of God. The world had not been created in six days in 4004 BC, as Archbishop Ussher had calculated by working out which ancient begat whom and when. Darwin was no outsider, however. He came from a well-established English family, had trained to become a clergyman and had married a young woman who was a devout Anglican.

It could be argued that the roots of Freud's creativity had less to do with being Jewish and able to cope with 'solitary opposition' than he imagined. Freud exposed the hidden tensions between children and their parents. The fact that he grew up in a complicated family meant he had sensed those tensions from when he was a little boy. When he analysed his dreams, their memories flooded back and gave him the material on which he built his theories.

Anti-Semitism and *la chose genitale*

Long before the Nazis came to power, Freud believed he understood the deep reasons for anti-Semitism. He was well aware of some of the obvious causes. But the fundamental reason came down to '*la chose genitale*', to use Charcot's phrase – specifically what happened to the genital thing eight days after Jewish boys were born.

The roots of anti-Semitism, Freud claimed, lay in the 'remotest past ages' and had nothing to do with physical differences. Jews did not look weird; they were not of a different colour and jibes about hooked or Hittite noses were silly – Julius Caesar had had a very hooked nose, after all. Jews were not 'fundamentally different' as they were 'essentially Mediterranean'. Freud also dismissed the idea that anti-Semitism was due to the fact that the Church blamed the Jews for betraying Christ.

Anti-Semitism was too emotional and ran so deep it had to have unconscious roots. Freud's analysis in the 1930s was based on his treatment of the only child he ever saw as a patient. Little Hans was the five-year-old son of his inevitably Jewish friend Max Graf, who was a composer and historian of music. Graf sent Freud reports about the boy's interest in anything sexual. Hans was growing up normally and then, suddenly, he developed a crippling phobia.

Little Hans would not leave the house. He would not step into the street. When his father asked why, Hans said that he was afraid a horse would bite him. Freud asked to see father and son, and the boy was brought to Berggasse. As Freud talked to him, he soon realised that the horse reminded the boy of his father. There were two visual details Freud made much of: Max Graf had a moustache and wore glasses. Those were very significant, he argued, because to Hans they made Max look like a horse. If Freud could have painted, it seems safe to imagine he would have become a Surrealist. Little Hans's phobic fear, that a horse might bite him, was a desperate compromise to try to solve the Oedipal conflict.

Hans loved his father but his father was also a rival for his mother's love. Such thoughts were forbidden, the little boy knew unconsciously, so he was a stew of guilt, repressions and fears. The lid would blow off his inner kettle any moment and Hans developed acute castration anxiety. When his sister was born, the anxiety got worse because he was jealous of her. The boy did say he wanted her dead – just as Freud had wanted his little brother Julius dead. But Hans could not say anything of the sort about his father. He had to repress his anger and aggression, and that repression made him fear that his father wanted to castrate him.

At the age of five, in his unconscious mind at least, Hans was a subtle strategist. It was not hard to avoid horses, because he did not have to go out into the street, but the real monster, Dad with the castrating knife, was at home. By being frightened of the horse, Hans could ward off the greater anxiety: that his father would cut off his penis. The horse phobia masked a deeper fear and actually helped the boy manage his terrors. It is a view of phobias which remains influential to this day.

To understand why Gentiles hated Jews, Freud wrote in a footnote to his paper on Little Hans, one also had to look to Genesis. God promised Abraham the Jews would be the chosen people. As a mark of that covenant, every male child was to be circumcised when he was eight days old, as Freud of course had been. But the snip reminded men of their primal fear: castration.

Freud wove this into a complex theory. Jews made themselves 'separate' and, of all the practices which made them so, 'circumcision has made a disagreeable uncanny impression'. Christians hated the Jews not because the Jews had Christ crucified but because they reminded them of the traumatic fear that makes men wriggle with discomfort. It was canny of St Paul to argue that what Christ demanded was circumcision of the heart, which is rather less traumatic than the real thing. As Charcot had said, it was all down to *la chose genitale*, the genital thing.

Freud also blamed Jewish pride. Genesis and Exodus constantly emphasise the covenant between God and Israel, the chosen people. So the Jews do not just evoke unconscious fears of castration; they also have the impertinence to claim a privileged relationship with God the father. For now he said little about that.

'I venture to assert that jealousy of the people which declared itself first-born, favourite child of God the father has not yet been surmounted among other people even today; it is as though they had thought there was truth in the claim.' Freud believed that before the Nazis came to power, but he did not dare utter these thoughts for many years.

Moses and Rome

Freud's lifelong interest in Moses was also a sign of how Jewish he felt. But his attitude to the prophet was complicated by his ambivalence about Rome. Freud adored the city, yet by the time he was 40 he had never visited it, though he had managed to get to London, Manchester, Paris, Nancy, Hamburg and Berlin. He even got to Trasimene, which is some 85 miles from Rome, but he did not press on. There was a reason for that, of course.

In 217 BC Hannibal defeated the Romans on the shores of Lake Trasimene. Freud identified with Hannibal, who brought elephants over the Alps. In *The Interpretation of Dreams* he wrote in a spirit of confession:

> I had actually been following in Hannibal's footsteps. Like him, I had been fated not to see Rome; and he too had moved into the Campagna when everyone had expected him in Rome. But Hannibal, whom I had come to resemble in these respects, had been the favourite hero of my later school days. Like so many boys of that age, I had sympathised in the Punic Wars not with the Romans but with the Carthaginians. And when in the higher classes I began to understand for the first time what it means to belong to an alien race, and anti-Semitic feelings among the other boys warned me that I must take up a definite position, the figure of the Semitic general rose still higher in my esteem. To my youthful mind Hannibal and Rome symbolised the conflict between the tenacity of Jewry and the organisation of the Catholic Church.

Hannibal's father, Hamilcar Barca, made his boy swear he would take vengeance on the Romans. If Hamilcar had had a hat, the Roman who dared knock it off his head would have found a sword down his throat. Freud wrote that Hannibal had had a place in his fantasies. For Hannibal, Rome meant the capital of the Empire; for Freud, Rome meant the captital of the Catholic Church, which often humiliated the Jews. In December 1897, Freud told Wilhelm Fliess, 'My longing for Rome is, by the way, deeply neurotic.'

After four years of self-analysis, Freud finally overcame his resistances. Jones reports this visit rather grandly, saying Freud 'triumphantly entered Rome', as if Sigmund marched into the city with a band of armed analysts. In fact, Freud and his younger brother, Alexander, travelled by the overnight train from Vienna and got a cab to the Hotel Eden much like ordinary tourists. One of the tourists was very excited. 'The visit was a high point of my life,' Freud wrote to Fliess. Freud was about to see a work of art he had studied in detail in photographs for years.

If you walk up the hill that overlooks the Colosseum, you snake up through lanes leading past a magnificent yellowing building, the School of Engineering of Rome University. Beyond the school, the lane opens out on to a modest piazza, but the church that dominates the piazza is anything but modest. The entrance of San Pietro in Vincoli, St Peter in Chains, is protected by a set of wrought-iron gates. Inside, the church is dramatically white, supported on each side by 10 white marble columns. The columns lead the eye to what looks like a giant four-poster bed, the baldachin, which covers the altar.

Lavish paintings and sculptures decorate the walls; there is a particularly macabre skull and a strange sculpture of a lobster. Just in front of the baldachin, a few steps lead down to a small alcove. This is what the devout come to see: a box which holds the chains that held St Peter. The chains gleam; no rust has ever tarnished them.

The chains are not the most remarkable of the trophies in the church. An alcove to the right houses a huge monument with seven life-size statues. There are marbles of Pope Julius II lying down, as well as of the Old Testament heroines Rachel and Leah. In the middle is a magnificent, imposing *Moses* by Michelangelo. This statue is more than life-size; *Moses* measures 2.35 metres. He is seated and holding the tablets of the law God gave him on Mount Sinai, his beard a spectacular flowing tangle of locks. The prophet looks slightly manic, partly due to the fact that two horns protrude from his head. According to Exodus 34:29–35, Moses had *karan* or 'rays on the skin of his face' because he was bathed in the Divine Light. The Hebrew is ambiguous, though. *Karan* can be translated either as 'radiated [light]' or 'grew horns'.

Michelangelo felt *Moses* was his most lifelike creation. According to one tradition, when he finished it, the sculptor hit the right knee and said, 'Now speak!' A scar on the statue's knee is thought to be the mark Michelangelo made with his hammer.

The tomb of Pope Julius II was designed for St Peter's Basilica in the Vatican and was supposed to contain 40 statues, but there were cash-flow issues as the rebuilding of St Peter's ran over budget. The negotiations about the size of the tomb took years. Finally, in 1542, Michelangelo agreed to reduce his 40 sculptures to seven. As a result, *Moses* dominates the structure even more.

Freud had read and reread Vasari's *Buonarroti Life of Michelangelo*, which was published in 1568. Vasari described the statue wonderfully:

Michelangelo finished the Moses in marble, a statue of five braccia, unequalled by any modern or ancient work. Seated in a serious attitude, he rests with one arm on the tables, and with the other holds his long glossy beard, the hairs, so difficult to render in sculpture, being so soft and downy that it seems as if the iron chisel must have become a brush. The beautiful face, like that of a saint and mighty prince, seems as one regards it to need the veil to cover it, so splendid and shining does it appear, and so well has the artist presented in the marble the divinity with which God had endowed that holy countenance. The Jews still go every Saturday in troops to visit and adore it as a divine, not a human thing.

Freud found this last phrase interesting enough to underline it in his guidebook. The statue awed him and sometimes he 'crept cautiously out of the half-gloom of the interior as though I myself belonged to the mob', by which he meant the mob of rebellious Jews who exasperated Moses by dancing round the Golden Calf. Freud expected to see it 'start up on its raised foot, dash the Tablets of Stone to the Ground and let fly its wrath'.

Michelangelo caught Moses just before he gets up to smash the tablets, Freud argued. The marble is alive with tension. The prophet stares to one side; the veins on his hands bulge. Freud went beyond Exodus, however. He claimed that Moses manages to control his anger and stop the tablets of the law slipping from his grasp. So when he did smash the tablets, he was in control of himself. That was an achievement to salute, as Exodus paints the prophet as a man given to anger and even violence.

Freud visited Rome seven more times after 1901. He usually stayed at the Hotel Eden and he seems to have had no problems in going back to the city. The last visit he made was in 1923 with his daughter Anna.

It would take Freud 13 years after his first visit to publish any of his ideas on Moses and then he did so anonymously. The paper was published in *Imago*, a psychoanalytic journal Freud controlled. There was even some effort to suggest the writer was not an analyst. The paper is a response to a great statue rather than an attempt to put Michelangelo's masterpiece in any analytic context; it reads more like art history.

One writer, Patrick Mahony, argues that Jones was rather cavalier in failing to explore why Freud identified so deeply with Moses. A great dream interpreter like Freud would, one might expect, identify rather with either Joseph or Daniel, the Bible's main dream diviners. But there was one key difference between Moses and these other two: Moses encountered God face to face and spoke with Him, not in a dream but on top of Mount Sinai.

In her sometimes obscure book *From Oedipus to Moses*, Marthe Robert argues that Freud was battling with his ambivalent feelings about his father. Jacob was not the strong father a clever boy was entitled to expect, so Freud looked for nobler father figures, picked some choice ones – and identified with them.

Carl Jung: The Crown Prince

Five years after he set foot in Rome, Freud met the most important of his disciples. Since Jung would ally himself with the Nazis and play a dishonourable role in Freud's last years, their tangled history needs to be told in brief.

Carl Gustav Jung was the son of a pastor in the Swiss Reformed Church. He studied medicine at Basle University and went to work under one of the great psychiatrists of the time, Eugen Bleuler at the Burghölzli Hospital, a major clinic in Zurich. Jung read Freud's *The Interpretation of Dreams* soon after it was published and it inspired him to devise the Word Association Test. Subjects were shown a card with a word on it and then had to produce an association.

The words might be neutral, like the colour RED, or have some emotional charge, like MOTHER. Subjects responded differently to neutral and emotional words. Sometimes they hesitated or were slow in producing the association. Jung attached his subjects to a galvanometer to measure the electrical resistance of the skin and watched where the needle peaked. A spike in electrical activity when someone was asked to associate to the name 'Mary', for example, showed the psychiatrist that there was something to investigate about what Mary meant to them. Delays or hesitations in producing associations suggested where the psychiatrist should probe. The 'psycho galvanometer', as Jung called it, was like those instruments prospectors used to locate buried treasure.

In 1906 Jung sent his work to Freud, who then sent Jung in return a collection of his latest essays. These exchanges marked the beginning of an intense correspondence and collaboration. Jung and Freud agreed on many issues; both believed that below the conscious mind there is another realm, that of the psyche, which both men called the unconscious.

By 1907 Freud had decided that Jung was to be his successor, even calling him his 'son and heir'. He told Jung that he was Joshua, who would enter the Promised Land – a privilege Moses had not been allowed. Both analysts saw themselves as prophets and neither could be said to suffer from low self-esteem. Ultimately, their relationship was doomed; only one ego could survive.

There were two critical moments. The first was when Freud fainted after he had bested Jung in an argument (it must be said that Freud had a tendency to faint). The causes of such behaviour went back a long way. On 3 October 1897 Freud wrote to Wilhelm Fliess about one of his insights during self-analysis: 'I greeted my one-year-younger brother' – he meant Julius – 'with adverse wishes and genuine childhood jealousy; and his death left the germ of [self-]reproaches in me.' Freud told Jones that all his fainting attacks 'could be traced to the effect on him of his young brother's death'. The young Sigmund had unconsciously wanted his little brother Julius to die because his mother loved the baby so much. And Julius did die. That death was Freud's first triumph. Any other triumph, like besting Jung in an argument, inevitably brought back unconscious guilty memories the death of Julius had aroused. The stress made him faint and the only reason he fainted was that he had proved Jung wrong. Jones accepted Freud's explanation without question.

There are simpler explanations, however. One is that Freud felt some homosexual attraction for his Swiss colleague and was embarrassed by that. A second is that he hated giving up the least shred of control or authority, which is precisely what Jung craved. Jung was a dominant personality too. To avoid a final battle, Freud fainted.

The second critical moment took place in 1909, when Jung sailed with Freud to America to attend the 20th anniversary celebrations of Clark University in Worcester, Massachusetts. Freud had been invited to make a key-note speech. As they travelled, Jung told Freud his dreams, which Freud duly analysed. Jung felt that since he had trusted Freud with these dreams, Freud should repay the trust and tell Jung his own dreams. But Freud refused to do so. No one would get the founder of psychoanalysis lying down on the couch to reveal his dreams. He'd done that already in print, where he could be in total control.

Far from being wonderfully mature, as Jones claimed, Freud reacted neurotically to any challenge to his authority, according to Jung. From then on, the two medicine men were at war. Freud expected an apology for Jung's impertinence; Jung did not think he had any reason to apologise. Disagreements about the importance of sex fuelled the tensions. For Jung, Freud stressed sex too much as a cause of neurosis. For Freud, Jung was a repressed Swiss Protestant who could not admit the importance of sex because the Christian tradition demonised the body. Sex within marriage is a gift from God for Jews, but some Christian saints went to extraordinary lengths to avoid contact with women – Simeon Stylites, to take one example, did so by spending years on top of a pillar. The letters between Freud and Jung became formal and bitter.

In May 1914 Jung resigned as the chairman of the International Psychoanalytic Association. The two men never spoke again and did not even exchange a letter. The rift was to have serious consequences 20 years later, when the Nazis came to power.

CHAPTER 4

Sex, Children and Family Secrets

Freud grew up in an extended family where there were jealousies and complex emotions. Leslie Adams, we have seen, claimed Freud had some sort of phantasy of his brother being his father. Marianne Krüll suggested his mother may have had an affair with his other half-brother. Both these are huge claims.

We are probably on firmer ground when it comes to a relationship between Freud and his sister-in-law Minna. After her fiancé died, she lived with her sister and Freud; she had never known a man. Consciously or unconsciously, Freud recreated a situation which resembled his stepfamily life when he had been a child. Minna lived with the Freuds from 1892 until her death. Her bedroom was next to the marital one and Paula Fichtl offered the morsel that to get to Minna's bedroom it was necessary to walk through that of her sister and brother-in-law.

The 'passionate side of marriage', as Jones put it, declined for Freud, and Jones did not hint at any sexual relationship with Minna. Soon after Minna moved in with Freud and his wife, however, Freud was thinking and dreaming of sex day and night as he started to write *The Interpretation of Dreams*. If Freud dreamed forbidden dreams of Minna – and he would hardly have been the first brother-in-law to do that – he did not write about them publicly. One of the most intriguing passages in Harry Freud's notes claims that Freud and Minna took a holiday by themselves in the early 1920s in Bad Gastein. Harry recounts this without drawing any inferences.

Freud was almost proud that his theory of the Oedipus Complex had first been dramatised by Sophocles. Sophocles knew it was a hugely powerful myth, but he was a teller of tales, not a finder of facts. So he deduced nothing from it, just as Shakespeare deduced nothing from Hamlet, who was as Oedipal as it is possible to be. Both stories haunted Freud all his life.

Oedipus arrives in Thebes as the city is being ravaged by plague. King Laius has been murdered. The Oracle says that the plague will not cease until someone solves the riddle of the Sphinx: 'What walks on four legs, then on two, then on three?' The answer is a human being, for a baby crawls on all fours, an adult stands on two legs and then, when old, uses a third leg in the form of a walking stick.

Oedipus solves the riddle, the plague vanishes and he is crowned king in place of Laius; he also marries the king's widow, Jocasta. Twelve years later, the plague returns and Oedipus determines to find out why. The blind seer Tiresias finally announces that Oedipus himself is the problem, as it was he who killed Laius. Jocasta now admits to Oedipus (apparently for the first time in their 12 years of marriage – clearly they did not talk much) how it was foretold that her son would kill his father and have children by his mother. To prevent such a calamity, she gave her baby son to a trusted servant and ordered him to leave the child exposed to the elements to die. But instead he was found and brought up by a shepherd. Oedipus had left Corinth to avoid killing the man he thought was his father, but he cannot avoid his destiny. In a fight, he kills King Laius, without knowing that Laius was his real father, and marries his mother, again without knowing her true identity. The end is appalling: Jocasta hangs herself, while before going into exile Oedipus puts out his eyes. This was symbolic of castration, Freud argued.

Oedipus did what every child unconsciously wants to do, Freud said, but he did not link this with another telling story, that of Lot and his daughters in the Bible – a perfect illustration of the Electra complex. Lot's daughters come with him out of the land of Zo'ar and settle in a cave. Genesis: 28–30 go on:

> And the first-born said to the younger, 'Our father is old, and there is not a man on earth to come in to us after the manner of all the earth. Come, let us make our father drink wine, and we will lie with him, that we may preserve offspring through our father.'

So the girls made Lot drunk. The first night his elder daughter lay with him, the second night his younger daughter. Drink did not make Lot impotent and he managed to father children on each of his girls without remembering any of the proceedings. Sodom and Gomorrah were razed because they were so sexually immoral, but no one is punished for this incest; Genesis never explains why. Both Lot's daughters give birth to sons. The son of his elder daughter is named Moab and Genesis adds, 'he is the father of the Moabites to this day'. The younger daughter's son 'is the father of the Ammonites to this day'. Just as Oedipus never talked to Jocasta about exactly where Laius had been murdered, Genesis does not tell us if Lot and his daughters ever discussed what had happened. The ancients were splendidly unconscious about their lack of inhibitions.

Oedipus and Lot's daughters reveal the psychological reality. Below consciousness, the id bubbles with primeval passions and we are all father killers and mother fuckers and, in the case of Lot's daughters, father fuckers. But we can't admit it to ourselves. As Freud noted: 'When I insist to one of my patients on the frequency of Oedipus dreams in which the dreamer has sexual intercourse with his own mother, he often replies, "I have no recollection of having had any such dream."'

These denials could not last long, because the Oedipal impulse was so powerful. Oedipal material kept forcing its way through the denials and defences. The conscious mind screened, censored, softened, deceived, fiddled, faddled and fudged, but it could not change the raw truths of the unconscious. 'Disguised dreams of sexual intercourse with the dreamer's mother are many times more frequent than straightforward ones,' Freud claimed.

But he knew that suggesting that his patients dreamed of committing incest with their parents did not endear psychoanalysis to the public, so he had the good sense to offer some independent evidence when he gave his lecture at Clark University in 1909.

Freud quoted a study of 2,500 observations of infants made by Sanford Bell and published in the *American Journal of Psychology* in 1902. Bell, who taught at Clark University himself, wrote, 'The emotion of sex love…does not make its appearance for the first time at the period of adolescence as has been thought.'

In Freud's opinion:

He [Bell] says of the signs by which this amorous condition manifests itself: 'The unprejudiced mind, in observing these manifestations in hundreds of children, cannot escape referring them to sex origin. The most exacting mind is satisfied when to these observations are added the confessions of those who have as children experienced the emotion to a marked degree of intensity, and whose memories of childhood are relatively distinct.'

He added that sceptics 'will be most astonished to hear that among those children who fell in love so early not a few are of the tender ages of three, four, and five years'. He also said that, as Bell was an American, 'it would not be surprising if you should believe the observations of a fellow-countryman rather than my own'.

Freud told his audience that some important psychiatrists, such as Eugen Bleuler, who ran the Burghölzli Hospital, 'said a few years ago openly that he faced my sexual theories incredulous and bewildered, and since that time by his own observations had substantiated them in their whole scope'. Doctors ignored this area because they had 'forgotten their own infantile sexual activity under the pressure of education for civilisation and do not care to be reminded now of the repressed material'. His audience should analyse their own dreams, which would soon lead them to 'an interpretation of your own childhood memories' simmering with sexual thoughts. The audience was more impressed than shocked.

Though Freud received an honorary doctorate and met great figures like the philosopher and psychologist William James, author of *The Varieties of Religious Experience*, he did not take to America. It was almost a visceral reaction. Freud blamed rich American food for intestinal troubles which had, in fact, started long before he set foot in the country. 'I often said to myself,' he once wrote, 'that whoever is not master of his Konrad should not set out on travels.' Konrad was the nickname he used for his bowels. The Americans had no understanding of the need for public toilets. Freud suffered from prostate troubles by 1909 and had to urinate often. But in America men were expected to have heroic bladders: 'They escort you along miles of corridors, and ultimately you are taken to the basement, where a marble palace awaits you – only just in time.' Freud never seems to have forgotten how uncomfortable not finding a convenient toilet could be. Or forgiven it.

A Treasure Trove of Family Letters

Given the amount of material which the Freud Archives have restricted, it is fortunate perhaps that some interesting material was not originally controlled by the archives. The John Rylands Library of the University of Manchester was given 248 letters, postcards and telegrams in 1958 after the death of Poppy Hartwig, the daughter of Emanuel Freud. I intend to call this branch of the family the Lancashire Freuds. The letters were written by Sigmund Freud to Poppy Hartwig's brother, Sam or Solomon Freud. Both were the children of Sigmund's half-brother Emanuel Freud, who had moved from Vienna to Manchester in 1860. He and his full brother, Philipp, had a memorable telegraphic address: Freud Manchester. Emanuel returned to Vienna a number of times. In 1900 Freud told Wilhelm Fliess that when Emanuel came to Vienna, 'He brought with him a real air of refreshment because he is a marvellous man, vigorous and mentally indefatigable despite his sixty-eight or sixty-nine years, who has always meant a great deal to me.' In 1908 Freud went back to Manchester to see Emanuel.

The letters between Sam and Freud reveal many interesting aspects of Freud, his affection for his complicated extended family and his worries about money, as well as nice trivia such as his fondness for cheese. Sam's German was not very good and Freud seems to have been quite happy to write to him in English. His use of the language was surprisingly free of mistakes. Crucially, these letters – and Sam's replies – also provide information about Freud's secret bank accounts. Sigmund Freud Copyrights were unaware for some time that these letters existed and so could not stop scholars consulting them. The letters to Sam date from 1914; the last one was written in 1938. Many of the issues that would concern Freud in his last years come up in these letters.

When I went to examine this material, I was told I was only the second person to ask to see it for as long as the librarian could remember. This is strange given the volumes and volumes of Freud scholarship. I kick myself because in 1982 I made a film for Channel 4 about English Jewry and much of that film was based around Manchester's Jewish community. Local historians never mentioned the fact that Freud's half-brothers had lived there. I suspect they just did not know; they certainly did not know of the correspondence in the university library. Ernest Jones, Freud's authorised biographer, knew of Sam Freud but never seems to have bothered to meet him, even though Sam lived just three hours away by train from London. One later author, Peter Gay, mentions the correspondence, but in a book of over 640 pages he has about eight sentences about it. Sam was, after all, neither a philosopher nor a psychiatrist but a cloth merchant. Snobbery would seem to have affected scholarship.

After Freud visited Manchester in 1875, Emanuel went to Vienna. There then seems to have been a long gap till Sam came to Vienna with his father, Emanuel, in 1900. Freud also spent four days in Manchester and Southport in 1908. He and Emanuel planned to go to the Isle of Man but the sea was too rough. Emanuel travelled down to London with him and they then crossed the Channel together.

Given that and Freud's liking for writing letters, it is hard to believe there were no letters written between 1876 and 1914. There is evidence that some other documents are missing. Leslie Adams, who was planning a biography of Freud, discovered that Emanuel Freud had taken out a British passport but the documents relating to this appear to have been lost. The archives at Manchester University have a photograph of two men who could be Freud's brothers in their thirties. One is dressed as an army officer and has a handlebar moustache; the other is wearing a kind of cowboy hat. Unfortunately the photographs are not properly labelled so it is not possible to be sure. Neither man is Sigmund Freud.

The first letter between Freud and his nephew Sam I have found dates from 1914. It does not start with an apology or a polite reason for resuming writing after years of silence. Freud had excellent manners – except when it came to dealing with some fellow analysts perhaps – and would have made some apology. Letters between Freud and his half-brothers may be restricted in the Library of Congress or, perhaps, not correctly catalogued under family correspondence. While at the library, I found two letters in the Harry Freud collection which had slipped into files where they should not have been.

The value of the letters to Sam is that Freud seemed able to say to his nephew things he could not say to analytic colleagues. They are quite emotional at times. In one of them, for example, he wrote that his son Martin was in some difficulties over his marriage as he had an 'unreasonable abnormal wife'. The material is a rich and untapped resource. It reveals a side of Freud that we do not often see: his pride in his family and his unhappiness about family tragedies. In one letter he tells Sam that there are many 'weak spots' in the family.

The letters also show frequent anxieties over money. In one of the first Freud talks about his family as Sam's 'poor relatives' because the 1914 war meant they lost so much. The letters also shed light on Freud's finances and especially on the secret bank accounts, which would become extremely important when Freud wanted to leave Vienna in 1938.

The first letter is dated 7 July 1914 and Freud had a very specific reason for writing. Anna was going to spend some time in England to learn the language better. Her father sent Sam £20 which she could draw on as she needed. 'I hope you will do the kindness to play the role of her banker,' he wrote. Sam agreed.

Freud added, 'I am glad to have learned by his handwriting that the great older man [which can only be Sam's father, Emanuel] – an old one I am myself – is unchanged and I hope that the ladies and your dear person are all right.' The ladies were Sam's aunts, who also lived in Manchester.

It was lucky the letter got through, because on 28 June the Archduke

Ferdinand was murdered in Sarajevo, starting the confusion of events which led to the First World War. In that war, the Freuds of Manchester and the Freuds of Vienna were, of course, on different sides.

Not long after this an event occurred which is still shrouded in mystery. The offices of Freud and Co. in Manchester were by then at 61 Bloom Street, in the middle of the textile district, and Emanuel had moved to Southport, an elegant suburb by the sea. He had not retired and still commuted to and from work. The tragedy took place on 17 October 1914. The following note appeared in the *Southport Guardian*:

> On Saturday afternoon just as an express train from Manchester to Southport passed Parbold station, it was noticed that one of the carriage doors had opened and a man lay on the line. He had apparently fallen out of the train in which he had been travelling alone. He was dead when he was picked up. He was identified as Emanuel Freud aged 82, residing at 21 Albert Road Southport.

Parbold today is still a small village. The railway station is tiny and next to a level crossing. The platform is not long enough for a train of more than three carriages. It is just possible that Emanuel opened the door thinking there would be a platform there and fell out on to the track, but he made the journey every day. He must have known the platform was short.

Jones mentions Emanuel's death but says nothing about the circumstances. It is hard to escape the conclusion that one reason was that Jones did not want to draw attention to the surprising number of unexplained and suspicious deaths, as well as breakdowns, in the Freud family between 1915 and 1930.

Freud just said to Sam 'your father died leaving the train'. Emanuel was 82 years old. Their father, Jacob, had died at 81. The timing of these deaths made Freud believe he would reach at the very most 80 or 81 years of age. He never raised the topic of how Emanuel had died again.

Emanuel died just as the First World War started. Hermann, Freud's nephew, was killed in action in 1917. Freud's sons fought in the war and saw the horrors. Some doctors who were analysts went to the front to treat casualties. Like many Austrians, the Freuds went hungry and were grateful for food parcels. Some were sent by Max Eitington, a wealthy analyst who helped Freud and his family in many practical ways during the hard times of the 1914–18 war.

The war made Freud rethink one of his ideas. The slaughter of millions in the trenches made him realise that the libido, the life-giving, life-making pleasure principle, was not the only motive for human behaviour. The libido had a dark mirror image, the Nirvana principle or death instinct, as it has come to be called. Life is hard. We want to stop struggling, so we escape into sex, drugs and booze, lose ourselves in books and movies, or sleep. At the most extreme, we flirt with suicide, and every year thousands of human beings do just that. Apart from lemmings, we seem to be the only species capable of self-slaughter.

The war made it impossible for the correspondence with Sam to continue and the next letter in the archive is dated 27 October 1919. Freud described the difficult situation in Vienna and mentioned that the fall in the value of money had hit 'the middle class and those who earn their living by intellectual work' particularly hard. A month later Freud announced that his son Martin had got married – 'a courageous deed in these times' – and also that they were freezing since it was impossible to get coal. Sam asked if there was anything he could do.

Bureaucracy was the problem, Freud explained. One needed a permit to receive parcels and he had not 'procured one because I have not the time to procure it'. The customs procedure was very slow and tedious. 'My time at least is still precious,' he said. Sam replied that he was 'deeply pained' to hear of the privations Freud faced in Vienna.

In January 1920 Freud told Sam, 'I assure you it is not money we are in need of, we have plenty of this bad stuff, and good sterling money cannot be brought here by post.' On the 20th there was a tragedy. Freud's second daughter, Sophie, died of pneumonia. Martha was distraught. Sophie was 27 years old, had been happily married and left two sons. Freud knew Sam would feel for the family 'in our mourning'. Sam replied that he remembered meeting Sophie in 1910 and he did not know what to say; he could imagine nothing worse.

It is a little shocking that three weeks later Freud was thinking about tailor-made suits, but bereavement can have curious effects. His next letter, dated 15 February 1920, reveals Freud the sharp dresser. He needed a new suit, according to his wife, and managed to send his nephew £4 to buy him the cloth. Martha wanted him to have a 'salt and pepper' suit or a 'tete de negre'. Freud also lamented that you could send anything to Vienna except tobacco. He had another source for that, a young cavalry officer who had analytic ambitions.

The letter also introduced a theme which would recur often during the next 20 years. Freud said he might visit Manchester again. 'I am assured of a good reception in England were I to come over but business is very brisk now and you will have to wait,' he wrote. In a separate letter to Sam, Freud's daughter Anna asked if Sam might be able to send her six tennis balls as she and her cousin wanted to learn the game. She wrote to him three weeks later to say that the convoluted bureaucracy had failed to provide the permit to allow the balls into the country. Anna apologised to Sam for putting him to the trouble.

On 22 April Freud told Sam of another family marriage. His third son, Ernst, was engaged to a 'Jewish girl of good family'. Also Eli Bernays, the father of Edward Bernays, was coming to Vienna. Freud added that Sam's 'pa', as he called Emanuel, would have made the crossing to Austria to see Eli. In November there was cheerful news. A niece who called herself Tom was marrying a clever Hebrew scholar, Jankele Seidmann. That would not turn out well, however. ·

In the letters, Freud often refers to his reputation: 'As for me you know I have a big name and plenty of work but I cannot gain enough and am eating up my reserves.' The economic situation in Vienna was 'so bad'. The economic prospects for psychoanalysis became even worse when one of Freud's first benefactors died. Austrians might need therapy but there was no way they could afford to pay for it.

Sam asked what food they needed, because he could send parcels of provisions. Freud was not too proud to reply that they needed 'corned beef, cocoa, English tea cakes and cheese'. He was very fond of good cheese and was dismayed that it could not be found.

In a letter of 15 October Freud said he had hoped to come to Manchester, as he had to attend a congress in The Hague and it would be easy to get a ferry from there. At the last minute, however, Freud sent Sam a telegram from the Hotel Paulez to say he would not be coming as there had been another death. Morris, whose name was sometimes written as Moritz or even Maurice, was the husband of Mitzi and so Freud's brother-in-law and distant cousin. He had a weak heart, had recovered from a period of heart strain but, it seems, then killed himself. Money was the cause, Freud suspected. Morris had been unable to pay his debts. Freud had to return to Berlin to console his sister and her children. It saddened Freud to cancel the trip to The Hague because 'it was an opportunity to come to Britain which is not likely to recur soon'.

Sam replied tersely, just saying 'Poor Maurice, it is all very sad.' His own business was going through hard times, because the price of cotton had fallen so much. A few weeks later, on 5 November 1920, Freud worried about how Sam might have taken some of his talk about his reputation. He did not want his nephew to think he was arrogant: 'I am anxious that you could misconstrue my question about my renown in England; I wanted to know how much of the noise has reached your quiet home. Popularity is utterly indifferent to me, it must be considered at the best a danger for more serious achievements.'

On 22 July 1921 Freud felt bothered by how much he was costing his nephew. He told Sam he had ordered the Bank of Lipman and Rosenthal in Holland to send £8 to pay for some of the provisions Sam had sent. This is the first specific mention of the foreign bank accounts which would play such a big part in Freud's last years. Till now, no one has been able to trace when Freud first set them up or why.

One parcel of cheese had been 'spoilated' – in these letters Freud sometimes seems to have enjoyed himself making deliberate mistakes in English – and he hoped his nephew would be able to get some of the insurance monies. As a result of being 'spoilated', the all-important cheese had developed mould. The picture of Freud slicing the mould off the much desired cheese is touching. Since Freud scholarship can be obsessed with minutiae, I better admit I am unable to say what kind of cheese it was that had become mouldy. But thanks to Fichtl's recipes, we know that Freud liked cheese soufflé.

Freud could reimburse Sam for the provisions because 'I have somewhat recovered by the treatment of foreign patients and am in possession of a deposit of good money in The Hague.' He was treating patients in English most of the time and it made him aware that he should have learned the language better. Life in his apartment with his wife was depressing. 'We live together, old people in a big dwelling. Grandma is very old.' It was upsetting that Morris had left a financial muddle after his suicide: 'The conditions in Berlin after Morris' death are so intricate that nobody can see how rich or rather how poor they are.' And he and Martha were suffering – a nice phrase – 'the whims of old age'.

Freud asked Sam to give his love to all his Manchester family and then added, 'Are they aware that my name in the world at large and in England too is far more respectable than riches?' Shortly after, Freud again reassured his nephew, 'I am accumulating money in Amsterdam and can send you from there any amount you spend for me.' He regretted not to have come over to England, as he had been expected in Cambridge, 'where they take great interest in my work'.

Sam often told his uncle how proud they were of him. He had seen a poem about Freud and Jung in *Punch* and an article in a magazine called *Jack London*. Some of the material was not flattering, but Sam does not seem to have realised that. D.H. Lawrence, who later wrote *Lady Chatterley's Lover*, published a small book called *Psychoanalysis and the Unconscious* in which he made fun of Freud's ideas. Lawrence was exuberantly rude. 'Oh, damn the miserable baby with its complicated ping-pong table of an unconscious,' he wrote. If children were inclined to be in love with their parents, parents should not encourage them too much:

> Oh, parents, see that your children get their dinners and clean sheets, but don't love them. Don't love them one single grain, and don't let anybody else love them. Give them their dinners and leave them alone. You've already loved them to perdition. Now leave them alone, to find their own way out.

Shortly afterwards, James Thurber and E.B. White published a wonderful satire called *Six Day Bicycle Riding as a Sex Substitute*. The title says it all: pedalling was even better than masturbation. Thurber poked fun at Freud over the next 20 years. He wrote spoof reviews of books brimming with daft therapeutic advice. He reserved special barbs for *Be Glad You're Neurotic*, *How to Worry Successfully* and *Growing into Life*. Millions of Americans were psychologically blocked and didn't understand the Science of Happiness. Thurber knew the jargon of analysis and joked that, for most wives, the latent content of their husbands' minds was manifest enough – especially at breakfast. He made fun of an analyst called Louis E. Bisch, who suggested that people like 'Mr. C', who got run over, had unconscious motives. Sexual hunger made 'Mr. C' leap out in front of automobiles, which, Thurber mocked, 'unquestionably have sex significance'. His satires in the *New Yorker* show how influential psychoanalysis had become in the 1920s and 1930s.

What Thurber would have written if he had been aware of Freud's cigar addiction is delicious to imagine.

The Cigar is a Nipple

In the Freud Museum in London, a mummified half-smoked cigar perches on the lip of an ashtray on one of the landings. It is a Montecristo but of less gargantuan size than the cigars Churchill smoked. Tobacco was an indispensable prop to Freud as he worked; he wrote and smoked, smoked and wrote. In 1920 Freud offered his nephew Harry a cigarette and a lecture: 'My boy, smoking is one of the greatest and cheapest enjoyments in life, and if you decide in advance not to smoke, I can only feel sorry for you.'

Freud often got through 20 cigars a day and was unwell if he did not have his daily nicotine. Even after he was diagnosed with cancer of the jaw, he continued to smoke. Without cigars his writing would not flow and he made no effort to stop.

Jones never asked why Freud smoked. A conventional analytic interpretation would be that cigars and cigarettes are 'nipple substitutes'. A man who can't do without them is fixated at the oral – which is the most infantile – level of development. Freud wrote that the pleasure he got from being in the company of his daughter Anna could be compared to the pleasure he got from smoking a good cigar. As a cigar is a rather obvious phallic symbol as well as a nipple substitute, this was a truly odd statement for a father to make. Jones did not mention this comment, however, let alone attempt any analytic interpretation. If he had done, he would have had to raise the bizarre issue of whether, at some symbolic level, Freud saw his own daughter as a nipple!

But there were more serious issues.

Untimely Deaths

Often in his letters to Sam, Freud mixed in more conventional family news. 'I am sorry to hear that Ma is losing her sight,' he consoled. His own mother, whom he called 'Grandma', was nearly deaf. 'There is no blessing in old age. I am ready to resign my claim on the longevity of our family,' he said stoically.

Families were all about growth and decay, like plants, a comparison that 'old Homer' had made. If 'Grandma' was ageing, Alexander's son was doing well. This is the first mention of Harry, who was then twenty-five years old. 'Harry is growing nicely. He is good and clever,' Freud told Sam. Harry was also learning the joys of smoking from his uncle. But Alexander was often very depressed, because he had lost so much money after the war.

There was no good political news, Freud complained to Sam. 'You will have gathered from the papers how desperate our public conditions are.' However, he went on, 'As long as I continue working I am sure to be free of financial cares.'

The Freud finances were being kept in good order by his British and American patients. On 25 July 1921 he told Sam, 'I listen and—' Unusually, Freud's next word is hard to read. It looks like 'talk', though Freud has missed out the cross on the t, so it looks at first like 'lick'. Those to whom he listened were 'Englishers four to five hours a week'. Freud knew that

'Englishers' was not the right word, but it was part of his game of using some inappropriate words: 'I will never learn the d—d language correctly.'

The family then had more devastating bad news. Freud's sister Pauline had to face the tragedy that her only daughter, Rose, who was 25 years old, had suffered 'a nervous collapse' and had to be sent to an asylum. So a year after his daughter had died and his brother-in-law committed suicide, Freud had to cope with the fact that his niece was committed. Freud seems not to have intervened, perhaps because he thought 'Rose was gifted but half crazy'. It is slightly shocking to find Freud using such slang.

There is a particularly sad sentence in one of Freud's letters. He had gone to Hamburg to see Sophie's widower and his two small sons. He held Heinz, the baby, 'all that is left of Sophie'.

One recurring theme is money. Freud commented on the mood in Vienna, where 'the general depression is felt in every household'. He was clearly never quite able to relax about money, even when he had plenty of patients. One difficulty was that Austrians still could not afford analysis. 'I can earn foreign money and am free of cares,' he told Sam. The wider family was still 'dependent on Eli', who had gone into advertising and sales and was now doing so well in New York.

The fees patients paid made it possible for Freud to arrange for Sam to get some money again. He was always nagging his nephew to ask how much he had cost him. Eventually Sam said that he had spent £40 on provisions and had received £12. It did not matter. Nevertheless, on 27 December 1921 Freud told his nephew he had sent him £28 through James Strachey, who translated many of Freud's books. The Manchester files include a letter from Strachey in which he confirms that he has sent Sam a cheque for £28. Sam joked to his uncle, 'your credit is good'.

Throughout, Sam does not seem to have asked Freud for anything, but now he wanted him to check the value of some old Austrian bonds he had found among his father's things. Their value was tiny and realising them meant going through much bureaucracy, Freud learned. It would hardly be worth it because, at most, they would produce a few schillings.

One of the reasons Freud sent the £28 becomes clear in a letter of 5 February 1922. He asked Sam if he could send him a pair of strong boots: 'My feet are normally configured but when I tried a new pair bought in Vienna I spoiled them. Nothing good can be obtained here.' Three months later, on 13 May, Freud told Sam he had an account at yet another bank, the Bank of Lissa and Korn in The Hague. He could send him some money from there to reimburse him for the cost of the boots.

Six months later Freud had to tell Sam about another suicide. His favourite niece, Cäcilie, had had an unhappy love affair and become pregnant. 'The poor girl was passionate, yet obstinate, and very secluded so we don't know what the exact motive is,' he wrote. It did not help that she could not call on her family in the crisis as they were on holiday out of Vienna. She could not face the shame and took an overdose of Veronal, dying on 18 August 1922. Sam replied that it was 'a pitiable ending'.

Freud had some consolation, life in the midst of death. He was very moving in describing how he adored his small grandson, Sophie's second son, Heinz, who was a 'charming devil of a boy'.

On 14 December Freud wrote, 'I am still earning foreign money.' He was doing that even though Vienna was 'left quiet and lonely. All eyes are turned to Germany and the impending collapse there.' He had ordered three new volumes of the *Encyclopaedia Britannica* because they were the ones in which 'psychoanalysis is first fully mentioned'.

Another relative was now causing concern. Lucy, the daughter of Freud's sister Anna and the bankrupt turned millionaire Eli Bernays, was 'as crazy and unreliable as ever', Freud told Sam. Good news followed bad and, seven weeks later, he announced that his second son, Oliver, was getting married and that he had another grandson, Lucian. Lucian Freud would become, of course, one of the major artists of the 20th century. 'You may wonder what a thriving tribe we are,' Freud rejoiced on 9 February 1923. He was perhaps accentuating the positive to convince and colsole himself after the deaths and suicides.

The optimism was short-lived. A few months later, Freud had to announce another untimely death, that of his grandson Heinz: 'The boy was the cleverest sweetest child I have met.' He wrote more about this death than about any other apart from the death of his father, once saying that Heinz was the last person he had fallen in love with. The news about his own health was poor too: he had to have a growth removed from his soft palate.

The year saw another family tragedy, though one that affected Freud less. His nephew Theodor or Teddy, the son of Mitzi, drowned while bathing in Berlin. 'The mother bears it with silent resignation,' Freud wrote to Sam. The toll Freud had had to cope with in six years included a death in combat, two suicides and two accidental deaths, as well as the death of his daughter and his grandson.

Six months later, Freud referred to the Nazis for the first time. 'The situation in Berlin is a very threatening one,' he told Sam. In 1923 Hitler tried to stage a putsch in Munich. He failed and was sent to jail, where he was kept in luxurious conditions. He used the time to dictate *Mein Kampf*, in which he set out his philosophy and his anti-Semitic programme. The famous philosopher Martin Heiddeger joined the Nazi Party 18 months later. Hitler's colleague Hermann Goering, who had been a famous pilot in the Luftwaffe during the 1914–18 war, was less lucky. He had to flee Germany and ended up addicted to morphine. Goering was placed in a lunatic asylum in Austria, often in a straitjacket. The experiences of Hitler and Goering, who had both been treated by psychiatrists, would play a part in the fortunes of analysis.

Freud told Sam that grieving for Heinz was still agonising. They had Heinz's elder brother staying with them but Freud 'did not find him a consolation to any amount'. He had bad medical news too, as he had not overcome the effects of his last operation to stem the cancer. His mouth hurt dreadfully, which made it agonising for him to swallow.

On 25 October 1923 Freud told Sam that, when he had returned from the sanatorium the day before, 'very much broken and enfeebled', it had cheered him to find his letter. The operation removed the greater part of the buccal mucous membrane and a skin graft was put in its place. Freud told Sam, 'If I recover and become movable to see all three of you would an enjoyment I would try to attain.'

Freud did not tell Sam the whole story. He was furious when he discovered that his physician, Felix Deutsch, and his surgeon, Markus Hajek, had not told him that cancer of the jaw had been found. By what right, he demanded to know, and at once dismissed them. For the next four years the only doctor he would see was his oral surgeon, Hans Pichler. Anna had to take on many nursing chores.

After the operation, Freud had to wear a prothesis in his mouth. It was painful but if he did not wear it he could not speak or eat properly. If he kept it in all the time it hurt, but if he took it out for long periods there was a serious risk that the device would shrink and not fit back properly. A small antiseptic room was set up in the apartment so that Anna – and it usually was Anna, unless she was travelling – could take it out, clean it and put it back every day. Freud always hoped someone would build a better prothesis. He could not write for a while with a pen and his letters are typed for the next six months. He told Sam that his speech 'may be impaired but my family and my patients say it is intelligible'.

Freud could not give up smoking, however. In the next 16 years, he had to have 30 operations to excise pre-cancerous lesions. He was lucky to have a brilliant and devoted surgeon who kept up to date with the latest technology. Nevertheless, 'the result was a life of endless torture,' Max Schur, his last doctor, noted in *Freud: Living and Dying*.

A second operation, Freud told Sam, had left him nearly drained of 'all confidence'. It had been costly too. 'I have lost a great deal of money, spent a great deal of money and expect to pay a high but well deserved fee to my physician,' he wrote on 19 December 1923. That physician was Pichler.

Freud had undergone another medical procedure on 17 November 1923, a peculiar 'rejuvenation' treatment which had a certain vogue in high society. An endocrinologist called Eugen Steinach had discovered the interstitial cells of the testicles produced the male sex hormones. Tying these sperm ducts up would atrophy the cells that produced the hormones. As cancer was thought to be the result of ageing, partly at least, rejuvenation treatment should help because it delayed the ageing process. The whole thing was, of course, a bizarre fantasy. Many years later, Max Schur asked Freud whose idea it was that he should go in for this treatment. His own idea, Freud insisted. He also revealed that he hoped it might revive his sexuality a little.

It is easy to offer a not very profound explanation. Freud had suffered two suicides as well as other deaths in his immediate family; he had been unable to help. He was trying to prolong his life and to feel more alive himself. Freud did not say anything to Sam about his sperm ducts.

Some family details were not covered by the letters. In 1923 Dorothy Burlingham, the granddaughter of the man who had founded the great jewellery store Tiffany's, came to Vienna. She wanted help for her four children. There is a touching photograph of her, a tall elegant woman, her hair parted in the middle, gazing down at a baby on her lap. She had married a surgeon called Robert Burlingham, but they often spent long periods apart as Robert stayed in America. He was depressed and the marriage was in deep trouble. Dorothy first met Anna because she wanted her to help her 'naughty' children. The two women became close friends. Anna introduced Dorothy to her father. Many Freudians deny the relationship between Anna and Dorothy ever became a sexual one. In any event, they were not the only apparently platonic lesbian couple Freud would be close to.

The next letter to Manchester asked how Sam's life had 'changed since Ma died'. At least her death was 'in time'. Eli Bernays, however, had died at the relatively young age of 61 after a sudden attack of appendicitis. He had left Vienna to escape his creditors but now his estate was worth $1 million. Freud wondered whether Eli had made any provisions 'for his indigent sisters for this time'.

Two days before his 68th birthday, on 6 May 1924, Freud was given the freedom of the city of Vienna. Sam congratulated him. Vienna might have a long history of anti-Semitism but it did now recognise one of its great Jews. This honour would make Freud feel all the more reluctant to leave the city.

On 21 August 1925 Freud's mother celebrated her 90th birthday. He rejoiced in her strength, but Minna was ill, he told Sam. Freud himself was approaching his 70th birthday. He felt rather inadequate compared to Grandpa, as he now called his own father, Jacob, who was 'journeying over the Continent after he was 70'. Freud was at least happy to note that he was 'considered a celebrity'. Jews all over the world were 'pairing me with Einstein. I have no reason to complain. After a long period of poverty I am earning money without hardship.'

Sam did not manage to come to Vienna for Freud's 70th birthday in May 1926, regretting that he could not leave Manchester. But if Sam could not make it, other relatives did. Perhaps the most interesting one who came to visit Freud was Edward Bernays, Eli's son. Edward arrived from New York to wish his famous uncle well. He was, Freud told Sam, 'a clever boy and a rich man and good natured but truly American'. Bernays was more than clever. If his uncle revolutionised psychiatry, Eli revolutionised public relations. After leaving Cornell University, he worked in the entertainment business. When he had to give a character reference for the famous tenor Enrico Caruso, Edward was asked what his profession was. He said 'counsel in public relations' and some historians say this was the first time anyone used the term 'public relations'. Edward had more serious ambitions than getting film stars on the front page. In his early twenties, he became a 'counsellor' to Woodrow Wilson. Edward founded the Committee on Public Information, which aimed to influence public opinion to support American participation in the First World War. A year before he came to visit Vienna, he published *Crystallizing Public Opinion*. Basing his views partly on his uncle's work, he wrote:

> If we understand the mechanism and motives of the group mind, is it not possible to control and regiment the masses according to our will without their knowing about it? The recent practice of propaganda has proved that it is possible, at least up to a certain point and within certain limits.

He called this scientific technique of opinion-moulding the 'engineering of consent'.

As historians have largely ignored the Manchester archive, they have not realised the influence Edward's visit may have had on one of Freud's last books. Bernays had been working for Woodrow Wilson and Freud was planning to write a book about the President with William Bullitt, an American diplomat whom he had treated and who had worked for the President. It seems likely that Freud discussed Woodrow Wilson with his clever nephew. He certainly discussed Wilson when Max Eastman came to interview him in 1926. As well as being a journalist, Eastman was a theorist of humour and had written a number of books on what made people laugh, a subject which always fascinated Freud. Eastman wrote a nice portrait of Freud at 70.

Crotchety Genius

The great man, one of twelve modern heroes interviewed, was smaller than Eastman had imagined. 'Slender limbed and more feminine apart from his nose' was how he described him. The Freud hooter looked 'as if somebody with brass knuckles had given him a good poke in the snoot'. In Freud's study the two men sparred about the state of America. Eastman joked that American intellectual leaders had stopped thinking at all.

'Why?' Freud asked.

'You know why people stop thinking,' Eastman said. 'It's because their thoughts would lead them where they don't want to go.'

That amused Freud and 'the whole of his gentleness came back including the delighted little crinkles at the corners of his eyes. He put his head back and laughed like a child.' Eastman added that Freud

> waggled his head and hands about all the time looking up at the ceiling and closing his eyes or making funny little pouts and wry faces when he was trying to think of a word or an idea. I never ceased feeling that underneath it all was an obdurate hard cranky streak but I also never ceased feeling his great charm.

Freud loved jokes and puns. He even revised his book on jokes when he was 72 years old. His interest was not just frivolous. As dreams did, jokes allowed dangerous taboo material to erupt into consciousness. Humour was like a blowtorch blasting its way through. Yet every portrait or picture of Freud shows him as a stern sage – never a man with a twinkle in his eyes or laugh. It is a shame no such picture was recorded for posterity.

Eastman asked why Freud hated America so much. A.A. Brill, who translated some of Freud's books, believed that Freud felt that he had not been well received during the 1909 visit.

'Hate America?' Freud said to Eastman. 'I don't hate America...I regret it.' He threw his head back and laughed hilariously. 'I regret that Columbus ever discovered it.'

Eastman laughed with Freud, a good journalistic move because that 'rather egged him on'. Freud went on say that America was an experiment that had gone bad.

'In what way bad?' Eastman asked.

'Oh, the prudery, the hypocrisy, the national lack of independence.'

Eastman countered that the young did show some spirit.

'Mostly among the Jews, isn't it?' Freud said.

'The Jews are not so free from prudery and hypocrisy,' Eastman replied.

To that Freud made no reply but changed the subject.

He even had a crack at John Watson, the founder of behaviourism. 'Perhaps you're a behaviourist? According to your John B. Watson, even consciousness does not exist. But that's just silly. Consciousness exists quite obviously and everywhere except perhaps in America.'

Finally Freud asked what Eastman's plans were. Eastman said he meant to write.

'I'll tell you what I want you to do,' Freud said. 'I want you to go home and write a book on America and I'll tell you what to call it. *Misgeburt.*'

He then paused and they debated how to translate the word properly. They rejected 'abortion' and then wondered about 'monster'.

Freud finally hit on the right word. 'The word is miscarriage. *The Miscarriage of American Civilisation* – that shall be the title of your book. That book will make you immortal. You may not be able to live in America any more, but you could go very happily and live elsewhere.' Freud laughed.

Eastman was delighted he had got a good quote.

Freud made Eastman promise to send him the book and said he would await it 'with happy memories of this conversation'.

Eastman returned to America and though he never published the book Freud had dreamed up for him, he did draw a vivid portrait of Freud at 70.

A Princess for a Patient

In 1926 Freud told Sam how proud he was of Anna, who was 'treating naughty American children, earning lots of money'. She had passed her 30th birthday and 'does not seem inclined to get married and who can say if her momentary interest will render her happy when she has to face life without her father'. The momentary interest seems to have been Freud's way of describing Anna's interest in child therapy.

Freud sent a proof copy of his 1925 *An Autobiographical Study*, which he inscribed specially for Sam (it is now in the John Rylands Library). Then, two months after he celebrated his 70th birthday, he wrote of his worries about his three sons: 'None of them can boast a satisfactory position or a good income.' Anna was the star among his children.

'Work is easier for me than enjoyment,' Freud told Sam on 28 July. But in these years some patients provided enjoyment too. A vital late relationship in Freud's life was that with Princess Marie Bonaparte, which started now. She was genuine royalty, as Napoleon had been her great-grandfather. Her paternal grandmother, Princess Pierre Bonaparte, was ruined at the time of the Paris Commune in 1871 but decided to restore her family fortune through an old aristocratic trick. She arranged for her son to marry an heiress whose father owned most of Monaco. The girl had money; the boy had class. Their only child, Marie, inherited a vast fortune.

A month after Marie was born, however, her mother died. Her father was not devoted, as he was more interested in glaciers – he was one of the world's experts on the subject – than in his daughter. Marie hardly ever saw him, because he was always up an Alp. Princess Pierre brought up her grand-daughter, but the Princess was a monstrous snob. It was out of the question for a girl who could trace her descent from Napoleon to play with ordinary children, so Marie had a lonely childhood. She developed night terrors, a morbid fear of illness and enough obsessional anxieties to keep an army of therapists fully occupied.

But if Marie was formidably neurotic she was also formidably intelligent. When she was seven, she started to write stories and draw pictures which expressed her problems. If she had been a boy, someone would have realised how talented she was and she would have got a proper education as a matter of course. But she was a girl with a harridan for a grandmother.

Marie was about as lucky in love as she was in her family. As a teenager she became infatuated with one of her father's assistants; the man promptly blackmailed her, threatening to publish the love letters she had written him. She also became convinced that she would die young, just like her mother had done.

When Marie was 25 years old, her father chose Prince George of Greece as a suitable husband. As a result she became related to the British royal family. George was about as suitable as a deckchair as he was as neurotic as Marie. He loved his uncle Valdemar more than any woman. On their wedding night, her new husband apologised to Marie: 'I hate it as much as you do. But we must do it if we want children.' It is astonishing they managed to have two children, but they were aristocrats and knew marriage was about breeding heirs.

Marie had the common sense to take lovers, including Aristide Briand, the Prime Minister of France. However, none of her lovers managed to excite her. She was frigid. Her problem was that 'she had a marked virility complex', a French psychiatrist, René Laforgue, told her. He suggested she see Freud.

Marie Bonaparte went to Vienna at once. It was inconceivable that Freud would not see a princess who was descended from Napoleon, had a prime minister for her lover and was fabulously rich. The princess and the analyst adored each other from the moment Marie walked into 19 Berggasse, and she had the presence of mind to keep notes about their sessions. He looked a bit tired when she first met him. He immediately accepted her as a patient and said her analytic hour would start at 11 o'clock.

Freud sensed that Marie would become very dependent. She reported that he told her, 'I am 69 years old and there are a few things that don't work so well. You must not get too attached to me.' Marie started to cry. Celia Bertin, Marie's biographer, describes the start of the analysis much like the start of a great love affair. In many ways it would become one.

Within a few days, Marie admitted she loved Freud. It was not all one way. Freud replied that though they had known each other a mere three weeks, 'I have told you more than I tell most people in two years'. He repeated that she should not get too attached. Marie wept, saying she could not bear to be let down by a man yet again. She held out her hand behind her – she was lying on the couch – and Freud took it. He promised not to let her down. He doubled her analytic time to two hours a day. There is no record of any other patient being so privileged.

Freud became convinced within weeks that, as a small child, Marie had witnessed the 'primal scene'. Marie hurried to see her wet nurse, who confessed that she and a groom had indeed made love in front of the baby Bonaparte. Freud had not let her down.

He discovered that his intellectual patient was interested in female sexuality and it was to her that he wrote his much quoted confession: 'The great question that has never been answered, and which I have not yet been able to answer, despite my thirty years of research into the feminine soul, is "What does a woman want?" '

As they shared so much, Freud told Marie he felt it was time that he had a new physician. Since the row with Felix Deutsch, he had relied just on Hans Pichler, his oral surgeon. Marie had found a good young doctor, Max Schur, and recommended him to Freud.

Freud invited Schur to meet him and was quite impressed. But before he appointed him, Freud insisted to Schur 'that he would always be told the truth. My response must have reassured him that I meant to keep such a promise. He then added searchingly, "Promise me when the time comes that you won't let me suffer unnecessarily."' Freud said this with simplicity, 'without a trace of pathos but also with complete authority'. Schur knew perfectly well what the 72-year-old man who had been diagnosed with cancer meant.

These two relationships, with Schur and Marie Bonaparte, would be vitally important as Freud got older.

On 3 August 1927 Freud told Sam, 'I am not very confident of the near future.' He was losing two American and two English patients who had been paying him in dollars and sterling. 'I expect an easier but a poorer life,' he wrote.

Jones said virtually nothing about Freud's frequent worries about money. Freud was, in fact, often very generous and loaned and even gave money to some young analysts. But like most people in Central Europe, he found the period after the First World War financially stressful and borrowed – or simply accepted – money from friends. Jones did not like to say very much about that because it might damage Freud's reputation and even upset Anna.

At the end of 1927 Freud wrote Sam a touching tribute to the women of his family: 'Whatever bodily power I save from this debacle [his cancer], I owe to the tender affection of my wife and my two daughters.' He was moody, though. On his 72nd birthday he complained, 'I do not enjoy life.' He was not 'better than a wreck in social respects', but at least the Freudian brain was still working. It is now time to look at the career of the man who would be accused of stealing from Freud.

The Young Sauerwald

In 1921 Anton Sauerwald met the girl who would become his wife, Marianne Talg. They were both still in their teens. In his twenties, Sauerwald lived in many different places and often went back to stay at home with his parents, in the house where he had been born. He also spent much time with his married sisters, who were older and did not seem to mind him staying. He was a restless young man.

After Sauerwald left school, he joined a fraternity called Burschenschaft Germania, which was anti-Semitic and had fascist tendencies. It had started some time in the 19th century. Only men were allowed to join and there were some odd traditions. Many of the fraternity liked fighting duels to prove themselves. The slightest excuse would do. That seems bizarre today, but the youngest man to ever be named a professor in Austria, the economist Joseph Schumpeter – whom some people think was more brilliant than John Maynard Keynes – fought a duel over who should be allowed into Vienna University library.

Sauerwald got good enough results to be admitted to Vienna University and, after toying with both law and medicine, settled for chemistry. He had one relative who was a chemist and had published two academic monographs on the properties of iron. His professor was Freud's friend Josef Herzig, who had worked out the stucture of a number of flavonids, including quercitin, fisetin and chrysin. He became famous among organic chemists for a special determination-reaction for methylimides: the Herzig-Mayer Reaction. When he taught Sauerwald, Herzig became interested in natural dyes such as galloflavin.

We have seen that Herzig courted Freud's sister Rosa. Though they did not marry and Herzig married another Jewish woman, Herzig was often a guest at 19 Berggasse. Sauerwald liked and admired his professor, who told him that he was a friend of Freud's. By 1923 it was something to boast about; Freud was a celebrity.

When Herzig died in 1924 at the age of 71, Sauerwald went to work under J. Pollak, who had been the professor's pupil. It took four years for Sauerwald to finish his doctoral thesis in organic chemistry. It was entitled 'Über die Einwirkung von p-Toluolsulfonsäure auf Dibromparaffin' (On the Effect of p-Tolulosulphate on Dibromparaffin). Sauerwald then published four papers in the reputable journal *Monatshefte für Chemie* in one year, a tribute to his energy. Two were shortened versions of ideas he had developed in his thesis, a third examined how nickel could be a catalyst at high temperatures, while the fourth was a synthesis on hexamethylenimins. The study of catalysts interested Sauerwald most of all.

After getting his doctorate, Sauerwald could have expected a successful academic career, but that did not happen. In none of the statements he provided after 1945 did Sauerwald explain whether he left the university out of choice or because he was not offered a position. What seems certain is that he did not leave as an embittered man – which would turn out to be lucky for Freud.

In the autumn of 1928, Sauerwald went to the Academy for Horticulture, not to study but to work as a jobbing gardener. It was a bizarre choice for a man with his qualifications and, after nine months, he got a job at a large company, Krupp Berndorf, as a chemist. We think of Krupp as an arms manufacturer central to the Nazi war effort, but the company also made knives, forks and lamps – or at least its subsidiary Krupp Berndorf did. They were famous for it. Krupp Berndorf were proud of being at the cutting edge of cutlery; the company had invented a process which made cheap metal look like good silver. In your humble home, you could pretend your 'silver' was real silver. Today Krupp Berndorf cutlery and tableware are regarded as good antiques. Although Sauerwald soon realised that he did not want to spend his life devising the best ways to give cutlery a rich-seeming gloss, there was a Depression. Better jobs were not easy to find.

A New Maid

The year 1929 also saw a change in the domestic arrangements at Berggasse. Paula Fichtl joined the Freud household as a maid. She was 26 years old and came from a small village near Salzburg. Her memoirs provide intimate details of Freud's routines, routines he tried to maintain as he got older. Fichtl arrived at a difficult time, when Freud had realised that his mother, Amalie, could not live much longer. She was 94 years old.

On 2 June Freud told Sam that his mother was 'somewhat forlorn'. He still went to Berchtesgaden for the summer and told Sam that Anna would be in Oxford for a congress. Maybe they could meet. They did not, because Anna was too tired to come to Manchester. Then, on 6 December, Freud faced something he found hard to bear – his dog got lost and was run over.

Freud did not usually discuss his work with Sam and so did not tell him that he had decided to write a book on Moses. I have argued that Freud did not see his father as much of a hero and that this may have pushed him to identify with great men of the past. Thirty years after his father's death, it was easier to fulfil the wish the old man had expressed in 1891 that his son should return to the traditions of their ancestors so that 'there will burst upon you the wellsprings of understanding, knowledge and wisdom'. For the next 10 years, Freud would work on and off at his book on Moses, building on the paper in which he had described Michelangelo's statue back in 1914.

As Freud's reputation grew, some of his friends tried to influence the jury who decided who should get the Nobel Prize. Discreetly Einstein was sounded out, but he said it was hard to be certain that Freud deserved this ultimate distinction. The only prize Freud could be awarded was the prize for medicine and Einstein was not sure that Freud's theories had been scientifically proved. Freud got a significant consolation prize, however. He was awarded the Goethe Prize, one of Germany's most prestigious literary awards. Freud noted to Sam he was 'a celebrity' and added that some people even compared him to Einstein. Einstein would not have appreciated the comparison.

In 1929 and 1930, there were two more suicides in the family. Jankele Seidmann, the clever Hebrew scholar, was 'an honest, nice and clever fellow' but he had foolishly decided to start a publishing company. He had no backing and was soon in desperate financial trouble. Unable to face it, he killed himself. His wife, Tom, had been 'half crazy before the disaster so you can imagine what she is like now', as Freud wrote to Sam. A few months later Tom took her own life, the second of Freud's nieces to do so.

The toll now was four suicides in 10 years among Freud's relatives, as well as a drowning and an unexplained death. The question of how Freud's half-brother Emanuel ended up falling from the train at Parbold cannot be answered 90 years after the event, but the list of tragedies is remarkable:

- Emanuel Freud, half-brother: fell from train, aged 80.
- Hermann, nephew: died in combat, aged 21.
- Rose, niece: serious nervous breakdown, aged 25.
- Cäcilie, niece: committed suicide, aged 24.
- Theodor, nephew: drowned, aged 23.
- Sophie Freud-Halberstadt, daughter: died, aged 27.
- Heinz Halberstadt, grandson: died, aged 6.
- Moritz Freud, cousin and brother-in-law: committed suicide, aged 64.
- Jankele Seidmann, husband of niece: committed suicide, aged 30.
- Tom Seidmann, niece: committed suicide, aged 30.

In the last 20 years, research has made very clear the impact of suicide and sudden deaths on surviving family and colleagues. Those who are left behind often ask themselves if they have failed to see something, if they could have done something to prevent the deaths. Guilt, remorse and asking if one should have listened more or better are frequent responses. Survivors sometimes feel very angry at the person who took their own life.

Freud had been analysing his own motives for years. He can hardly have failed to ask himself why close members of his family had not turned to him when they were in acute distress. But he never wrote about that except for the few lines to Sam. I cannot help wondering if some of the material in the Bernays files in the Library of Congress, which we have been assured contain no 'horrors', does not deal with these deaths. There is no evidence of a history of suicide in either Jacob Freud's or Eli Bernays's family. For all their faults, both had survived adversity, change and scandal.

There were other crises. We have seen that Anna started to treat Dorothy Burlingham's four children and then she and Dorothy became friends and, at the least, a platonic couple. This did not stop Freud from accepting Dorothy as a patient. A little later, her estranged husband arrived in Vienna. Robert Burlingham suffered from depression, which was perhaps not that surprising as his wife had left him and taken an apartment above the Freuds to be close to Anna. Dorothy made it hard for Robert to see his children; he needed a good divorce lawyer but also ended up being analysed by Freud.

Freud was very careful in sessions with Robert because he knew perfectly well that Anna did not want Dorothy to go back to her marriage. Robert's father warned his son that he was now in a very dangerous position, as he had put himself in the hands of a man whose daughter 'wanted' his wife. The historian Paul Roazen suggests that Freud contributed to the final breakdown of the marriage by insisiting on 'an absolute barrier' between Robert Burlingham and his wife – which was in all likelihood just what Anna wanted.

Fifteen years after they had started writing to each other, Freud admitted to Sam that it was not likely they would ever see each other again. The journey was just 'too hard', but Harry Freud did arrive in Manchester and went to visit Sam. Freud said his nephew was 'a clever boy and affectionate'. Sam enjoyed the visit.

Harry still lived in Vienna. Paula Fichtl, who had few romantic entanglements, fell madly in love with him, but she was not impressed with his brains. She said that he was one member of the family whose intelligence did not intimidate her. She was as clever as he was, she thought. Indeed, her letters to him show her to have been an intelligent, quite literate young woman. But Harry did not seem interested in her, so she bottled up her love. Paula believed that Freud did not know how she felt about his nephew.

Harry might reject her, but Paula was liked by Anna and accompanied her at least once when she and Dorothy went on holiday. In her memoirs, Paula was asked about the relationship between the two women. Her ghostwriter says that by the time she talked to her, Paula was too old to even hear the word 'lesbian'.

The year ended well in two ways. Freud and Stefan Zweig had corresponded since 1908. Zweig had become famous as the author of *The Royal Game*, *Amok* and *Beware of Pity* and of biographies of Erasmus, Magellan and Marie Antoinette. He now published *Mental Healers*, which appeared in German in 1931 and English in 1933. The book contained a flattering though far from full biography of Freud, as it also covered – as we have seen – Mesmer and Mary Baker Eddy. Having explained Freud's ideas and how they developed, Zweig wrote perceptively that the whole aim of psychoanalysis was 'to effect disillusionment and to dispel ungrounded fantasies...It makes no promises at all, offers no consolation and is silent when asked for one or the other.' Zweig praised the candour of Freud, which made his work 'amazing in its moral significance'.

Zweig did not see the twinkling charmer Eastman had identified. In fact, he thought that Freud had 'a dash of Old Testament grimness'. But he praised Freud as an 'indefatigable worker'. Over 50 years Freud had seen a procession of 'complaining, questioning, eager and excited, hysterical and irate; always the sick, the oppressed, the tormented, the mentally disordered'. Zweig liked the rhythm of lists. In his enthusiasm he added one judgement which feels wrong. He said, 'Like Jehovah, he [Freud] is less likely to pardon a lukewarm supporter than an outspoken renegade.' Zweig was being tactful given how aggressive Freud was to those analysts he fell out with.

The second honour was that Freud's birthplace, Freiberg in Moravia, was going to erect a plaque in his honour. 'Jacob would have been 116 years old,' he told Sam. Anna was sent to represent her father. This accolade did not mean he could stop worrying about money, though. Freud's son Ernst still had to rely on an allowance from his father, he told Sam, 'and on what he gets from his well-off mother-in-law'.

Freud faced a cash-flow problem too. The publishing firm he had set up in 1919, the Internationaler Psychoanalytischer Verlag, was on the brink of bankruptcy. He wrote to some of his rich friends, although he did not really think that in the middle of a Depression many would help. However, he was wrong and several societies and individuals responded with generosity. A.A. Brill sent $2,500 and the wealthy Edith Jackson contributed $2,000. Both the New York and British societies sent substantial gifts. It is impossible to understand the rest of Freud's life without understanding the economic problems he and the world faced as unemployment and despair grew in Europe and America. A good example of the mood comes from John B. Watson, the founder of behaviourism. He lost a fortune in the crash and wrote an article called 'Why I Don't Commit Suicide' for *Cosmopolitan*. He wrote to 100 people who had suffered and asked them to explain their state of mind. He was disappointed so many were in despair, arguing that even those who had lost everything should struggle on. The article was rejected by the editor of *Cosmopolitan* because it was too optimistic; the editor killed himself a few months later, having been ruined in the crash.

The French Detectives and the Bankers

Early in 1932 two French detectives entered a hotel near the Champs-Elysées. They had been given a useful tip-off about potential tax evaders.

At the time, France faced a huge budget deficit. Three years after the Wall Street crash, the world economy was in a deep Depression. Edouard Herriot led a coalition government which included a number of socialist ministers. The socialists had a clear programme for dealing with the crisis. They wanted to reduce French military spending and to nationalise banks and railways. These measures were too extreme, Herriot thought, and instead proposed an austerity programme. If he were going to get that through Parliament, the last thing Herriot needed was a financial scandal that exposed the fact that the rich avoided the taxes everyone else had to pay.

The French detectives entered the hotel rooms of the president and vice-president of the Commercial Bank of Basle. It did not take them long to discover interesting and nicely incriminating documents. The bank officials had a list of 2,000 French clients who had got money to Switzerland illegally. It did not require much ingenuity. Even today the border near Geneva is guarded by just one customs post at Ferney-Voltaire; there are now, and were then, many other ways of getting goods into Switzerland. When I made a film about a sinister cult called the Order of the Solar Temple, which was based near Geneva, one informant (who had worked for the Rothschilds) explained to me that the Swiss deliberately do not patrol the border well because it would be bad for business. Smuggling money, jewels or even sculptures had to be made possible.

The French tax 'cheats' included senators, a former minister, bishops, generals and industrialists, the cream of French society. Many of those who preached public austerity were practising private greed. After news of the police raid leaked out, there was a furious debate in the Chamber of Deputies. The socialist Fabien Albertin had good contacts with the tax and customs departments and got hold of a copy of the list of 2,000 cheats. He took great pleasure in reading out some of the names of the 'great and good' fiddlers. The upper class was as greedy as ever, Albertin told his fellow deputies. France had lost 9 million francs in tax – at least. He called for agreements with other countries to pursue the cheats and recover the money.

Predictable political posturing followed. The left called for all the assets of French taxpayers to be declared. The right denounced this as a cheap ploy to justify passing an austerity budget. The right-wing paper *Le Figaro* oozed morality and reminded its readers that the deputies in the Chamber paid tax on only half their income. The Communist paper *L'Humanité* denounced the '2,000 bourgeois compromised in a massive organised tax fraud scandal'. Satirists joined in the fun as *Le Temps* joked, 'Contraband is not something to be reprimanded.' Tax cheats should be congratulated for their initiative. The government could hardly refuse to prosecute the tax cheats. It announced the immediate start of negotiations with the Swiss government.

The arrest of two top bankers in Paris was no joke for the Swiss, however. Jesus might have thrown the money changers out of the temple but, by 1540, many Protestants believed being rich was a sign of being one of the elect. Heaven beckoned those with a fat purse. Four centuries on, the Swiss believed banks had their God-given duties; the state of one's account was as sacred as the state of one's soul. Priests could not reveal what was said in confession and bankers could not reveal what was in accounts. Swiss newspapers complained about the arrogance of the French.

To find a way out of the crisis, Swiss banks turned to the Swiss Federal Court, which ruled obligingly that banks had to keep their clients' files utterly confidential. The battle between the French and the Swiss became bitter. The French Prime Minister, Herriot, had to pacify his socialist allies, so he promised to give the tax authorities the right to scrutinise all bank operations. No one would be able to open an account, write a cheque, rent a safe or send a single sou abroad without a French bureaucrat knowing about it.

The Swiss thought they had won the battle when, on 18 December 1932, the Herriot government fell. To make sure their banks could never face such embarrassment again, the Swiss framed a new law. Article 47b of the Swiss banking act of 1933 introduced the notion of banking secrecy. Any bank official who revealed the identity of the holder of a numbered account was committing a crime and could be imprisoned. Bank customers could be sure of complete confidentiality.

It was not just French socialists who complained about Article 47b. A month after Herriot's government fell, Hitler became Chancellor of Germany. This new Swiss law would allow Jews and other 'enemies of the state' to hide their money, the Nazis protested. The international Jewish conspiracy was triumphing once again. The Nazis, believing that all Jews cheated the German people, preached violence, hatred and revenge. Jews were beaten up and their shops and businesses attacked: the nightmare had started.

At this point I should like to add some personal history so that readers can understand the pressures Jews were under – and the solutions they found. My mother's family fled Romania in 1938. The country was ruled by the anti-Semitic General Ion Antonescu. After the war one of my uncles,

Zoltan Gruber, to whose memory I have dedicated this book, became a money smuggler. If, for example, you wanted funds in France, you gave money to someone Zoltan trusted in England and, no questions asked, you would meet someone in Paris who handed you your money minus a small commission. From 1950 to the end of the 1980s, many countries made it hard to send money abroad and this informal system worked well.

My uncle had a soft spot for my mother and he sometimes sent her bank drafts which she could cash at the bank of Julius Baer. The bank has just one branch in London and just one cashier. They were not used to dealing in the small sums my uncle sent, but they always treated my mother with great courtesy. The head of the bank would have much to say as late as 2007 about the history of the secret bank accounts. It was a story which had to be forced out, detail by detail.

Freud's secret bank accounts were not discussed in the biographies. We now know their origin. Anna Freud was aware of them, as were Freud's other children, especially Martin, who had qualified as a lawyer. But the accounts were a secret, and the kind of secret anti-Semites would say was typical of Jews. There were reasons why no one wrote about Freud's accounts, even if there was some evidence of their existence. First, it seemed shameful for a distinguished Jew to be too concerned with money. But after the First World War Freud, like millions of Central Europeans, was in financial straits. Money was losing its value. Freud told Sam that the Austrian schilling had lost 95 per cent of its value.

Long before they conceived of the gas chambers, the Nazis aimed to rob the Jews of everything they owned. Adolf Eichmann, the architect of the Final Solution, provides excellent evidence of this in his memos, which were written to Berlin as leading Nazis discussed the best way to fleece Jews. In such circumstances Jews did what they had to do so that they, their children and their grandchildren would survive. There was no dishonour in that.

When he asked for contributions to keep the Internationaler Psycho-analytischer Verlag going, Freud also urged cooperation between German psychoanalysts and those in the rest of the world. 'Let us not be blinded by the apparent lessening of hostility towards our analysis,' he wrote. 'It is more an improvement in tone than in reality. More "modo" than "re". Yet for some time it will be necessary for the analysts to stick together, more closely together, than the closely related groups of neurologists, psychiatrists and psycho-therapists.'

One of the contributors to the Verlag was Marie Bonaparte. They had stayed in regular touch. After seeing Freud in 1927, she decided to try something different to cure her frigidity. She had an operation which moved her clitoris closer to her vaginal orifice. She believed in Freud's theory of the vaginal orgasm and he did not discourage her. The procedure did nothing for her sex life, which continued to distress her. Now she wrote Freud a letter which showed how extreme she could be. She was thinking of committing incest with her son. Did Freud think that was a good idea?

CHAPTER 5

The Rise of the Nazis

After the Allies defeated Germany in 1919, France and Britain demanded enormous payments by way of reparation. The American President, Woodrow Wilson, complained that the Allies were too vengeful, but he gave way when faced by Lloyd George and Clemenceau. Germany suffered crippling inflation; at its peak, money had to be carted about in wheelbarrows.

Winston Churchill in *The Gathering Storm* described a 'little corporal' who had 'been temporarily blinded by mustard gas in a British attack' and whose 'personal failure merged with the disaster of the whole German people'. As a result 'an agony consumed his being'. The little corporal left hospital to find his country in chaos and an 'atmosphere of despair and frenzy'. The little corporal was, of course, Adolf Hitler. Churchill pictured him as the fog of war turned into the misery of peace in 1919; for Hitler, 'as in a dream, everything suddenly became clear, Germany had been stabbed in the back and clawed down by the Jews, by the profiteers and intriguers…by the accursed Bolsheviks'. Churchill's next sentence has a Freudian ring, because he imagines Hitler having a daydream which motivates him: 'Shining before him he saw his duty, to save Germany from these plagues, to avenge her wrongs. And lead the master race to its long decreed destiny.'

There are more esoteric accounts of Hitler's psychology. In a 1936 biography, *Hitler the Pawn*, Berlin journalist Rudolf Olden argued that Hitler was deliberately vague about his career as a corporal because he suffered from psychological problems. Hitler became clincally depressed and 'came under the spell of an excommunicated man who animated a small circle of friends with messages from a saintly spirit, always ending up with

the command to break the fetters of Versailles'. Hitler had become involved
with spiritualists and let himself be manipulated by sinister anti-Semites. But
Olden had not discovered the whole truth.

In 1918 Hitler was indeed depressed and underwent treatment by hypnosis
at a special military hospital called Pasewalk. He was treated there for
hysterical blindness by a Dutch psychiatrist, Edmund Forster. Usually Forster
would bully shell-shocked soldiers into returning to active duty, but Hitler
was not trying to shirk. He was eager to get back to the front line and very
distressed that he could not while he was blind. Forster observed Hitler for
a week and became certain he was a very unusual case. He had gone blind
not out of funk but because he could not bear to see what had happened
to Germany.

According to a psychologist, David Lewis, Forster thought the most
effective treatment for this blindness would be to convince Hitler he might
play a part in the salvation of Germany. He could do that only if he recovered
his sight. A detailed account of how Forster treated Hitler can be found,
Lewis argues, in a novel by Ernst Weiss called *The Eyewitness*, which
examines how a character called A.H. is cured of blindness. Weiss had been
given Forster's notes in which he detailed the treatment. Forster also was
consulted by Hermann Goering for help with his morphine addiction. Such
details help to explain the particularly tangled nature of the relationship
between the Nazis and psychotherapy. Hitler and Goering had positive
experiences of forms of therapy which were influenced by Freud's work.
They wanted to hide that they had ever been in the hands of psychiatrists,
but they had the sense to see therapy could help.

Germany itself could have been diagnosed as being neurotic after the
inflation and unrest of the 1920s. The great German writer Thomas Mann
understood why the Nazis had taken such a hold; they had induced a
psychotic state in their fellow citizens:

> This fantastic state of mind, of a humanity that has outrun its ideas, is
> matched by a political scene in the grotesque style, with Salvation Army
> methods, hallelujahs and bell-ringing and dervishlike repetition of
> monotonous catchwords, until everybody foams at the mouth.
> Fanaticism turns into a means of salvation, enthusiasm into epileptic
> ecstasy, politics becomes an opiate for the masses, a proletarian
> eschatology; and reason veils her face.

Mann's phrase 'reason veils her face' was all too apt. For educated Jews,
there was a particular problem. For over 50 years, in Germany more than in

Austria, many had been successful and seemed to be accepted. Freud told Stefan Zweig, 'And we certainly have our Germanness in common – only it's a Germanness of the past it seems to me.' Zweig replied that he had thought a great deal about 'my relationship to Germany and to my Germanness, and my relationship to the Jews, to the Jewishness in me and in the world, and to Palestine'.

On 18 August 1932 Freud answered, saying that he had heard of the Nazi threats against Zweig, but he encouraged his friend to go on with their correspondence and their regular exchange of manuscripts: 'So perhaps the Nazis are playing into my hands for once. When you tell me about your thoughts, I can relieve you of the illusion that one has to be a German. Should we not leave this God-forsaken nation to themselves?'

By the autumn of 1932, the grotesque style, as Mann had described it, was winning but it had not yet gained control. In October Hitler went to see the German President, Hindenberg, to try to get himself appointed Chancellor. The President thought, as many upper-class Germans did, that Hitler was a puffed-up little corporal. Hitler had a good sense of how Hindenberg viewed him and took Hermann Goering with him to the meeting. Goering had been a heroic pilot in the 1914–18 war and, perhaps, could persuade Hindenberg that Hitler was a substantial figure. Unusually, Hitler let Goering do most of the talking. Goering had thought Hitler was a genius from the moment he first heard him speak, but he failed to convince Hindenberg.

Hindenberg called new elections for the end of November, hoping that the Nazis would lose seats in the Reichstag. But he had read the mood of the country badly. Hitler's Nazi Party won 35 per cent of the votes, more than any other party. Hindenberg had no option but to offer Hitler the chance to form a government. At the end of January 1933, Hitler took power. The fury against the Jews which Churchill had described was about to be unleashed with total venom.

As soon as Hitler became Chancellor, Jones wrote to Freud, 'You must be glad that Austria is not part of Germany.' Freud replied that he expected 'the Hitler movement' to spread to Austria but he had faith in the guarantees given to minorities in the Treaty of Versailles. Austrians 'were not inclined to German brutality', partly because they were so lazy.

Some scholars have argued that Freud only discovered how Jewish he felt in the 1920s and 1930s as the Nazis became more powerful. Freud himself wrote that he was lukewarm in his attachment to Judaism 'until I noticed the growth of anti-Semitic prejudice in Germany and German Austria'. The historian Peter Gay argues that:

in the poisonous atmosphere of the late 1920s and early 1930s he did more than refuse to deny his Jewish origins. He trumpeted them. As he got older, he became more inclined not just to assert his Jewishness against anti-Semites, but also to express a strong positive emotional attachment to it.

Gay suggests that this was partly nostalgia, partly gratitude for the sense of community Freud's Jewish identity gave him in a hostile world.

Yosef Yerushalmi also argues that Hitler's rise to power made Freud feel more Jewish and take a greater interest in Jewish issues. Jung had a different and perhaps more accurate view. He had sniped years earlier that Freud had 'the common Jewish sensitivity to the slightest hint of anti-Semitism'.

Freud's approach was historical and psychoanalytic rather than frankly political. He did not dwell much, even in private, on the reasons why the Nazis now attracted so much support. Only two analysts grappled with this issue in political as well as psychoanalytic terms, Otto Fenichel and Wilhelm Reich. Both were socialists.

Fenichel explained the rise of the Nazis as a response to fear of uncertainty. But Reich was the more glittering character. Freud was so impressed by Reich that he let him start treating patients when the young man was only 23 years old. Reich was friends with Anna Freud, who wrote 'back then in Vienna we were all so excited, full of energy: it was as if a whole new continent was being explored, and we were the explorers, and we now had a chance to change things'.

In 1925 Reich became deputy director of Freud's Psychoanalytic Polyclinic. He moved to Berlin three years later and set up clinics which offered advice on sex, contraception, venereal diseases and even homosexuality to young people. At first Freud approved but then, not for the first time, he turned against a colleague. He started to be annoyed by his prodigy and, especially, by Reich's ideas about sex, which seemed too crude and too literal. Reich did not help by raising questions about the Nirvana principle or death wish.

Reich's *The Mass Psychology of Fascism* made this conflict worse. Reich could never be bothered to be tactful and suggested that Freud had been unwilling to pursue his ideas to their logical end. Society suppressed the sexuality of children not to socialise them but to make them docile citizens:

The moral inhibition of the child's natural sexuality, the last stage of which is the severe impairment of the child's genital sexuality, makes the child afraid, shy, fearful of authority, obedient, 'good' and 'docile' in the authoritarian sense of the words. It has a crippling effect on man's rebellious forces because every vital life-impulse is now burdened with severe fear; and since sex is a forbidden subject, thought in general and man's critical faculty also become inhibited.

The Nazis created 'severe fear' expertly, Reich added. 'The result is conservatism, fear of freedom, in a word, reactionary thinking. And sexual frustration makes one vulnerable.'

Nazi parades were almost disguised orgies:

The sexual effect of a uniform, the erotically provocative effect of rhythmically executed goose-stepping, the exhibitionistic nature of militaristic procedures, have been more practically comprehended by a salesgirl or an average secretary than by our most erudite politicians.

It was inspired of the Nazis to design flashy uniforms for the men and to put the recruiting into the hands of attractive women. Reich recalled that recruitment posters for the Royal Navy in the 1914–18 war 'ran something as follows: "Travel to foreign countries – join the Royal Navy!" and the foreign countries were portrayed by exotic women'. Why are these posters effective? Reich asked. 'Because our youth has become sexually starved owing to sexual suppression,' he answered.

The left had to understand 'why the masses proved to be accessible to deception, befogging, and a psychotic situation'; only his mass psychology could explain 'why would millions upon millions affirm their own suppression'.

The Mass Psychology of Fascism had the distinction of being loathed both by the Nazis and by Freud. Anna Freud said that she got along with Reich better than most 'because I tried to treat him well instead of offending him. It helps a bit and would help more if he were a sane person, which he is not.'

But Reich was far from insane in assessing the risks he was running. He said he had not written about such issues earlier 'simply because I feared the consequences. Again and again I hesitated to put my ideas down on paper.' Once the Nazis were in power, it might 'have a highly dangerous potential as things now stand'. He left Germany before the book was published. Today some see it as a classic.

The only public statement Freud made about politics at the same time was far more vague and he wrote it at the request of Einstein.

Why War?

In July 1932, when an official of the League of Nations came to see him, Freud was unusually diffident. Leon Steinig believed that Freud and Einstein should have a public exchange on the causes of war, an exchange that might help avoid another one.

Freud listened sceptically, then told Steinig that all his life he had had to tell 'people truths that were difficult to swallow. Now that I am old, I certainly do not want to fool them.' He doubted anyone would want to publish his pessimistic views. The League of Nations 'had not paid the slightest interest in our work', Freud complained. But he agreed to work with Einstein, even though he knew by now that Einstein had been against his getting the Nobel Prize.

Why War? was an exchange between the great physicist and the great psychiatrist, a major event. Freud was right in guessing that no one would want to listen. The demoralised and incompetent League of Nations printed only 2,000 copies.

Freud told Einstein that there was just 'one sure way of ending war and that is the establishment, by common consent, of a central control which shall have the last word in every conflict of interests'. The problem with the League of Nations was that it had 'no force at its disposal and can only get it if the members of the new body, its constituent nations, furnish it. And, as things are, this is a forlorn hope.' But it would be very 'shortsighted' to ignore the League, as it was an experiment that had never before been tried in history.

Freud then discussed his theory of the death instinct, adding that, 'As a rule several motives of similar composition concur to bring about' any action. He then cited Professor G.C. Lichtenberg, one-time Professor of Physics at Göttingen, and said that the man was perhaps an even better psychologist than a physicist, having developed a subtle 'Compass-card of Motives'. Lichtenberg wrote, 'The efficient motives impelling man to act can be classified like the thirty-two winds and described in the same manner: e.g., Food-Food-Fame or Fame-Fame-Food.' Freud listed the 'whole gamut of human motives that may respond when political leaders summon their citizens to war'. There were greed and idealism, cruelty and heroism. Idealism was often disguised as a lust for destruction. 'All this may give you the impression that our theories amount to a species of mythology and a gloomy one at that! But does not every natural science lead ultimately to this – a sort of mythology? Is it otherwise today with your physical sciences?'

Freud saw no hope of curbing human aggression. He did not believe that 'in some happy corners of the earth, they say, where nature brings forth abundantly whatever man desires, there flourish races whose lives go gently by; unknowing of aggression or constraint'. No chance! Freud said he 'would like further details about these happy folk', whom Reich would no doubt have imagined spending their happy hours in happy sex play. The best hope, Freud believed, lay not in sex, but in culture. 'On the psychological side, two of the most important phenomena of culture are, firstly, a strengthening of the intellect, which tends to master our instinctive life, and, secondly, an introversion of the aggressive impulse.' We might become intelligent enough to avoid war.

The average IQ score has risen by 10 points since 1930, but it does not seem to have made us pacifists, incidentally. Freud did hope that as war 'runs most emphatically counter to the psychic disposition imposed on us by the growth of culture; we are therefore bound to resent war, to find it utterly intolerable'. He then described himself and Einstein as pacifists who were simply revolted not just by the atrocities of war but by 'the aesthetic ignominies of warfare'. This is a curious phrase; war is too ugly. His sons who fought in 1914 told him what conditions were like, as did doctors who were at the front.

Einstein was apparently not disappointed when he got Freud's reply. He answered on 3 December 1932:

You have made a most gratifying gift to the League of Nations and me with your truly classic reply. You have earned my gratitude and the gratitude of all men for having devoted all your strength to the search for truth and for having shown the rarest courage in professing your convictions all your life.

The Nazis loathed the pamphlet. It confirmed their views. Psychoanalysis polluted the noble Aryan mind and soul. It was typical Jewish thought, with its 'degenerate capacity to poison the sources of idealism and feeling for race and nation and, especially, to strike the Nordic races at their most vulnerable point, their sexual life,' said *Deutsche Volksegesundheit aus Blut und Boden*, a journal whose title can be translated as *The Health of the German People from Blood and Land*.

Many Jews, like Stefan Zweig and Einstein, saw that there was no future for them in Germany. In March 1933 Einstein announced he would never return to Germany. The Nazis confiscated his bank account, his wife's safe-deposit box and his house in Caputh. On 28 March Einstein resigned from the Prussian Academy of Sciences and, four days later, from the Bavarian

Academy of Sciences. He also renounced his German citizenship, managing to do this before the Nazis revoked it. On 12 April 1933 he told the Prussian Academy that he had refused 'to put in a good word for the German people as to do so would have been a repudiation of all those notions of justice and liberty for which I have stood all my life'. He continued, 'I should have been contributing even if only indirectly to moral corruption and the destruction of all existing cultural values.'

Einstein made for America, while Stefan Zweig headed for Palestine, the first of Freud's friends to try to live the Zionist dream. Zweig wrote to Freud, 'This land of religions can, after all, be seen from other points of view than just as a land of delusions and desires.' Freud disagreed – for now.

The Nazis might hate *Why War?* but there was one similarity between psychoanalysis and Nazi ideology, however. Both believed human beings could be improved. Freud claimed the purpose of analysis was to heal people so they could 'love and work'. A few Nazis realised that some type of therapy might be just the tool they needed to produce a more efficient *Volk*, as long as it was clear that the treatment did not owe anything to Jews or to Freud. Such ambivalences made the relationship between the Nazis and psycho-analysis complicated and controversial.

Nazi hostility could not damage Freud's position, however. He remained the most important figure in psychoanalysis. Analysts from Germany, Hungary, Britain, Holland and Scandinavia visited him. Yet though the Nazis became more vicious and violent against Jews in Germany, Freud remained cautious in public. That did not go unnoticed. Ernest Jones, who was about to become president of the International Psychoanalytic Association, did not denounce the Nazis either. Freud had made bitter enemies – Carl Jung was the most prominent – and they felt they now had their chance to take revenge. And some analysts succumbed to their anxieties as well as to Nazi threats.

Historians have debated the reasons why so many analysts were rather meek in this crisis. Geoffrey Cocks, for example, claims that the com-promises reached in the extreme circumstances of the 1930s can be easily understood and even forgiven. Others disagree. The reaction of the analysts was also confused because of their own often bitter in-fighting. We know more than ever before about their conflicts because Otto Fenichel, the socialist, circulated letters between some analysts. Few realised these *Rundbriefe*, or round-robins, existed until they were published in 1998. They show some analysts in a less than flattering light. Freud had been right to dismiss some of his colleagues at least as 'a gang'.

The situation was politically, ethically and psychotically odd. Four different groups were involved in the negotiations that started soon after the Nazis took power in Germany. Members of the International Psychoanalytic Association included analysts from Britain, North and South America, Europe, India and even Japan. The German Psychoanalytic Society represented all German analysts. Then there were local bodies like the Berlin Psychoanalytic Institute. It had fewer than 100 members but ran a major training institute. With offices on the Potsdamerstrasse, it had been founded in 1920 by Max Eitingon and Ernst Simmel, who was a socialist. Eitingon provided financial support and nearly all the state-of-the-art modern furniture. The Institute had 36 members, 12 teaching staff and nearly 50 students. Members, mainly Jewish, met every week to hear lectures; many of them had been influenced by Marx's ideas. The Berlin Institute made no secret of its ambition to make psychoanalysis, or at least psychotherapy, available not just to the rich but to working people who had problems. Freud supported that ambition at first.

Several Berlin analysts – most notably the radical Edith Jacobson – took part in 'illegal' resistance against the Nazis and were detained by the Gestapo. The best known of these socialists, Wilhelm Reich and Otto Fenichel, only escaped that fate because they had already left Germany.

The Über Whites

Only two of the Berlin Institute's governing council were not Jewish: Felix Boehm and Carl Müller-Braunschweig. Both men knew Freud well and were part of the analytic circle. Josine, Müller-Braunschweig's wife, was also an analyst, who published a number of papers on girls' concepts of the vagina. The fourth important Christian was Karen Horney, who left Vienna in the late 1930s.

When the Nazis took power, Boehm was 51 years old. He had studied medicine in Geneva, Freiburg im Breisgau and Munich. In 1913 he became a member of the Munich regional group of the International Psychoanalytic Association. In the First World War he served as a volunteer doctor and acted as a psychiatric expert in at least one war tribunal. After the war, Boehm started a training analysis with Karl Abraham, one of Freud's close friends and a Jew. Boehm then taught at the Berlin Psychoanalytic Institute from 1923 to 1933 and, while he was there, put his daughters into analysis with Melanie Klein. He made an interesting study of when girls first become aware of their vagina, a major theoretical issue for analysts, because Freud believed all women suffered from penis envy. Boehm also studied perversions and had written a book with Otto Fenichel, *On the Oedipus Complex*, though his fellow author was far to the left.

No one would have expected Boehm to betray the cause, even though his family had Nazi connections. His father and his uncles knew Alfred Rosenberg, who developed the racist ideas of eccentric thinkers like Arthur de Gobineau and Houston Stewart Chamberlain into a hierarchy of human races. Blacks and Jews were at the bottom; the 'Aryan' race was at the top. It was not enough to be white to be Aryan. The masters of the master race, the über whites, were the Scandinavians, northern Germans, Dutch, British and those of pure Baltic stock. Rosenberg couldn't even be consistent in his eugenic fantasies, for he argued that the Berbers of North Africa (many of whom were both black and Jewish) also belonged to the Aryans. Rosenberg ranted against homosexuality as well, as in his pamphlet 'Der Sumpf' ('The Swamp'). Homosexuality was not just a perversion; it stopped the breeding of the glorious Nordic race.

Carl Müller-Braunschweig was the other key player in the negotiations with the Nazis. After writing his doctoral thesis on the philosopher Immanuel Kant, he switched to medicine and also had a training analysis with Karl Abraham. Müller-Braunschweig became a member of the executive committee of the International Psychoanalytic Association in 1925 and regularly wrote in the *Internationale Zeitschrift für Psychoanalyse*, in journals on sexual science and in *Imago*. He published a glowing review of Freud's short *An Autobiographical Study* (1925) which said Freud 'gives the subject new and fresh applications' and that every psychoanalyst 'will take particular pleasure in Freud's pithy phrases'. He corresponded with Anna Freud regularly.

The Vienna Psychoanalytic Society had grown out of the meetings which started in Freud's apartment in 1902. Most of the 149 members were Jewish. Freud's only official position was here, but no important decisions about psychoanalysis in Europe were made without his being consulted. In effect, he could stop any development of which he did not approve.

In March 1933 Max Eitingon went to Vienna to consult Freud on the developments in Germany. He left Felix Boehm and Carl Müller-Braunschweig in charge. Behind his back, the two non-Jewish analysts immediately started to try to negotiate with the Nazis. They had a simple plan. As he was a Jew, Eitingon would have to resign as the leader of the German Psychoanalytic Society, as would all the Jewish members. Only then could they strike a deal with the Nazis to save psychoanalysis.

Boehm and Müller-Braunschweig intended to argue to the Nazis that it was an accident that psychoanalysis had been invented by a Jew and that the fact that nearly every major analyst was a Jew did not make the enterprise a 'Jewish science'. Ernest Jones did not object; his letters show he was committed to protecting the interests of German psychoanalysis at least as much as he was to protecting Jewish analysts.

When Eitingon returned from Vienna he found the others had decided Felix Boehm should become president of the German Psychoanalytic Society. Very soon afterwards Eitingon agreed to that, partly because he had decided, like Zweig, to emigrate to Palestine. Boehm went to Vienna to discuss the possibility that he would become president with Freud; even those who were negotiating with the Nazis felt they needed him to approve.

Freud was supremely calm to Boehm's face. He said that if Boehm could get a majority of analysts to vote for him, he would not stand in his way. But a second version of these events suggests Freud took the initiative to some extent as he knew Eitingon had decided to go to Palestine.

There is no dispute, however, about the conditions that Boehm had to fulfil if Freud were not to oppose him. First, Boehm had to expel Reich from the Society; Freud now described his once prodigy as a 'Bolshevist attacker' and wrote to Eitingon on 17 April 1933 that he wanted Reich expelled from the German Psychoanalytic Society and the International Psychoanalytic Association: 'I desire it on scientific grounds but have nothing against its coming about on political grounds – I do not begrudge him the role of martyr.' The scientific grounds had to do with Reich's objections to Freud's death-wish theory.

Secondly, Boehm would have to fight against 'inside opponents' such as Harald Schultz-Hencke, who had criticised Freud's libido theory and his ideas on the structure of the unconscious. As a result, he had been forbidden to teach training analysts. After Eitingon returned to Berlin Freud wrote to him, saying that he wanted to ensure that Schultz-Hencke did not take advantage of the 'present situation to promote his theories'.

Demonstrations

One of the less likely consequences of Hitler taking power was that Sigmund Freud started to read the *Manchester Guardian*, as German papers did not provide a true picture of events. Information was fragmentary and many things were not reported, Freud wrote to Sam, while the *Manchester Guardian* provided good coverage. No paper in Germany had reported, for example, that 150 Nazis broke into the house where Marx had been born.

On Friday 10 March 1933 it reported that Nazis had started to picket large shops owned by Jews. The article continued:

> During the busiest shopping hour this evening the following scene could be witnessed outside the Kadewe, the largest department store of the West End. A detachment of Storm Troops marched up to the shop, formed a cordon in front of the entrance, and put up a large notice, 'Germans! Don't buy from Jews.' The people inside the shop left hurriedly and no others were allowed to go in. The police looked on with apparent indifference. Many people who had assembled outside seemed to be favourably impressed by this demonstration, and talked cheerfully to the Storm Troopers, who assured them that they would put an end to the Jewish shops.

The *Manchester Guardian* described similar scenes in front of Rosenheim's in the Kurfürstendamm, a shop which sold high-class leather goods. As it was such an exclusive shop, it could hardly be accused of unfair competition. 'It was closed simply because it belongs to a Jew,' the paper reported. Such demonstrations had propaganda value for the Nazi Party, they added. Anti-Semitism was not just talk; small shopkeepers often supported Hitler and welcomed the attack on big department stores.

Attacks on department stores were the start of a long campaign of hatred. Anna Freud and Jones both heard from a Dutch analyst, J. van Ophuijsen, who visited Berlin and told them, 'Germany is at present a hell for German Jews.' Only four or five analysts stayed in Berlin. Jones wrote to the analyst Smith Ely Jelliffe in New York, 'The persecution has been much worse than you seem to think and has really lived up to the Middle Ages in reputation.'

Austria did not remain untouched by the situation in Germany and nor did Anton Sauerwald.

Sauerwald the Bomb Maker

In 1932, Anton Sauerwald resigned from the cutlery maker Krupp Berndorf and set up a chemicals business of his own. He was 28 years old when he did so and had financial help from his parents. This was a brave move, as the German and Austrian chemical industries were suffering in the Depression. Subsidies to academics from large companies like I.G. Farben were being cut.

Nevertheless, Sauerwald took premises at 19 Gelbergasse. His company specialised in catalysts, the preparation of patent applications and, in essence, anything chemical. He employed an old friend, Emil Rothleitner, whom he had known at the University of Vienna and in the Burschenschaft Germania fraternity. Rothleitner described himself as someone whose job it was to carry out 'practical undertakings' directed by his 'chief'. Rothleitner was the same age as Sauerwald but he was not as well qualified academically. In one respect, however, the employee did much more than carry out Sauerwald's instructions. Rothleitner was heavily involved in Nazi Party activity in Vienna from the early 1930s. There, he led and Sauerwald followed.

On 4 March 1933 Chancellor Engelbert Dollfuss suspended the Austrian Parliament and blocked all attempts to reconvene it. Dollfuss was concerned by the rise of the Nazis in Austria. He used a 1917 emergency law which had been enacted to protect the state 'against the economic dangers associated with a disturbance of public peace, order, and security'. Dollfuss said that both the Nazis and the socialists threatened the country's stability. From then on he ruled by decree.

On 19 June Dollfuss outlawed the German National-Socialist or Nazi Party. The Nazis' response was to start a campaign of terror. Six days later, they tried to assassinate 10 senior Austrian officials. Crowds of Nazi students gathered in front of the university; mounted police chased them down the Ringstrasse. It was the start of days of rioting. Usually the Nazis targeted Jews.

A huge bomb tore out the inside of one of the Nazis' favourite targets, a department store owned by a Jewish family. One elderly Jewish lady died in a different part of the city. *Time* covered the story well. Frau Futterweit was standing in the doorway of her little jewellery shop when a passenger in a car threw an old silk stocking stuffed with newspapers and a hand grenade at her. With great presence of mind, Frau Futterweit tried to throw it back, but the grenade burst in her hands and killed her instantly. Eight passers-by were wounded, one dying later in hospital.

There is good evidence that Anton Sauerwald was involved in this violence. The company he had set up in 1932 also made explosives – and we have seen that his assistant Emil Rothleitner was involved in Nazi cells. To the authorities, Sauerwald said he was supplying chemicals to, for example, construction companies for demolition. He did do this legitimately, but it has been claimed that the business was also the perfect front for making bombs for Nazi groups. In his book *Freud: Living and Dying*, Max Schur insists (in a footnote) that Sauerwald boasted to Freud's younger brother, Alexander, that he had played a very subtle game in the 1930s. We have seen that Sauerwald had been successful as an academic chemist, with four papers in *Monatshefte für Chemie*. That made him well qualified to work as an explosives expert for the Vienna police. So he became a kind of double agent: on the one hand he was retained by the police and on the other he was making bombs for Austrian Nazi groups. Sauerwald would manufacture bombs, the Nazis would plant them, the bombs would explode and then the witless police would bring Sauerwald the fragments so that he could use his forensic skills to analyse them. It sounds like a black comedy and it would have been funny but for the fact that people died.

The unrest in Vienna continued to June 1933, when the Austrian government arrested 1,142 Nazis. It suspected Berlin had ordered the violence. The Austrians then refused to grant diplomatic immunity to Hitler's personal envoy to Vienna. The man 'was routed out of bed at six in the morning. Police seized numbers of incriminating documents,' *Time* reported, adding, 'Berlin replied to this with typical Nazi bumbling.' German police called at the house of the Austrian press attaché in Berlin, Dr Erwin Wasserback. The doctor picked up the telephone and called Chancellor Dollfuss, who happened to be in London.

'Excellency,' Wasserback cried, 'the police are knocking at the door, what shall I do?'

'Don't do anything till they threaten force. Then let them in,' Dollfuss was reported to have said with some humour.

The Nazis had not chosen their victim cleverly. Wasserback was a priest as well as a doctor, which gave Dollfuss a nice opportunity. The Chancellor arranged for a formal protest from the Papal Nuncio in Berlin. Dr Wasserback was released quickly and Dollfuss transferred him to London, so that he could tell British diplomats how the Nazis behaved. Hitler had fans in Britain like Lloyd George, who had insisted on the huge German reparations after the First World War.

Dollfuss told a conference in London soon after the riots, 'While I do not charge the German Government with any such intention, the danger exists that irresponsible elements might march into Austria from Bavaria. If that happened we would have Czechoslovak and Jugoslav troops marching in to protect the interests of the Little Entente and a virtual war with my poor country as the battlefield. That is what I fear.'

Dollfuss returned to Vienna with a substantial prize, a loan for $29,975,000 from the League of Nations, which had money at least. He didn't have long to enjoy his success. Vienna was still in chaos. Nazi sympathisers were throwing grenades at policemen. Freud warned his son Ernst that Dollfuss 'probably won't be able to curb the dangerous fools in Heimwehr', who were the Austrian National Guard.

In the midst of all these upheavals, Sauerwald finally married Marianne Talg. She said that from that moment on he told her everything. The marriage did not calm a certain restlessness in Sauerwald.

After the war Sauerwald was asked where he had lived after the Nazi Party was declared illegal. He gave five different addresses:

- Vienna, 79 Hauptstrasse, 17th district.
- Vienna, 41 Semperstrasse, 18th district.
- London, Kingston Hall.
- Vienna, 20 Wettehauergasse, 18th district.
- Rosenheim, southern Germany, near the Tyrol border, 121/2 Aiblingerstrasse.

Rosenheim was a centre of Nazi activity. Hermann Goering was born there.

Sauerwald's time in London is intriguing. Freud's doctor Max Schur suggested that the only reason for Sauerwald to have come to England was that he had been sent as a spy by the Nazi Party. The files in the Austrian State Archives do not confirm Schur's suspicions. There is no mention of Sauerwald in the British National Archives. But the address Sauerwald gave, Kingston Hall, is something of a mystery. There was such a place in the London suburb of Kingston upon Thames, but it was pulled down around 1900. There is still a Kingston Hall Road, however. There was also Kingsley Hall, a kind of superior hostel founded in 1926 where some celebrities lodged while in London – Gandhi stayed there; it had socialist connections. It is possible that Sauerwald lied about his London address because he was on a Nazi mission, but there is no proof of it.

6 May 1933 and the Einstein of Sex

On 6 May 1933 Freud celebrated his 77th birthday. It would turn out to be a momentous day – and a very upsetting one.

On that day the Nazis closed down another institute some of whose members had links with Freud. We tend to think Alfred Kinsey was the first scientist to study human sexual behaviour. From 1919 onwards, however, regular visitors to Magnus Hirschfeld's Institute of Sex and to the Museum of Sex in Berlin were asked to fill in questionnaires about their sexual behaviour. Hirschfeld was Jewish, had been studying sexology for 30 years and was nicknamed the Einstein of Sex. He had an international reputation. Jawaharlal Nehru had visited his museum, as had a 1923 commission from

the Ministry of Health in Russia. The poet W.H. Auden came during his trip
to Berlin in 1929. Hirschfeld even published a book on homosexuality
among German high society, including the military.

The Institute was affiliated with the University of Berlin. It had a huge
library of 20,000 volumes, 35,000 pictures and 40,000 biographies, as well
as patients' records and a variety of rare objects and art.

On the morning of 6 May trucks drove up and about 100 students, all of
them committed Nazis, jumped out. Then, bizarrely, a brass band marched
to the front of the building. The students stormed it and took away many
documents while the band played on. Staff were kept locked up while the
students took the documents, which mainly dealt with 'intersexual' or
homosexual cases. The band kept on playing. This assault to loud music
soon attracted a large crowd.

At noon the leader of the students made a long speech and then they left,
singing a particularly vulgar song and the Horst-Wessel song, the Nazi
anthem. In the afternoon a second group of students returned to loot more
patient records. There were bonfires as usual. Some of the staff at the
Institute suspected that more than 'mere' anti-Semitism and homophobia
were involved. The Nazis feared that the Institute 'knew too much' about
party officials who had come to be treated for their un-Aryan problem; they
were homosexual. More files, 'Jewish filth', were burned in Opera Square.

On 7 May, with Freud's blessing, Max Eitingon resigned as president of
the Berlin Institute. Three days later, students from the Wilhelm Humboldt
University took books from their university library to the Franz Joseph
Platz. They also lit a bonfire and, once again, a band was playing. The
students then threw books by 58 authors into a huge bonfire. The writers
whose books went up in flames included H.G. Wells, Ernest Hemingway,
Karl Marx, Sigrid Unset, Albert Einstein, Thomas Mann, Jack London,
Erich Maria Remarque and, of course, Freud himself. There was some
ceremony as students consigned his books one by one to the flames. Freud
dared to see into their minds and was one of the most detested of these
writers.

The event was hardly spontaneous, as the Propaganda Minister, Joseph
Goebbels, was on hand to give a speech. The students sang Nazi songs round
the bonfire. Over the next few days, other university libraries were ransacked
and more books were burned all over Germany. The international press was
outraged; international politicians said nothing.

'Hundred thousand march here in six-hour protest over Nazi policies,' ran
the headline of the *New York Times* on 11 May. With uncanny prescience,
Newsweek called the burning 'a holocaust of books'. Many papers quoted

a warning by the 19th-century German Jewish poet Heinrich Heine, one of Freud's favourite writers. In his 1821 play about the Spanish Inquisition, *Almansor*, one of Heine's characters says, 'This is but the prologue. Where books are burnt, people in the end are burnt too.' Unusually, the *New York Times* allowed its Berlin correspondent to comment: 'This evening a significant part of ancient German liberalism – if that still existed – burnt along with the books.'

Walter Lippmann, one of the leading liberal journalists of the time, understood, like Heine, that this was the beginning, not the end. He wrote:

> The Nazis deliberately and systematically mean to turn the minds of the German people to war. These acts symbolise the moral and intellectual character of the Nazi regime. For these bonfires are not the work of schoolboys or mobs but of the present German Government acting through its Minister of Propaganda and Public Enlightenment. The ominous symbolism of these bonfires is that there is a Government in Germany which means to teach its people that their salvation lies in violence.

With some gallows humour, Freud noted that the Nazi action represented moral progress. In the Middle Ages, they would have burned him but now they were just content to burn his books. Some of those who corresponded with Freud did not manage the black humour. The Protestant pastor and analyst Oskar Pfister wrote to Freud that he been infected with 'disgust' in Germany and he would not easily rid himself of it for a long time: 'Proletarian militarism stinks even more rottenly than the blue-blooded Junker spirit of the time of the Kaiser.'

Freud replied, 'our horizon has become darkly clouded by events in Germany' and added that 'hatred for Judaism is at bottom hatred for Christianity itself'. He believed that 'only this Catholicism protects us against Nazism'. But Jews would have to be prudent and 'we naturally hesitate to do anything that would be bound to arouse the Church's hostility. This is not cowardice but prudence.'

The violence made Freud consider a possibility he dreaded and he told Pfister, 'Three members of our family with their families are looking for a new country and still have not found one. Switzerland is not among the hospitable countries. My judgement of human nature, especially of the Christian Aryan variety, has little reason to change.' A few weeks later, however, he wrote, 'flight would only be justified if there was a direct danger to life'. It was the first time he talked of leaving Vienna.

Freud's son Ernst now decided to leave Austria. His brother, Oliver, 'was also looking for a place to live in France somewhere near St Briac'. Analysts who wanted to escape did not find it easy, however. Britain, for example, was not in a mood to accept refugees and only four analysts went to Britain in 1933. One was Walter Schmideberg. He had been a cavalry officer in the 1914 war and was the man who had managed to keep Freud supplied with cigars. Walter came to join his wife, Melitta, the daughter of the child analyst Melanie Klein. I interviewed Melitta Schmideberg in 1980, when I was making a film on depression. She was an irrepressible old lady whose house near Marylebone station was crammed with antiques, rather like Freud's had been. She took great pleasure in showing me a spoon which Freud had given her. Life among the analysts made her very sceptical, she told me. She had long ago realised that talking and chicken soup were as effective as complicated analytic techniques.

Freud still hoped he and Martha could remain in Vienna, but he knew it was precarious. 'We are living here in a Catholic country under the protection of that Church, uncertain how long that protection will hold out,' he wrote. The Italian dictator Mussolini was doing more than France or England to protect Austria against the Nazis. 'Our bit of the civil war wasn't pretty at all,' Freud told Arnold Zweig. 'One couldn't go out into the street.'

It was hardly surprising that in Germany the analysts tried to find some accommodation with the Nazis.

Towards a Nazi Psychotherapy

In September 1933 Boehm and Müller-Braunschweig met with the Nazi Ministry of Culture to discuss the conditions under which the German Psychoanalytic Society could continue its work. They hoped to persuade Nazi officials that psychoanalysis did not have to be 'Jewish' but could be used to help the Reich. Boehm again told officials that it was not especially relevant that a Jew had invented psychoanalysis. The technique had its merits and the Nazis were wrong to believe it was 'subversive'. He had 'never known psychoanalysis to have a destructive effect on love of country,' Boehm assured them.

Müller-Braunschweig went even further. He wrote a 'Memorandum' on psychoanalysis for the Nazis and published it in a slightly adapted form in October 1933 as 'Psychoanalysis and Weltanschauung' in *Reichswart*, a 'rabid anti-Semitic publication'. He claimed it was wrong to see sexuality as the central issue; rather, psychoanalysis tried to heal the conflicts between our wild, reckless instincts and our egos, which struggled to keep everything under control. It was orthodox Freud, but Müller-Braunschweig cleverly framed these ideas in talk of 'mastery', which the Nazis lapped up. The unconscious could be 'mastered', he said; the patient could 'master' himself. He went on to write what some see as a passage which was a great betrayal:

> Psychoanalysis works to remodel incapable weaklings into people who can cope with life, the inhibited into confident types, those divorced from reality into human beings who can look reality in the face, those enslaved by their instincts into their masters, loveless, selfish people into people capable of love and sacrifice, those indifferent to the totality of life into those willing to serve the whole. Thus it does outstanding work in education, and is able to give valuable service to the principles, only now mapped out anew, of a heroic, constructive conception of life, attuned to reality.

Müller-Braunschweig reassured the men at the Ministry of Culture that a modified form of analysis, with decent Teutonic elements, could boost psychological health, which he defined 'in terms of blood, strong will, proficiency, discipline'.

But Boehm and Müller-Braunschweig feared that fine words wouldn't be enough; it might make all the difference to have a cousin of one of Hitler's strongmen as their ally. Both knew Matthias Goering, the cousin of Hermann, Hitler's deputy.

The Goerings

During the 1923 failed putsch, Hermann Goering was wounded and some accounts say he was saved by a Jewish doctor. Hermann had to flee Germany. We have seen how he was put in an insane asylum, but he loved his wife Emma and she loved him. With her help, he recovered and returned to Germany in 1927. So Hermann knew from all too personal experience that it was possible for psychiatric treatment to help. This created a bond between him and his cousin Matthias.

Matthias studied law at the University of Freiburg and travelled to Palestine, India and Ceylon. Jerusalem fascinated him. In 1907 he got his doctorate and went to work for one of the great psychiatrists of the time,

Emil Kraeplin. Matthias became interested in psychotherapy and hypnosis. As Freud had once done, he believed hypnosis could lay bare a patient's repressions and secrets and help heal him or her. Matthias was a convinced Christian and always carried a Bible with him. Photographs taken when he was in his fifties show a man with a long white beard. His patients called him Papi or Father Christmas. Treating the mentally ill seemed to reinforce his sense of the presence of God.

In 1929 Matthias set up a study group of psychotherapists in Wuppertal, but that did not mean he had become a Freudian. Where Freud stressed the libido, Goering emphasised the power of 'community feeling', as well as faith – faith in God and in the German nation. He does not seem to have seen any contradiction between faith in Christ and faith in Hitler, writing, 'External drill does not suffice. The core of man must be grasped as the Führer has repeatedly emphasised, and treated instinctively so that our subconscious is directed on the right path.'

Matthias once told Werner Kemper, an orthodox Freudian analyst, that it was not just sex that he objected to in psychoanalysis; it was also the couch. Freud made patients lie down while the analyst sat behind them and looked down on them. The unseen analyst had all the power. Eye contact was vital, Matthias believed. Helper and helped had to face each other honestly, in the spirit of Christ.

In his book on the relationship between the founder of individual psychoanalysis, Alfred Adler, and religion, Matthias wrote, 'To love means to be able to merge into another, to understand one's fellow man and to desire to help him in an effective manner.'

In *Psychotherapy in the Third Reich*, Geoffrey Cocks cannot decide whether or not Matthias was an anti-Semite. He did see Jewish patients, though he felt unable to help them because of 'social differences'. Yet it seems likely that, after Anna Freud asked him, he helped at least one analyst, Eva Rothmann, to escape from Germany.

It would not be totally out of character for a member of the Goering family to be sympathetic to Jews. Goering's other cousin, Hermann's younger brother, Albert Goering, hated everything Hitler stood for and left Germany for Vienna in 1928. He spoke out against the Nazis from the beginning. Albert's doctor, Laszlo Kovacs, recalled hearing Albert say, 'I defy Hitler, my brother and all the National Socialists.' This was not just talk. Albert gave Kovacs money to set up a secret bank account at the Bank Orelli in Bern, which he instructed Kovacs to use to help Jewish refugees to get to Lisbon. In 1939, during the war, he was stationed in Bucharest. When two Nazi officers recognised him as the brother of Hermann Goering and saluted him with the normal 'Heil Hitler', Albert replied, 'You can kiss my arse.' Despite their different political views, Albert and Hermann got on well. Hermann often protected him loyally and Albert often put pressure on Hermann to let some Jews escape.

After Albert came to live in Vienna, he took a house in Grinzig, which is where Freud liked to spend his summers. They had some acquaintances in common. Did the two men meet? There was much café life in the resort, so it is not improbable. The question is intriguing, because the Goering family was to have so much influence on the fate of psychoanalysis in Germany from 1933 onwards.

Now, with the approval of Jones, Boehm and Müller-Braunschweig offered Matthias the leadership of the German 'psychotherapists'. The pious Christian did not hesitate and had no trouble justifying his decision:

> In the interests of our society I wish to accept your offer, because I am a National Socialist not in name only but wholeheartedly in the spirit of Adolf Hitler, because moreover I bear the name of the Prussian Minister-President and am related to him. Also in the interests of National Socialism I must not refuse, for I believe that we psychotherapists have a great mission in the new state...we are called to educate children and adults in the right spirit.

From the very start, therefore, the psychotherapists in the Third Reich pinned their colours to a masthead already painted in the Nazi red and black. But the great mission could hardly proceed when so many analysts were Jewish and others, like Reich and Fenichel, were socialists. Boehm was well aware of the problem. He complained that 'Reich had often come out publicly as a Communist and as a psychoanalyst, presenting his opinions as the results of psychoanalysis...I had to fight against this prejudice.' Anna Freud, who, as we have seen, once befriended Reich, now wrote to Jones:

> Here we are all prepared to take risks for psychoanalysis but not for Reich's ideas, with which nobody is in agreement. My father's opinion on this matter is: If psychoanalysis is to be prohibited, it should be prohibited for what it is, and not for the mixture of politics and psychoanalysis which Reich represents. My father can't wait to get rid of him inasmuch as he attaches himself to psychoanalysis; what my father finds offensive in Reich is the fact that he has forced psychoanalysis to become political; psychoanalysis has no part in politics.

At a board meeting in the summer of 1933, Ernst Simmel, who had founded the Berlin Institute with Eitingon, had proposed Reich's expulsion. Eitingon wanted this postponed until the next general meeting, at the beginning of October 1933. By that time, he would be in Palestine.

Reich should have been warned of the moves against him and given a chance to defend himself, but he had already fled to Denmark, so the board decided it was not 'opportune' to contact him. Freud does not seem to have objected to keeping Reich in the dark.

On 7 December 1933 Freud wrote to Marie Bonaparte that he felt 'too cold'. He was smoking just one 'denerved cigar daily' and worrying about the book on Woodrow Wilson he was writing with William Bullitt. 'From Bullitt no direct news. Our book will never see the light of day,' he lamented to her. Freud also wrote to Sam in Manchester that 'life in Germany had become impossible'. He assumed that Sam would be reading about how the Nazis were behaving, so 'you know how unassured our situation is'. But he added, 'we are determined to stick it out'. Freud had become stubborn and his stubbornness made him a little blind.

What remains striking is how private Freud kept his views about the Nazis. *Why War?* had not attacked the Nazis, for example. An excellent indication of Freud's attitude is a letter he wrote to George Sylvester Viereck that year in response to a letter Viereck had written to the *New York Herald Tribune*.

Viereck had befriended Freud during the 1914–18 war and was one of those who sent him food parcels. He published an interview with the 'Columbus of the Unconscious' in 1923; Einstein also granted Viereck an interview, thinking the journalist was Jewish. But by the mid 1930s, both great men were disillusioned with the writer. The reason was that Viereck was a cousin of the Habsburg Crown Prince who had been supporting Hitler. By the early 1930s, Viereck had become an apologist for the new Germany.

The Crown Prince had assured the press that no one in Germany suffered injustice on account of their religion. Astutely, in support of this claim, the Crown Prince offered Neville Chamberlain's statement that he was not concerned with the alleged atrocities but would heed official Nazi announcements. At the time Chamberlain was Great Britain's Chancellor of the Exchequer.

Freud knew Viereck wanted him to comment and told him he would have done so 'and it would have been quite extensive were I not concerned that you might somehow use it for publicity'. He told Viereck that he replied on the understanding the letter would stay private. Viereck had 'debased' himself 'by siding with those wretched lies in your royal cousin's letter,' Freud said sharply. But he made the point privately.

CHAPTER 6

The Poet and the Analyst

By sticking it out, as he put it to Sam, Freud meant continuing to work as normal. We are lucky to have a vivid description of Freud at work in his last years from notes taken by the American poet H.D. (Hilda Doolittle) which she worked up into a small book, *Tribute to Freud*.

Doolittle was an immensely gifted writer who obviously intended to document her own analysis. Freud was hardly the first great man she met. She was friends with the great poets Ezra Pound and William Carlos Williams. Pound, who had helped T.S. Eliot, quickly recognised her talent as a poet. In 1919 Doolittle started what would be a 42-year-long affair with Annie Ellerman, who dramatically called herself Bryher, after one of the Scilly Islands. Bryher was given to dramatising herself.

Bryher was the daughter of an English financier and shipping tycoon, John Ellerman. She helped found the POOL Group, a small film production company, and she published *Film Problems of Soviet Russia*, a critique of Eisenstein and other Russian directors. She also started *Close-up*, probably the first magazine to look at film as an art form. POOL Productions made several experimental films, including *Borderline* (1930), which starred Paul Robeson and his wife, Essie, as well as Doolittle. Bryher astutely compared the pleasures of film production to childhood play, noting, 'I think it is because studios are nurseries on a large scale, with full-size blocks, trains, people, etc., to play with.' We all know Hollywood is a Wendy house.

In 1927 Bryher did something typically impulsive. She was in Venice when she 'saw a flight to Vienna and back, advertised at a moderate price, and smelt adventure'. Meeting Freud would be a great adventure. Bryher brought a letter of introduction from the pioneer sexologist Havelock Ellis. When she told Freud she had seen a storm as they flew, 'I knew that he wished that he had been with us himself.' Freud actually took a plane two years later, the only time he ever flew, though all he did was to circle Vienna.

When Doolittle went to see Freud, she had a complicated life and a complicated history in analysis. Her daughter Perdita Schaffner described Doolittle and Bryher as platonic lesbians. Their letters to one another suggest affection and emotional intimacy rather than lust. If they were lovers, it did not stop them sleeping with men. H.D. had a number of lovers, while Bryher would marry twice. Still the two women were bonded for life.

When Doolittle said she was unhappy in her analysis with Mary Chadwick, an English analyst who was also involved with POOL, Bryher suggested that she go into analysis with Hans Sachs, one of Freud's closest friends. Sachs was, however, not the right analyst for her. He tended to mix discussions of film and social chit-chat in with his interpretations. Doolittle was suspicious of him and wrote to Bryher – they wrote every day when they were apart – that she wondered if Sachs was motivated by 'your dollars, my analysis, or my beaux yeaux-es' (given Doolittle's eccentric spelling, there's no slur on readers' French if they don't get that means beautiful eyes). And Sachs clearly wanted rather more from his patient than he should; to her horror, he arranged for her to stay on the same floor of the same hotel as he was. Doolittle then asked him for an introduction to Freud. Sachs could hardly refuse.

Doolittle does not give this background in *Tribute to Freud*. She merely explains that she went to see Freud because she hoped 'to fortify and equip myself to face the war when it came', which apparently meant understanding her neuroses.

The book Doolittle wrote is not, as she confesses, 'a historical sequence'. She digresses into the reasons for own neuroses and flip-flops between the two periods when she spent time with Freud – 1933–4 and 1938, once he came to London. Like Eastman earlier, she gives a vivid portrait of Freud.

Though poetically vague about the dates, Doolittle clearly came at a time when there had been disturbances in Vienna. The hall porter at her hotel warned her not to get involved in any political discussion and advised her not to go out at all. Doolittle ignored him, but it soon became clear how sensible his advice had been. She was stopped by a group of armed men who wanted to know where she was going. She said in her 'sketchy' German that she was going to the opera and they gave her 'almost a guard of honour' to its steps.

Doolittle's 'sketchy' German meant that she and Freud spoke in English.

When she arrived, Paula Fichtl, 'the little maid', peered through a crack in the door. Doolittle was a good reporter when she was not on one of her journeys into her own interior and described the consulting rooms in detail. The furniture was heavy; small statues and figurines stood on every table and bookcase. She noticed the framed photographs of Havelock Ellis and of Sachs. The honorary diploma from Clark University from 1909 hung on the wall. A bizarre and horrifying engraving of some nightmare, 'a *Buried Alive* or some such thing done in Düreresque symbolic detail', caught her eye.

More than most of Freud's patients, Doolittle could detach herself and look. She knew that she would turn this experience into material. She told Walter, Melitta Schmideberg's husband, she was making notes of her analysis. And the notes started while she was waiting to see Freud for the first time: 'I look around the room. A lover of Greek art.' No one had told her that Freud's room was 'lined with treasures'. A door at one end of the room opened in from the little waiting room. That was the way to the inner sanctum. Another door at right angles, the exit door, led through a rather dark passage or 'a little room that suggests a pantry or laboratory'. Then there was the hall 'beyond it where we hang our coats on pegs that somehow suggest school or college'.

Freud eventually appeared and asked Doolittle why she had come. In her account, she often reports what Freud said in rather lengthy quotes. No one can be sure that she remembered what he had said perfectly or that she did not invent passages, but the words she attributes to Freud feel authentic. She gets his tone, one feels. Freud comes over as a little quirky, even crotchety.

Doolittle had come expecting to greet 'the Old Man of the sea but no one had told me of the treasures that he had salvaged from the sea depth'. She felt he was part and parcel of these treasures 'and immensely old, old' because he is 'weighing the soul in the balance'.

Freud was struck by how interested she was in her surroundings: 'You are the only person who has ever come into this room and looked at the things in the room before looking at me.' At this point 'a lioness' – Doolittle quickly admitted she was just a chow – ran out from under the couch. Doolittle bent down to greet the little dog.

Freud warned, 'Do not touch her – she snaps – she is very difficult with strangers.'

The chow, Jofi (it seems unlikely that Freud did not realise her name meant 'pretty' in Hebrew, incidentally), was not afraid of Doolittle. The dog snuggled her nose into Doolittle's hand. While Jofi snuffled, Doolittle carried on a dialogue in her own mind: 'You call me a stranger, do you?' Doolittle was determined to show that she was no such thing. The fact that his chow had snuggled into her hand proved that.

Freud said nothing while his dog and his patient sniffed each other out. In Doolittle's mind, however, a little instant self-analysis was proceeding. She was riffing to herself: 'You are a very great man. I am overwhelmed with embarrassment. I am shy and frightened and gauche as an over-grown school girl.' But she was damned if she was going to show it; her stream of challenging consciousness bubbled on: 'You are a man. Jofi is a dog. I am a woman. If this dog and this woman take to each other it will prove that beyond your caustic implied criticism there is another region of cause and effect.'

Doolittle saw that Freud was not jealous because Jofi liked her. Good dog, good sage. His new patient realised Freud's dog was the way to Freud's heart.

When he asked her why she had come to see him, she thought, 'What did he expect me to say?'

But they were still at the polite stage. She said she felt she would benefit from analysis; her analysis with Mary Chadwick had been less than satisfactory. Freud replied, in Oracle mode, 'we never know what is important or unimportant until after. We must be impartial, play fair to ourselves.' Doolittle does not report saying anything about Sachs.

Freud had great respect for artists and their relationship was surprisingly equal. Doolittle soon stopped being the overwhelmed schoolgirl. Freud thought that her play *Ion* was a masterpiece. Doolittle was flattered that Freud treated her as an intellectual equal. They shared a passion for archaeology, mythology and for Athena, the goddess of wisdom and warfare. Freud had a number of statuettes of Athena and showed Doolittle which one was his ultimate favourite.

Freud often would say 'but of course you understand' and then offer Doolittle a 'rare discovery, some priceless finding'. Doolittle's mood often changed during her sessions. They were sessions but she makes them sound far more free-flowing, like musical improvisations, than textbook analytic sessions should be. She could be challenging one moment, nervous the next. Sometimes her nervousness made her clumsy; once she dropped the rug that she had wrapped round herself from the floor. Would Freud comment on this? she fretted. He did not. Doolittle was also embarrassed because the couch was slightly too small for her.

Very early, the poet had the kind of dream patients dream in order to please their analyst. It was a dream of Moses as a baby in a basket. Freud asked her if she saw Batya, the Pharaoh's daughter. The prophet was obviously on his mind.

Doolittle's description of being in analysis is often quite playful even though she had harrowing issues to deal with. She offers the nice image of doing analysis as a 'jigsaw' and remarks on how she and Freud would play 'hide and seek, hunt the slipper, hunt the thimble and patiently and meticulously patch together odds and ends of our picture puzzle'. As they tried to complete the jigsaw that was Doolittle, familiar themes emerged: 'Freud insisted that I myself wanted to be Moses.' There were implications from that: 'Not only did I want to be a boy but I wanted to be a hero.' She had better read Otto Rank's book *The Birth of the Hero*, Freud suggested. It would give her perspective.

Fairly early, they seemed to have made considerable progress into Doolittle's problems, which included difficulties with men, something of a fixation on her father and her relationship with Bryher. One day Freud said, 'Today we have struck very deep.' Another day Doolittle reports him saying, 'I struck oil.' She also noted that 'He used the slang of the counting house or of Wall Street.' Freud went on to tell her that the contents of the oil wells, her oil wells, her hidden depths, had only just been sampled. 'There is oil but there is enough left for 100 years or more,' Freud said.

Doolittle commented acidly that the profits of the oil went to someone else. 'There are astute doctors,' she said, 'who will squeeze you dry with their exorbitant fees for prolonged...treatments.'

One of the many useful insights that Paula Fichtl provides is information about fees. Freud charged $25 an hour, which was frankly a fortune. That was £6 an hour at the exchange rate of the time. You could buy a small house in London for £1,000. So you could have about 167 hours of Freud or a house. An analyst today would have to charge about £2,500 an hour to match that.

When Doolittle raised the question of fees, however, Freud was utterly unconcerned: 'Do not worry about that. That is my concern. I want you to feel at home.' In fact, of course, Bryher would have paid Doolittle's fees, but it seems Freud did not want to take more money from Bryher, as she had sent money to help out with the Internationaler Psychoanalytischer Verlag.

Just as with Marie Bonaparte, Freud did not play by the analytic rules he had invented. He was not the impenetrable blank sitting behind the couch, revealing nothing of himself. He was worried about how he and his family would cope in the political turmoil. She said, 'I am also concerned but I do not openly admit this, about the Professor's attitude to a future life. One day I was deeply distressed when the Professor spoke to me about his grand-children – what would become of them? He asked me that as if the future of his immediate family were the only future to be considered.' She had no idea of the deaths and suicides. She was the awed patient who saw that 'he knew he was among those who would be counted as immortal' and also that he was very concerned about a 'more imminent, a more immediate future'.

In one session they discussed Time. 'When I said to him that time went too quickly he struck a semi comic attitude,' Doolittle said.

'Time,' Freud said. 'The word was uttered in his inimitable two edged manner.' Doolittle thought that he managed to pack into that word a 'store of contradictory emotions': irony, entreaty, defiance, with a vague and tender pathos. He also had a surprisingly delicate voice.

'Time,' Freud repeated. 'Time gallops.'

She then added a riff on time in Shakespeare. Time gallops with a thief to the gallows. Time and the gallows, images of death and of age.

Doolittle had read Freud's *An Autobiographical Study* of 1925, in which he recorded one of his few positive experiences in the United States. He went for a walk with the pioneer psychologist William James. James stopped, 'handed me a bag and asked me to walk on saying he would catch up with me as soon as he had got through an attack of angina pectoris'. His courage impressed Freud. 'I have always wished I might be as fearless as he was in the face of approaching death,' he wrote.

Death was a presence in the room, like a thousand particles of dust, as Freud and Doolittle talked. Among his books there were some plays and one of them was *Alcestis*; she could not recall who had written that, but it did not matter as

the play is going on now – at any rate we are acting it, the old Professor and I. The old professor doubles the part. He is Hercules struggling with Death and he is the beloved, about to die. Moreover he himself in his own character has made the dead live, has summoned a host of dead and dying children from the living tomb.

Freud sensed how attached to him Doolittle was becoming and insisted on one point: 'Please, never – I mean never at any time in any circumstance, endeavour to defend me, if and when you hear abusive remarks about my work.' If she tried to do that, 'the anger or the frustration of the assailant will be driven deeper...You will drive the hatred or the fear or the prejudice in deeper.' Defending him would do no good, for 'antagonism once taking hold cannot be rooted out from above the surface and it thrives in a way on heated argument and digs in deeper'.

Much of Freud's behaviour was not very Freudian. He did not insist that Doolittle always lie on the couch; he stood up himself sometimes rather than sitting unseen behind her. He 'rarely used any of the now rather overworked technical terms invented by himself'. She complained about the way that 'some doctors, psychologists and nerve specialists who form the somewhat formidable body of the International Psychoanalytic Association' use them. Freud was wry about this.

Once she raised a topic and commented, 'I suppose you would say it was a matter of ambivalence.'

Freud did not say anything.

'Or do you say am-bi-valence?' Doolittle added. 'I don't know whether it's pronounced ambi-valence or am-bi-valence.'

Freud's arm shot forward, as it often did when he wanted to stress something. Then, 'in his curiously casual ironical manner', he said, 'Do you know I myself have always wondered? I often wish that I could find someone to explain these matters to me.'

The sage takes the Zen-like attitude. With her at least, he could make fun of the pretensions of other analysts.

He could keep it simple too. At one point, when she had revealed some traumatic events that had happened to her, Freud just said, 'Perhaps you are not happy.'

She found herself unable to explain.

'It is not a question of happiness. It is the happiness of the quest,' he insisted.

Freud told her he felt she was impatient with him because she felt sensibly enough that it was not worth her while to love a man as old as he was.

Two Women, an Analyst and a Dog

Freud was fascinated by Doolittle and by her relationship with Bryher. That was hardly surprising. It had some similarities to his daughter's close friendship with Dorothy Burlingham, who was also living in 19 Berggasse. Bryher was wily too, and had no intention of being excluded. She sent books to Freud and also questions about dogs.

Bryher commiserated with Doolittle when Freud's chow Jofi suffered a painful pregnancy, which reminded Doolittle of her own first pregnancy, in which she had lost the baby. Bryher drily contrasted her domestic dilemmas with Doolittle's analytic explorations: 'I'm glad I'm "male" in your uncons. MY unc keeps losing key of wine cupboard.'

At the end of April 1933 Bryher had a major dilemma. How did one turn down a gift from Freud without seeming rude? He knew Bryher loved dogs and wanted to repay her for helping with the Verlag, so he offered her one of Jofi's puppies. But she did not like chows. Bryher and Doolittle discussed how to refuse without giving offence. Finally, Bryher wrote to Freud and apologised. Her father was very ill and so she had to turn down his kind offer. It would be irresponsible to take the puppy as she was not sure she could provide proper puppy-sitting in London.

After Doolittle left Vienna, she and Freud wrote sporadically to each other, but she had no intention of letting the old master die without seeing him again.

The Promised Land

The rise of the Nazis made many Jews sympathetic to Zionism, but Freud was ambivalent. In 1932 Freud had pointed out to Arnold Zweig that Palestine had produced nothing but religions and 'presumptuous attempts to conquer the world of appearances by the inner world of inner feelings'. Now that he knew what life was really like there, there was also the problem that one could not be sure of a hot bath. Letters from friends constantly complained about how primitive their life had become.

On 21 January 1934 Zweig wrote from Tel Aviv:

> At one moment the central heating did not function, at another the oil stove smelt. We are not prepared to give up our standard of living and this country is not yet prepared to satisfy it [...] I don't care any more about 'the land of my fathers'. I don't have any more Zionistic illusions either. I view the necessity of living here among Jews without enthusiasm, without any false hopes and even without the desire to scoff.

Seven days later, Freud replied, 'I have long waited eagerly for your letter [...] I am eager to read it, now that I know you are cured of your unhappy love for your so-called Fatherland. Such a passion is not for the likes of us.' Quite what he meant by the last sentence is not clear.

But Freud did not manage to dissuade another friend from emigrating. On 9 January 1934 Max Eitingon gave all the modern furniture he had loaned them to the Berlin Institute and took the train for the French Riviera, the first leg of his journey to Palestine. He stayed a few days in the expensive resort of Cap Ferrat, then caught a train to Marseilles and from there boarded a ship to Haifa. Soon after he got to the Promised Land, he founded the Palestinian Psychoanalytic Society. He was disappointed that no Arabs or Orthodox Jews were interested. Eitingon saw just four patients in his first year and never saw more than 20 patients a year. Virtually all of them were Jews from Central Europe. The rather sad letters he wrote to Freud about life in Palestine – almost no cafés, almost no cultural life – would not have encouraged anyone to leave Vienna for the Promised Land, even if the Nazis were baying across the border.

We owe to another of Freud's Jewish friends, Stefan Zweig, one of the best descriptions of how the Nazis plotted in Austria; it is to be found in his short story 'The Royal Game'. Zweig is reckoned by many to be one of the greatest 20th-century writers but he has been little read in Britain. The story centres round a chess game, one of whose players is a doctor, Dr B, who lives in Vienna. Given that Zweig and Freud were in constant correspondence and that Zweig lived in London after 1938, when Freud was there, it seems likely that Zweig based Dr B partly at least on Freud. Dr B described how the Nazis had started to position themselves to take power:

> The Nazis had begun long before they rearmed their military forces to organise another army – just as dangerous and well trained – in all the neighbouring countries, the legion of the underprivileged, the downtrodden and the maladjusted. In every office, in every business, they established their so called cells in every government department up to the private offices of Dollfuss.

The Nazi cells did not remain in hiding for long. On 12 February 1934 a force of Nazis searched the Hotel Schiff in Linz, which was owned by the Social Democratic Party. Shooting started; the police and the regular Federal Army became involved. Fighting spread to Vienna. Members of the socialist Schutzbund (safety group) barricaded themselves in housing estates, including one named after Karl Marx. The socialists had only small arms but Dollfuss ordered the army to use artillery. Many buildings were destroyed before the socialists surrendered on 13 February. Several hundred people died and more than 1,000 were wounded. The police made over 1,500 arrests and executed nine socialist leaders. It was not easy to get precise information, though.

On 19 February 1934 Freud wrote to Marie Bonaparte, 'If the Nazis come here and bring with them the same lawlessness as in Germany then of course one must leave.' The next day he wrote to his son Ernst, 'thanks to the guiding principle of all journalistic reportage – of making as much noise as possible – it is probably not easy to learn from the papers what is really happening in a city where shooting is going on. What affected us most was that we were without electric light.' But the matches worked at least, Freud joked. The victors were bound to make 'every error that can be committed in such a situation'.

After these disturbances, Dollfuss established a quasi-dictatorship, but he was a devout Catholic and had no intention of attacking the Church. In Germany, however, the Nazis were becoming less restrained against the Jews. They passed edict after edict, restriction after restriction and committed violence after violence. Kosher slaughter was banned. Jews were banned from the army even if they had served with distinction in the First World War. Jews were banned from the civil service. New laws were going to outlaw sex between Jews and non Jews.

At least German Jews were not being forcibly sterilised yet. As analysts at the Goering Institute helped with this shameful policy, it has to be explained. Seven months after he took power, Hitler forced through a 'Law for the Prevention of Hereditarily Diseased Offspring'. Anyone who suffered from schizophrenia, epilepsy, 'imbecility' and chronic alcoholism would be sterilised. The Interior Ministry set up special Hereditary Health Courts to examine inmates of nursing homes, asylums, prisons and aged care homes. About 360,000 disabled and mentally ill people were sterilised. Most German doctors blithely forgot the Hippocratic Oath, which insists that the first duty of a doctor is to do no harm.

Hitler passionately hated those he thought 'unworthy of life'. His doctor, Dr Karl Brandt, and the head of the Reich Chancellery, Hans Lammers, said Hitler had told them sterlisation was just the first step. Killing the incurably ill made more sense, but public opinion would not accept this in peacetime. 'Such a problem could be more smoothly and easily carried out in war,' Hitler judged, and he intended 'in the event of a war radically to solve the problem of the mental asylums'.

'The future is uncertain,' Freud wrote to his son Martin. It would be either Austrian fascism or the 'swastika'. Native fascism would be just about tolerable, as he did not believe Austrian Nazis would be as brutal as their German counterparts. The alternative, going to live in a foreign country, would not be pleasant, Freud added.

Daily Life at the Freuds

Life in a new country would be unpleasant because it would mean change and Freud was an old man who had his routines. Paula Fichtl described them

in detail. She was the first person to be up in 19 Berggasse because she had
to switch on the boiler for hot water. Freud would wake up at 7a.m. You
could set a clock by him. Freud and Martha shared a big brown wooden
double bed. Almost the first thing Freud would do was take his bath and
that gave their housekeeper an unexpected insight into their relationship.
Once Paula went into the bathroom, to find 'the Professor who was utterly
naked' while Martha was towelling him dry. She was using a rough towel
because Freud got itchy and liked to have his back scratched. Paula ran out
flustered, but not just because she had trespassed; she had also noticed that
Herr Professor had a large member, as she said daringly in her memoirs.

The double bed and the towelling make it clear that even if Jones was right
and the 'passionate side of the marriage faded after Freud turned forty', the
couple were still physically affectionate even in their seventies.

After Freud had had his bath, he and Martha had breakfast in the dining
room. Then the barber would come to shave Freud and trim his beard. The
Professor hated the smell of the aftershave. Fichtl would nearly always pay
the barber a schilling. Because Freud smoked so heavily, his suits were
flecked with tobacco and the smell made Paula slightly sick; her job was to
keep his clothes looking impeccable. She sometimes hung his suits out to dry
in the window at Berggasse. Freud had many fine suits and took some care
choosing which one to wear every day. His socks were a problem because his
long, sharp toenails meant they were full of holes and needed constant
darning.

After breakfast, Freud would go to his study to write or see patients. The
room was impeccable. Fichtl dusted his study, his statues and the analytic
couch every morning. The dog sat at his feet. Fichtl then offers a shocking
detail: Freud kept two urine bottles by his desk and was clearly in the habit
of pissing in them. This is very strange, as there was perfectly good plumbing
in the apartment about five metres away. Fichtl had to empty the bottles and
clean them. This was not her only personal-hygiene task. Martha had
explained to her when she started the job that Fichtl would sometimes find
flecks of blood and faecal matter on the bedsheets, on the Professor's side.
She had to make sure the sheets were clean. The rest of the bedlinen,
however, was just changed every two weeks.

Lunch was always served at 1p.m. Freud liked Paula's vegetable soup
because the prosthesis made it hard to chew. Often he did not finish his lunch
and gave some of it to the dog, who sat by the table. Sometimes Freud had
a short nap after lunch, snoozing on the analytic couch. He often hummed
to the dog while resting.

He frequently worked late into the night, which, of course, helps explain how productive he was to the end of his life. Paula always laid out his pyjamas for him. He liked to read both in the study and in bed. His tastes were eclectic. He loved Dickens, Thackeray and detective novels, including those of Sir Arthur Conan Doyle, Dorothy L. Sayers and Agatha Christie. He thought he always knew who the murderer was, or should be, and got extremely annoyed if he did not guess right. He was a fast reader and very rarely needed more than an evening to finish a book. If he was in the middle of one, he used a matchstick to mark the page he was at.

Paula got on well with Freud, who was obviously not stand-offish and chatted to her at times during the day. Once she broke a statue of an angel and offered to pay to have it fixed. The Professor would have none of it. When the angel came back restored, he joked that it was 'now presentable again'. At Christmas, Freud gave her gold coins, which she treasured and often did not spend.

She also noticed, as the 1930s progressed, that the Freuds were more worried about money. At the start of the decade, a tailor used to come every second month to measure Freud for a new suit. But that stopped around 1934, she realised.

Paula loved Martha but had problems with Minna, who became jealous of 'the little maid' who performed many quite personal tasks. Minna felt she had been partially replaced as the third woman in Freud's home. Paula was not being paranoid. Harry Freud recalled that Tom Sidemann, Paula's nephew, observed that being an aunt 'did not mean being an ice-box'. The home was, Paula said, 'quiet but not happy'. Freud talked about his work more to Minna than to his wife. Sometimes when Minna answered the phone, an instrument Freud loathed, she gave the impression that she was his wife.

It is lucky for us that Freud hated the phone and therefore put so much energy into letter writing. On 20 February 1934 Freud wrote to his son Ernst, 'Our attitude to the two political possibilities for Austria's future can only be summed up in Mercutio's line in *Romeo and Juliet*: "a plague on both your houses".' Freud did not send the letter at once. The next day, when martial law in Vienna was repealed, he added a sentence: 'Our government and our Cardinal expect a great deal from God's assistance.' Despite his lack of belief in God, Freud was quite capable of invoking the Almighty. In a letter to Arnold Zweig he spoke of the power of the Nazis and concluded, 'God has much to put right there.'

The choices were few. On 25 February 1934 Freud told Zweig:

You are quite right in your expectation that we intend to stick it out here resignedly. For where should I go in my state of dependence and physical helplessness? And everywhere abroad is so inhospitable. Only if there really were a satrap of Hitler's ruling in Vienna I would no doubt have to go, no matter where.

More Analytical Battles

At the start of 1934 Ernest Jones became president of the International Psychoanalytic Association. He believed it was vital to keep politics out of psychoanalysis so that it would survive in Germany. If Germany were expelled from the Association it would provoke a huge crisis. Preventing expulsion would not be easy, however, Jones told Boehm, because of the 'storm of indignation and opposition' coming from some members, especially the 'exiles from Germany'.

Jones consoled Müller-Braunschweig:

You will know that I myself regard these emotions and ultra Jewish attitudes very unsympathetically and it is plain to me that you and your colleagues are being made a dumping ground for much emotion and resentment which belongs elsewhere and has been displaced in your direction.

Brenda Maddox, Jones's biographer, is forced to defend one of his letters in which he said that a Jewish analyst, Isidor Sadger, should be sent to a 'concentration camp'. (Sadger had written a memoir about Freud which was not unflattering but highlighted a few differences between them.) When Jones wrote this in 1934, Maddox is at pains to point out, concentration camps did not mean what they came to mean later. Perhaps, but they were still brutal places of arbitrary detention.

That same month, Jones warned Boehm that he might be attacked at the forthcoming international psychoanalytic congress because he had tried to negotiate with the Nazi Ministry of Culture. Jones insisted, 'My only concern is for the good of psychoanalysis itself, and I shall defend the view, which I confidently hold, that your actions have been actuated only by the same motive.'

The good of psychoanalysis could be compromised by Reich. Boehm, Müller-Braunschweig and Jones knew there would be no hope of reaching any compromise with the Nazis if Reich were still a member of the German Psychoanalytic Society. But many analysts saw Reich more as a victim than a viper. Worse, no one had bothered to tell him that he had been expelled from the International Association. Edith Jacobson was supposed to have informed him but had chosen not to. So Reich travelled from Norway to attend the Lucerne Congress on 26 August 1934, expecting to take part. When he got there, it was left to Müller-Braunschweig to tell him that he had been expelled.

Max Eitingon arrived for the congress from Palestine – he had few patients to treat there, after all – and persuaded Jones it would be only right to have a special arrangement for those analysts who had been forced out of Germany or had fled for their own safety. They should be allowed to have individual membership of the International Association if they were now in a country with no national association. Jones was persuaded to set up an emigration office to keep track of where analysts were settling.

Freud was kept in touch with all the developments. Anna Freud and Jones were writing to each other. Soon after the congress ended they were both alarmed by the arrest of Edith Jacobson in Berlin. She was accused of treating patients who were Communists, whose party the Nazis had outlawed. Jones flew to the city, intending to help her, but Boehm told him that one of her patients had been killed and that if he tried to intervene on her behalf psychoanalysis would suffer. Jones promptly returned to Britain.

The success of the Nazis also affected the ways analysts behaved to each other. Fenichel saw that Boehm had started to identify with the dictatorial style of the new masters: 'I told him that he was already infected with the modern Führer principle.' Boehm often said that he was 'the Führer of psychoanalysis', but Fenichel enjoyed bursting his balloon, pointing out that the Führer of the couches was 'a leader who in many respects trembled with more anxiety than many other leaders'.

Anxiety did make some seek analysis and consult Freud. On 23 April 1934 Arnold Zweig wrote:

Dear Father Freud
    I am taking up my analysis again. I just cannot shake off the whole Hitler business. My affect has shifted to someone who looked after our affairs for us in 1933 under difficulties. But this affect of mine is an obsession. I don't live in the present, but am absent.

In the summer of 1934, Freud left Vienna as usual for his holidays in Grinzig, but he did not enjoy a peaceful summer. No one did. On 25 July 1934 a group of Nazis stormed the Chancellery in Vienna and killed Dollfuss. Many Viennese thought Hitler would invade at once, but Mussolini sent troops to the border to warn the Germans against crossing into Austria. The Western Allies, however, hardly protested at the murder.

Kurt von Schuschnigg succeeded Dollfuss. The new Chancellor was 36 years old and had been in Parliament for only seven years, although he had already been Minister of Education and Minister of Justice. Schuschnigg tried to keep his options open. He talked to Austria's neighbours about creating an anti-German alliance; he talked to Otto von Habsburg about restoring the Habsburg dynasty; he talked to Franz von Papen, the German envoy to Vienna, about closer links with Berlin and the Nazis. He wanted at all costs to preserve Austria's independence.

The political uncertainty meant that Freud had fewer patients than before and so he had time to return to a subject he had never stopped thinking about: Moses. He told Arnold Zweig in September 1934, 'In a time of relative freedom and at a loss to know what to do with my surplus leisure' he had written something and 'it has taken such a hold of me that everything else has been left undone'. He had to admit that circumstances compelled him when it came to Moses 'to keep the completed essay secret'.

On 6 November 1934 Freud told Zweig, 'I have written to Eitingon that you are right in your view that it would be a risk to get my Moses published.' The Catholic Church had to be appeased to protect psychoanalysis but that was not simple. Freud now had an enemy to focus on. 'It is said that the politics of our country are made by a Father Schmidt,' Freud wrote.

Schmidt was a monk at the monastery of St Gabriel near Mödling and had published papers on the religious beliefs of primitive peoples. He had made 'no secret of his horror of psychoanalysis' and in particular of the totem and taboo theory. The monk had proved, to his own and the Vatican's satisfaction at least, that many primitive tribes had some sense that there was just one God; it was absurd to suggest, as Freud had done in *Totem and Taboo*, that primitive savages behaved like the 'modern sex ridden neurotics' Freud treated. The savages were much more civilised.

Schmidt was not some lowly monk in the Austrian Alps. He had the ear of the Pope. Eduardo Weiss, who had 'direct access' to Mussolini, found that the *Italian Journal of Psychoanalysis* was forced to stop publishing. He told Freud, 'The ban is said to come straight from the Vatican. And Father Schmidt is said to be responsible.'

Schmidt could not stop Freud publishing his book on Moses, of course, but the publication would 'be bound to create a sensation and it would not escape the attention of the inimical priest'. Freud would not care if he was the only one to be hurt, but he suspected other analysts would suffer. He had no right to 'deprive all our members in Vienna of their livelihood'.

Paying customers were scarce enough. It was not 'quite the proper occasion for martyrdom'. Freud was honest enough, however, to admit that he also had his doubts about his work and that 'this historical novel won't stand up to my own criticism'.

A few weeks after he had fumed about Schmidt, Freud was even more depressed. 'Don't say any more about the Moses book,' he wrote to Arnold Zweig on 12 December. He was making no progress and he had a new worry; he was fretting because 'my memory of recent events is no longer reliable'. Freud blamed the radium treatment he had received for the cancer that had been diagnosed eleven years earlier: 'I react to this diabolical stuff with the most frightful pain.' In French he added that he often thought the game no longer worth the candle. 'Resolutions' and willpower did not help in the face of unremitting agony.

But Moses would not let him rest. On 14 March 1935, Freud wrote to Zweig that he had read a new book by a German scholar, Elias Auerbach, but it was disappointing. Auerbach provided no support for Freud's heretical ideas (which are discussed later when considering *Moses and Monotheism*). The book did not argue that Moses was an Egyptian prince or a 'fusion' of that prince and a Midianite priest. Auerbach had not broken with tradition. Instead of being relieved that the new book had not stolen his thunder, Freud was upset because he had hoped Auerbach would provide some basis for his own ideas, making his work more historical and less of a novel.

Electro-coagulation

It seemed that Freud's medical problems might force the family to change their usual holiday plans and not go to Grinzig. On 23 March 1935 Pichler performed electro-coagulation on tissue at the back of the mouth, which involved applying a high-frequency electrical current locally with a needle to stop the bleeding. This was a cutting-edge procedure, less hard to bear than the radium, and it did lessen the pain. That was a blessing as Freud prepared for his 79th birthday.

Arnold Zweig was one of many friends to send their best wishes. Despite his own problems, Freud was still very aware of other people's difficulties. He worried about the state of Zweig's eyes and wondered if the optician he had recommended had helped.

Freud was resilient but realistic. On 2 May 1935 he wrote to the other Zweig, Stefan, and admitted that his hope of enjoying spring on Mount Carmel was a mere fantasy now as even 'supported by my faithful Anna

Antigone I could not embark on a further journey'. He went on to complain, 'since I can no longer smoke, I no longer want to write,' but he was restless, as 'Moses won't let go my imagination'.

Freud remained very alert to archaeological developments. He learned of an excavation report on a desert site in Egypt, Tell el-Amarna, which mentioned a mysterious Prince Thothmes, about whom nothing was known: 'If I were a millionaire in pounds I would finance the continued excavations. This Thothmes could be my Moses and I would be able to boast I had guessed right.'

By his birthday on 6 May, Freud was still in pain and complained to fellow analyst Lou Andreas-Salomé, 'What an amount of good nature and good humour it takes to endure the gruesome business of growing old.' She should not expect 'anything intelligent' from him, as coping with his own poor health took time and energy. He quoted Mephistopheles in Goethe's *Faust*:

> In the end we depend
> On the creatures we made.

Again he praised Anna: 'It was very wise to have made her.' Even his farewell, 'your old Freud', was mournful.

The pressure of events was making Freud more willing to confide in friends and risk the authority he always worried about compromising. On 13 June he admitted to Arnold Zweig that he told him many things that he withheld from other people. He disliked having so much free time because he had very few hours of analytic practice. He was also noticing that 'as far as my own productivity goes it is like what happened in analysis'. He had repressed working on Moses because of his doubts, but 'nothing could take its place. The field of vision remains empty.' He was always tinkering with the text, however, and looked forward to reading his manuscript to Zweig if he came to Vienna. He also told Zweig that he had worries about money.

But there was some good news. Freud had just been made an honorary member of the British Royal Society of Medicine and that, he noted, would make 'a good impression on the world'. Sometimes one detects the influence of his nephew Edward Bernays, the world's first public relations counsel. The image of psychoanalysis could do with a boost. Dictators and devious divines like Father Schmidt might respect it more and persecute it less. 'Analysis can flourish no better under Fascism than under Communism or National Socialism,' Freud said.

Freud came to a pessimistic conclusion. Arnold Zweig had been writing a novel called *Education before Verdun*, named after one of the battles of the First World War, which Anna had been discussing with her father. Freud told his friend how much he admired the book and the lessons he drew from it:

> Today one says to oneself, if I had drawn the right conclusions about Verdun then I should have known that I could not live among these people. We all thought it was the war and not the people but other nations went through the war as well and nevertheless behaved differently. We did not want to believe it at the time but it was true what the other nations said about the Boches [French slang for Germans].

Just as Freud was honoured by the Royal Society of Medicine, Carl Jung (who could be seen as half 'Boche', as he was German-Swiss) chose to make trouble. There has been much controversy about Jung's behaviour and at times he has been accused of being a secret Nazi, an open Nazi and an anti-Semite; what is evident is that he exploited the situation. He now accepted the editorship of a leading psychoanalytic journal and became president of the German Society for Medical Psychotherapy. He also became involved in the plan to take over German psychoanalysis. He later claimed he was not motivated by revenge.

Without telling Jones, Boehm and Müller-Braunschweig arranged meetings with Jungians. Jung himself stayed away. They talked about setting up a new institute that would be headed by Matthias Goering, who was drawn to Jung's ideas. This seems to have been the decisive moment.

From then on, Boehm collaborated fully with the Nazis. He advocated harsher racial laws and expelled Jews from the German Psychoanalytic Society in December 1935. Jones became suspicious of Boehm and thought he was now 'pure black': in other words, a total Nazi supporter. He told Anna Freud that Boehm was a weak and inadequate leader: 'He has neither the personality required to manage a group nor a sufficiently quick grasp of the essentials of the strategic situation.'

Jones also criticised Müller-Braunschweig, who, he said, was 'busy coquetting with the idea of combining a philosophy of Psycho-Analysis with a quasi-theological conception of National-Socialistic ideology...no doubt he will proceed further along these lines, and he is definitely anti-Semitic, which Boehm is certainly not.'

But Jones was himself a little duplicitous at times. In November and December 1935 he sent telegrams urging Jewish analysts to resign from the International Psychoanalytic Association, as ever for the good of the cause. What Jones did not say was that the Nazis were keen to keep the German group in the International Psychoanalytic Association because 1936 would see the Olympics held in Berlin and they wanted the event to go smoothly. Jones did not go into detail about the way Goering's Institute took over the German Psychoanalytic Society, perhaps because by the time he wrote the biography in 1953, he questioned how he himself had behaved.

Otto Fenichel was especially critical, as usual. He noticed how his colleagues had changed. The 'Aryan' members of the Germany Psycho-analytic Society 'are avoiding any contact – both the slightest professional contact as well as personal contact – with their non-Aryan colleagues: an almost incredible example of the devil, who will grab your whole hand when you stretch out your little finger,' he wrote.

The non-Jewish analysts might seem surprisingly easy to influence but they were hardly the only ones. Hitler had some surprising fans even among liberals. In 1936 David Lloyd George, the British Prime Minister at the time of the Treaty of Versailles, argued that Germany was benign, even a marvel of social progress. The Communists would triumph if Hitler were to be overthrown. Lloyd George may well have felt he had demanded too many concessions at Versailles and now told the House of Commons, 'Do not let us be in a hurry to condemn Germany. We should be welcoming Germany as our friend.' He wrote an article in the *Daily Express* in which he called Hitler 'the George Washington of Germany', and said: 'The idea of a Germany intimidating Europe with a threat that its irresistible army might march across frontiers forms no part in the new vision' and 'the Germans have definitely made up their minds never to quarrel with us again'.

Like most Jews, Freud worried about where he could seek refuge if matters came to a head. He warned Arnold Zweig on 21 February 1936 not to be tempted by America, even though life in Palestine made Zweig feel 'isolated' and 'ill at ease'. Tel Aviv might not have a good café life, culture or even constant hot water, but 'at any rate you have your personal safety and your human rights'. Freud felt that America would be 'from all my impressions far more unbearable'. Zweig would have to give up 'not an article of clothing but your own skin', by which Freud meant that he would have to stop speaking German.

After that, the letter became strangely optimistic, however. Freud also believed that 'the prospect of having access to Germany in a few years really does exist'. The country would have changed, but 'one will be able to participate in the clearing up process'.

The Analysts' Final Compromise

In February 1936 the German Ministry of Culture told Boehm that psychoanalysis would be allowed to continue only if the Berlin Psychoanalytic Institute came under Goering's leadership as part of a new body that would forge a 'New German Psychotherapy'. It shows the confusion and the anxieties people felt that Anna Freud saw Boehm. She wrote to Jones on 10 March 1936, telling him that she and Boehm had discussed the German Psychoanalytic Society joining Goering's institute: 'I can understand why he wishes to make this attempt. If it fails, analysis has lost nothing [...] If he *saves* a little workgroup for the future then all to the good.' Anna would never have written that if her father disagreed.

The Nazis demanded many compromises for their very partial support. Boehm had to let Goering take over the German assets of the International Psychoanalytic publishing house, the Verlag. Goering also arranged for the library of the Berlin Psychoanalytic Institute to be confiscated. The new Nazified German Institute for Psychological Research and Psychotherapy began with a good deal of property, much of which belonged to Jewish analysts.

On 19 July Goering, Boehm and Müller-Braunschweig met Jones and A.A. Brill, who had done much to introduce psychoanalysis to America. Both sides had anxieties. The plotters were well aware of Freud's presence and power. Bizarrely, some Nazis had a grudging respect for psychoanalysis and even a little for him. The analysts were still doctors and doctors had high status in German society. Goering went so far as to promise Jones and Brill that psychoanalysis would remain an independent faculty within the new Institute. Jones believed him, writing:

> I found Goering a fairly amiable and amenable person, but it turned out later that he was not in a position to fulfil the promises he made to me about the degree of freedom that was to be allowed the psychoanalytical group. No doubt in the meantime the Jewish origin of psychoanalysis had been fully explained to him.

This was a strange claim. Matthias Goering had known Freud's work for over 20 years and the Nazis had been attacking it since the late 1920s. After that meeting, Jones and Goering exchanged letters, but Matthias had the sense not to end these letters with his customary 'Heil Hitler'.

The new Institute began work on 26 May 1936 and soon became known as the Goering Institute. Matthias did nothing to discourage that. In his inaugural lecture in October, he told his audience the new German psychotherapy would flourish but on a non-Freudian, pro-Nazi and anti-Semitic basis. Students who wanted to train as analysts would have to read that penetrating work of psychology *Mein Kampf*. According to Ellen Bartens, who worked at the Institute as a secretary, 'Freud's name was never mentioned, and his books were kept in a locked bookcase.' Freudian terms were renamed; the Oedipus Complex, for example, became the 'family complex'. But while the words were different, the concepts were much the same.

Freud could have issued a strong statement condemning the new Institute, but he did not do so. It might have made a difference. Even Boehm did not want to be excommunicated by Freud and went to Vienna to assure him of his loyalty. He had not really sinned, but Freud told him:

> Different peoples, with different destinies, have developed a capacity, varying in strength, of holding on to their convictions, even if they have to be abandoned on the outside. Our Jewish people have had the misfortune, or fortune, of accumulating a host of experiences of this kind...Other peoples are less capable of resisting, and when they give in on the outside, they eventually give in on the inside too. It will all depend on what you hold on to inside.

But no one outside the inner circle of the analysts knew Freud had said this. We only know of this conversation now because Fenichel recorded it in his *Rundbriefe*. After Boehm left 19 Berggasse, Freud said he did not believe psychoanalysis would survive in Germany. 'They are a submissive people,' he said, according to one of Fenichel's round-robins of 30 November 1936. Freud had made the same judgement when discussing Zweig's *Education before Verdun*.

Matthias Goering made good use of his family connections. In 1937 he established close links with the Health Department of the Reich Interior Ministry, as well as having contacts with the Hitler Youth, the League of German Girls, the SS Lebensborn and Reich Criminal Police Office. The flourishing Institute set up local branches in Munich, Stuttgart, Düsseldorf, Wuppertal and Frankfurt am Main. However, Goering remained suspicious of Boehm, assuming that he had been closer to Freud than was the case. Matthias banned him from teaching.

The Institute even had a bit of a fan in Hitler, who had been appalled when he learned how many German doctors were Jewish. The worst statistics from a Nazi point of view concerned paediatricians: 72 per cent were Jewish. On

14 June 1937 Hitler explained to Martin Bormann how important it was to move against Jewish doctors, 'since the duty of the physician is or should be one of racial leadership'. It was important to wean the Aryans off their dependency on Jewish doctors.

The Institute turned out to have a surprisingly important place in the Third Reich. Goering persuaded many of the Nazi leadership that it could serve the needs of the German people by developing a 'Nazified' psychotherapy. Neurotic Nazis would become more efficient. This was just what Müller-Braunschweig had suggested in 1933 and Goering appointed him to run the Vienna Psychoanalytic Society, the Berlin polyclinic and its publications. It turned out to be a bad choice from a Nazi point of view.

Goering was rewarded for his efforts. When the second conference of the German General Medical Society for Psychotherapy, as the German Psychoanalytic Society had been renamed, took place in Düsseldorf in 1938, Hitler sent a telegram thanking the Society for its 'vow of fidelity and for the announcement of the establishment of a German Institute for Psychological Research and Psychotherapy'. He wished it 'great success in [its] work'. After all, it was a psychiatrist who had knowledge of Freud's use of hypnosis who had given him treatment at a key moment, treatment that helped turn him from the insignificant corporal who had no leadership qualities into the Führer.

There is no way of knowing if Freud ever learned of this telegram, but he would have enjoyed the irony. The Nazis who loathed psychoanalysis were supporting an Institute which publicly condemned him but privately kept on using many of his ideas and techniques. Geoffrey Cocks claims that, though Jews were formally excluded, a tiny number somehow kept working in the Institute until the end of the war. Harald Schultz-Hencke, though his wife was Jewish, did not just survive in the Institute but became chief psychiatrist to the German army.

During the war, the Goering Institute would play a role which shows again how ambivalent the Nazis were towards therapy: it provided treatment for Luftwaffe pilots after flying missions. In Britain, however, no one imagined it would help pilots to talk about their feelings after they had battled up in the air.

An even more curious example of the tangled relations between the Nazis and the analysts was the dream of Georg Groddeck, who had written about the id. Groddeck developed the idea that if he could only get to meet Hitler and persuade him to agree to analysis by a Jew, the reasons for his anti-Semitic paranoia would soon become clear. Then the Führer could be healed. Groddeck's close friend the analyst Karen Horney spent hours trying to explain to him why this was not a practical proposal and would almost certainly end with Groddeck being murdered. Horney left for Chicago soon after she had restrained Groddeck.

More Jewish Than Ever

As the decade progressed, it would seem that Freud became more Jewish than ever. A memoir by Joseph Wortis, one of Freud's patients, shows how loyal Freud was to Jews.

Wortis had been reading about Einstein and told Freud that, though Einstein seemed likeable, 'I confess I am not easily in sympathy with his or your Jewish nationalism.' Wortis wondered, 'How far ought I to let my allegiance to Jews bring me?'

'That is not a problem for Jews,' Freud replied, 'because the Gentiles make it unnecessary to decide; as long as Jews are not admitted into Gentile circles they have no choice but to band together.' He added, 'Ruthless egotism is much more common among Gentiles while family and intellectual life are on a higher plane among Jews.'

Rather amazed, Wortis replied, 'You seem to think that the Jews are a superior people.'

'I think nowadays they are,' Freud said. To emphasise the point, he asked Wortis to consider the high number who had won Nobel Prizes.

Freud also now became more interested in Zionism – and sympathetic to those who believed in it. He was struck by the fact that Eitingon and Zweig remained in Palestine. After *Why War?* Einstein and Chaim Weizmann (who was a famous chemist and had also been a friend of Lord Balfour, the British Foreign Secretary who signed the Balfour Declaration, which promised the Jews a homeland) persuaded Freud to become a trustee of the Hebrew University in Jerusalem. For Freud, Palestine was no longer just a place for people with religious delusions. He even wrote to Stefan Zweig a little mystically about the Land of Israel: 'we hail from there. Our forebears lived there for perhaps a whole millennium and it is impossible to say what heritage from this land we have taken over into our blood and nerves.'

He also wrote very warmly of David Eder, an English analyst and author of *War Shock*, who moved to Palestine, where he worked with Weizmann. Eder was elected to the Zionist Executive there and served from 1921 to 1927. When Eder died in 1936, Freud confided to Eder's sister-in-law, British analyst Barbara Low, that he represented 'a rare blend of courage and an absolute love of truth, together with tolerance and a great capacity to love'.

Eder remained a firm Zionist to the day he died. Freud's attitude, on the other hand, changed. It would be quite wrong to suggest he had become a Zionist, but it no longer seemed to him deluded for Jews to want to build something in a land to which they had a claim. However, even if he had been totally healthy, Freud would have hesitated to go to Palestine, just as he had hesitated to go to Rome. Jehovah did not allow Moses to set foot in the Holy Land, after all.

The French writer Marthe Robert claims that Freud's work on Moses was also a last attempt to deal with his relationship with his father. Freud began to fear he was becoming more and more like Jacob. From his youth Freud had loved the works of the great German romantic writer Goethe, and he now noted, 'even the great Goethe who in his years of storm and stress had undoubtedly looked down on his unbending and pedantic father developed traits that formed part of his father's personality'. Freud had not identified with his father when he was a little boy, Robert suggests, because Jacob was not strong enough. Now, as an old man, Freud might finally do what little boys did to resolve their Oedipus Complex and identify with his father. His book on Moses was key to that, she argues.

By the end of 1935 Freud had a draft of his Moses book but it was a draft he was too frightened to publish. He had never expected to find himself in such a quandary as he neared his 80th birthday.

CHAPTER 7

Freud's 80th Birthday

Freud wrote four letters at the end of 1935 and in January 1936 which show how weary and anxious he had become. 'It goes so overall bad in the world why should psychoanalysis have it any easier?' he told Oskar Pfister at the end of November 1935. A month later Freud complained to Hilda Doolittle that Vienna was gloomy: 'it reminds me of those bygone days when I was still able to move around and visit the sunshine and beauty of southern nature myself.' The plant she had given him was a relative of the tobacco plant which 'used to do so much for me in former times but now can do little'.

Just after the New Year, Freud wrote to the dramatist and poet Richard Beer-Hofmann, 'Life has gone by in the endless tension of demanding work and now that I have more leisure time, there's not much I feel like doing any more.' Freud could not even face contributing to a Festschrift for the 70th birthday of his old friend Romain Rolland, the art historian and essayist. The two men had been corresponding for 15 years, but Freud told Victor Wittkowski, who was putting together the Festschrift, 'I would like to give but have nothing to give.' He had reached the point where it was impossible to write something because an occasion required it.

But some of Freud's loyal followers had no intention of letting him wallow in misery as his birthday neared. A Polish-born psychologist and student of Yiddish culture, A.A. Roback, was one of his devotees. Roback wanted to publish a testimonial to mark Freud's 80th. He invited many luminaries to contribute, including George Bernard Shaw, H.G. Wells, President Masaryk of Czechoslovakia, the psychiatrist Adolf Meyer (who had worked with the behaviourist J.B. Watson, whom Freud thought was so daft for denying the existence of consciousness), as well as the psychologist William MacDougall.

The replies from most of these luminaries were not encouraging but, worst of all, Freud 'frowned upon the project'. Ernest Jones rebuked Roback, who replied, 'I was not aware that anyone could possibly object to a Festschrift in his honour.'

Freud had a sensible reason for doing so, however. He told Roback the list of possible contributors included many people who had no connection with psychoanalysis, some who knew nothing about it and others who were 'declared enemies of it'. Freud hoped no one would contribute. Roback's idea of bringing out a volume for the 50th anniversary of the creation of psychoanalysis was also a fantasy: 'I don't know what ignorant journalist is responsible for this fairy tale,' Freud snapped. Analysis was born between 1895 and 1900; by 1945 or 1950, when it would be 50 years old, Freud was sure he would no longer be around. He then seems to have remembered that it was rather rude to scold and said he regretted that 'a meritorious man' like Roback should find himself involved with such a project.

Freud did not feel like celebrating and admitted as much to a man he respected more than Roback. He told Romain Rolland that his days of glory were long past. He recalled that he had had a 'passionate desire to travel and see the world' when he was a boy. Seeing the world was also escaping the poverty that he had grown up in, as well as the limitations of his family. Freud was always aware of natural beauty: 'When one first sees the sea, dips the toe in the ocean, looks at the sights in foreign cities, fulfilling what had long seemed unattainable things of desire, one feels oneself like a hero who has performed feats of improbable greatness.' His days of greatness were behind him now.

On 20 February Max Schur was concerned by the state of Freud's jaw and commented, 'It doesn't look good.' Hans Pichler was worried that the operation he performed three weeks later had not gone far enough. His notes said, 'It was probably enough to destroy the whole mucous membrane but at the edge there were still problems'. Two weeks later Freud started to suffer migraines, which was unusual for him, and to lose things. That did not put him in a happy frame of mind for turning 80. 'Everyone will expect something from me and I shall not be capable of doing it,' he told Marie Bonaparte. Then, as if to prove the point, he addressed his letter to the wrong street. It was sent to Rue Yvon Adolphe rather than to the correct Rue Adolphe Yvon. Readers can decide which of the following interpretation is truer. Was Freud trying to prove (unconsciously of course) that he was unwell or was the slip more serious? He said Marie lived on Rue Yvon Adolphe; he could not bear to put Hitler's Christian name, Adolphe, first.

Freud had cancelled one birthday party when he turned 50: 'We only made a fuss about celebrating landmarks such as our 60th, 70th and 80th birthdays as a way of fooling ourselves about the fact that none of us can avoid death.' So he was not in the mood and made sure there was no party. Paula Fichtl had to receive many bouquets of flowers and other presents.

Einstein sent congratulations, which pleased Freud, especially as he said that he was coming to see the truth of analytic ideas more. Freud replied that he had known that Einstein only admired him 'out of politeness' and had been convinced by few of his theories. He was very happy that Einstein seemed more positive towards analysis now. Einstein was much younger, of course, and Freud dared to hope that by the time he reached the age of 80, he would have become a disciple. Deftly, Freud then poked fun at his own wish, quoting Goethe, who had written of 'the lofty bliss' of anticipation. It was a charming letter. The press even produced a caricature of Freud and Einstein. The Swiss psychiatrist Ludwig Binswanger wrote to Freud, 'As is well known one can put up with any amount of praise.'

On 6 May 1936 Freud turned 80. The Austrian Minister of Education sent congratulations, but the government ordered newspapers not to report his kind words in case they upset the Nazis. Freud told Arnold Zweig that he had received 'not many numerous' presents of antiques but that he was especially pleased with the signet ring Zweig sent him. Like a wise but disappointed child, Freud added that, for all the birthday celebrations, 'I am the same as before.'

Three great novelists paid tribute: Selma Lagerlöf, the first woman to win the Nobel Prize for Literature, Stefan Zweig and the great German writer Thomas Mann. Zweig produced a glowing tribute in the *Sunday Times* and Mann gave a lecture two days later at the Vienna Academy of Medicine. Before giving it in public, Mann read his lecture to Freud in the apartment, a performance Freud rather enjoyed. Mann called the lecture 'Freud and the Future' and he felt sure the future would be glowing. One day, he said, Freud's work would be seen as the foundation 'of a new anthropology and of a new structure, to which many stones are being brought up today, which shall be the future dwelling of a wiser and freer humanity'. The science of the unconscious was a therapeutic method but it was more than that: 'Call this, if you choose, a poet's utopia.' Mann knew that Freud believed the future 'would probably judge the significance of psychoanalysis as a science of the unconscious to be much greater than its value as a treatment. But even as a science of the unconscious psychoanalysis is still a treatment, a super individual treatment, a treatment of great style.' Freud was touched and called Mann a noble *goy* – Yiddish, as we have seen, for a Gentile; he had doubted such a creature existed, he said to Stefan Zweig.

Freud got so many good wishes that he had a card printed that read: 'My sincere thanks for your kind remembrance on the observance of my 80th birthday. Your Freud'. The cards were signed. To Hilda Doolittle, Freud added the hope that she would forgive him 'this barbaric reaction to such loving expressions of friendship'. He then went into dog-lover mode. Jofi came into his bedroom to show him her affection in her own fashion, something she had never done before or since. Freud, the soppy dog lover, asked, 'How does a little animal know when a birthday comes around.'

On 18 May Freud thanked Stefan Zweig for his tribute and said he and Mann's lecture 'almost reconciled me to growing old'. Almost, but not quite, as he found it hard to accept 'the wretchedness and helplessness of old age'. He had been 'exceptionally happy' with his wife and his children, especially Anna. But death would come in the end. He 'could not spare his loved ones the pain of separation'. At the same time, Freud had to deal with a thorny request from the other Zweig.

Arnold Zweig wanted to write a biography but Freud was having none of it. 'I am too fond of you to permit such a thing. Anyone who writes a biography is committed to lies, concealments, hypocrisy, flattering and even to hiding his own lack of understanding, for biographical truth does not exist and, if it did, we could not use it.' He was 'not the most interesting person in your wax museum' and, with a reference to his beloved Hamlet, he added, 'Was the prince not right when he asks who would escape whipping were he used after his desserts'?

Zweig accepted Freud's verdict and never asked again. The Hamlet quote led to a discussion of Shakespeare. Zweig also gently poked fun at Freud's belief that Earl de Vere had written all of Shakespeare's plays. Freud had been convinced by the work of an author with the all too telling name of Thomas Looney. Then, in a letter on 17 June, Freud had fun at the expense of the venomous monk Father Schmidt. He thought it was to their credit, he told Zweig, that 'our arch enemy' Schmidt had received a decoration from the Austrian government for 'his pious lies' in the field of ethnology. Freud sniped that he imagined this would be some consolation for Schmidt for having to deal with the trauma that Freud had survived to the age of 80. But his father and his half-brother Emanuel had not lived much beyond their 80th birthdays, Freud told Zweig. Death was very much on his mind. And with good reason.

The Cancer Gets Worse

Early in July 1936, it was clear that Freud's cancer had not been beaten. The electro-coagulation Pichler had performed had given only temporary relief. Freud told Marie Bonaparte in a letter in December that he kept brooding on whether he would reach the age his father and brother had reached. On 12 December Pichler performed another operation, using 'short waves treatments with a portable machine'. This was a considerable innovation, Schur noted with some admiration.

Freud now faced a crisis that related to the early days of analysis. His one-time friend Wilhelm Fliess had died and his widow wanted to sell the letters Freud had written to him. Freud was very upset, because he felt they would be used against him. In them he had talked of various mistakes, even tragedies, that had occurred early in his career, one of which concerned Dora, the cousin of Elsa Foges (whose material is restricted until 2057 in the Library of Congress). But Freud did not have the means to buy the letters. Fliess's widow wrote to Marie Bonaparte next.

Freud's failure to cure Marie's frigidity – and even his advice that it was probably not wise to commit incest with her son – had not diminished her loyalty to him. She had started to translate his works into French and to take on patients herself. Her methods were even more unorthodox than those of her mentor. Patients were brought by chauffeurs in splendid automobiles to her house in Saint-Cloud, where they were often analysed in the garden, with the therapist reclining on a chaise longue behind the analytic couch and crocheting while she listened. When she travelled to Athens or Saint-Tropez, she encouraged her patients to come with her and put them up in her villas.

When the Princess heard Freud's letters to Fliess were for sale, she bought them. Freud wanted them destroyed but she refused. They were of great historical importance, she said. Freud was very annoyed but, for once, had to defer to her. It did not damage their friendship, as became clear in an extraordinary episode.

At the end of 1936 Freud congratulated Marie Bonaparte on the book she had just finished writing. It was 'moving and genuine' and revealed the 'analyst's thirst for truth and knowledge', Freud told her.

The book was not about female sexuality, which so concerned Marie, but about her dog. *Topsy* is a touching and at times frankly loopy memoir which tells how her chow suffered from cancer and how she faced the possibility of her pet's death. Freud recognised that the book was an odd love story, but he agreed to translate it into German. He even asked Marie whether Topsy realised she was being translated. The memoirs of Topsy would eventually appear in French, German and English.

Some of the chapter headings sound like parodies – 'Topsy and Shakespeare', 'On the Frontiers of Your Species' and 'Implorations to the God of the Rays'. I am not going to suggest that Freud identified with the dog, but there is little doubt that what made the memoir touching for him was not just that he loved dogs himself but that Topsy had cancer, as he did. The book started: 'Somewhere in Paris there is a huge house where steel apparatus of a fiendish appearance glitters in the dim light of armour-plated rooms. They produce mysterious rays which sometimes heal poor human suffering from the most horrible diseases.'

Marie asked why she had not interceded for Topsy with the deity 'who reigns over these realms' and she knew the answer. Dogs were not supposed to receive the most advanced radiotherapy. She would later bring the doctor who treated Topsy to London to examine Freud. Topsy might be a dog but 'life, august life, dwells in her humble body'.

After Topsy was X-rayed, Marie had to wait to see if the rays worked their magic. Did they destroy 'the death dealing cells' or did the cancer survive, so that these necrotic cells 'grafted themselves on her breathing lungs'. Freud knew these issues all too well.

Freud told Marie she had managed to explain something he had also experienced – why it was possible to love an animal like Topsy or his own dog Jofi with extraordinary intensity. In a 1936 letter to Stefan Zweig, Freud had discussed the sensitivities of his dog and also made a reference which again suggests Freud knew more Hebrew than he admitted. He told Zweig that his beloved dog Jofi 'is a stickler for accuracy'. The dog did not like being called Zofi, as Zweig had called her. Her real name was Jofi: 'Jo as in Jew,' Freud added.

Topsy allowed Marie to weave a cocoon. Shut in the garden of the villa in Saint-Cloud, mistress and dog were completely happy, 'a kind of unique self-absorbed couple'. In his response to Marie, Freud even quoted an aria from *Don Giovanni* and the line 'a bond of friendship unites us both'. Their mutual dog-admiration society knew few limits.

The world might be embattled, nations might go to war, stock markets might crash, as Wall Street had done, but the dog had the right attitude – she took absolutely no notice of such things and continued her doggy existence. 'That is why your presence in the sun-streaked shade of the garden was so calm and comforting to me,' the book said. 'Topsy knew nothing of the complication of human quarrels and only knew how to love me.' Topsy offered 'respite from human ambiguity. You either hate, as you hate cats, frankly, totally without limit, or you love bouncing with joy when I return.'

Freud even made sure that *Topsy* was published in German by Albert de Lange, who published many of his own books. Freud devoted time to this when he was quite ill and pain was making him 'grumpy'. This time the post-operative recovery was especially long.

On 2 February 1937 Freud learned of the death of his old friend Lou Andreas-Salomé, to whom he had been close though their friendship had become less crucial to him. He took it as another reminder that he did not have long to live.

But there were some consolations, especially his grandchildren. Clement Freud recalled being taken by his father to Vienna, where he had pillow fights with Paula and sat dutifully at meals. Once he went on a walk with his grandfather,

> me holding one hand, the leash of his Alsatian dog in the other. On that walk we came across a man having an epileptic fit. The man's hat had fallen from his head and, as he twitched and salivated, people placed money into the hat as a token of sympathy. We walked away, grandfather, the dog and I. Why did you not give him any money, I asked. Grandfather looked at me and said: 'He did not do it well enough.'

Freud had not lost his wit.

Freud had also been working on an old problem. As early as 1900, he had written to Fliess about a patient called Herr E. His patient was making good progress, but there were issues with transference. Herr E had a difficult choice to make, as he could get better but he could also persist in being ill. Freud tried to end the analysis but there were resistances; the patient did not want to let go. The sheer length of analysis had led to much criticism. It was not supposed to be a life-long procedure. Freud now published 'Analysis Terminable and Interminable', a paper which confronted the issue, and he did so in combative style. The origins lay in a quarrel with Otto Rank, who had once been close to Freud.

Rank claimed he could finish an analysis in four months. It was an act of defiance that led to another question, Freud felt: 'Is there such a thing as a natural end to an analysis?' Analysis should only end if the patient has been cured of symptoms, inhibitions and anxieties, he insisted. That would be possible only if enough repressed material had been made conscious and if enough resistances had been overcome; otherwise the symptoms could return.

If the main problem was some underlying trauma, it should be possible to work towards a 'definitively terminated' analysis. In one of his most famous cases, Freud had cured his patient the Rat Man of his obsessional neuroses in just over a year. But if it was not just a trauma, ending the analysis would be trickier. Other negative factors might make it harder to end an analysis: for example, if a patient had very powerful instincts, if he was very aggressive and if he was rigid in his attitudes.

The paper shows Freud's rather depressed mood in 1937. At the very end, Freud refers to another paper written 10 years earlier by the Hungarian analyst Sandor Ferenczi. Ferenczi had ended by saying that analysis 'is not an endless process'. If the analyst had enough skill and patience, it should be possible to bring an analysis to a 'natural end'. A good analyst should have learned from mistakes and also would have 'got the better' of the weak points in his or her own personalities. The trouble, Freud admitted, was the imperfection of analysts, who 'in their own personalities have not invariably come up to the standard of the psychical normality to which they wish to educate their patients'.

Normal was not an adjective that applied to that many analysts, Freud thought. Jung was repressed and deceitful; Adler had left the Vienna group because he could not bear deferring to Freud; the brilliant young analyst Victor Tausk had committed suicide; Jones had endless difficulties with girls; Reich had even more difficulties with girls and thought sexual energy rained down from outer space in the form of orgone dust. As Freud had complained to Binswanger, 'what a gang'. But his complaining had nearly always been private. In public, as in the 1937 paper, Freud insisted that no one expected doctors to be utterly healthy. A surgeon whose lungs were not in tip-top shape could still operate on diseased lungs. Analysts had 'a particular art' and they should be allowed 'to be human beings like anyone else'.

Freud offered the analyst sympathy 'in the very exacting demands' he had to deal with. He compared the job to two other 'impossible professions [which] are teaching and government'. Part of the problem was that training analyses were too short. They had to be concluded quickly so that the fledgling analyst could start work on patients.

Less than perfect analysts was not the only reason some analyses lasted too long, but Freud said little of another issue. Every analyst was supposed to judge when the cure had been achieved. There were no objective criteria. Freud had never allowed any study to be made of how successful analysis was, which might have led to some agreement as to when the treatment could be stopped. This was the legacy of Uncle Josef and his forgeries, Rand and Torok argue.

Just after the paper was published, Freud wrote to Marie Bonaparte that he hoped, when he died, 'you will quickly console yourself and let me live in your friendly memory – the only form of limited immortality I recognise'. He had not lost his black sense of humour, however, as he described an American ad which he considered 'the boldest and most successful' example of American publicity he had ever seen. It was for a cemetery and read: 'Why live if you can be buried for ten dollars?'

The political anxieties continued. In March 1937 Freud wrote to Jones that there was probably no way of preventing the Nazis invading Austria: 'My only hope is that I shall not live to see it. It is a similar situation to 1681 when the Turks were besieging Vienna…If our town falls, the Prussian barbarians will flood over Europe.'

One of Anna's oldest and closest friends now tried to persuade the Freuds to flee while they still could. Anny Rosenberg Katan had splashed Anna with water when both girls were seven; the memory of the incident apparently made Anna hesitate about analysing Anny when Anny asked her to do so in the 1920s. By 1934 Anny was married, divorced, remarried and realistic. She and her husband left for Holland. Anny wrote a nicely waspish account of her conversations with the Freuds:

> I tried to warn them before I left Vienna…Freud's humorous fantasy was that the Austrians were so disorderly that they would also be disorderly in applying Hitler's ideas, views and laws. I told him that the disorderliness of the Austrians would play no role because the Germans would follow. I could not persuade him. Freud and Anna really tried to prove that nothing would happen. It shows what a great role denial can play even in personalities like Professor Freud and Anna.

After a gap of five years, the correspondence with the Lancashire Freuds suddenly started again and the news was bad. Poppy Hartwig wrote to tell Freud that Sam was ill. Freud thanked her and said that he was sorry he had not been a *fürstlicher* – noble – uncle, but life was so full and England was far away. The last time he had seen her was when she was two years old. He had evidently not seen her when he visited Emanuel, around 1908. He was not even sure of Poppy's address, so he hoped the letter would reach her somehow.

Ernst and his family were in London; he then wrote to Sam 'in a flying visit' (getting his preposition wrong) and, in a peculiarly modern turn of phrase, added that they 'may turn up at yours'.

Despite all these problems, in August 1937 Freud finished what he called

'Moses II' and put most of it aside, though he did publish some fragments in *Imago*. He wanted to produce a third full and final version, but he found it hard to concentrate and he was afraid: 'I am so little used to concealing my ideas and taking into account various foreign considerations [i.e. political ones] that I do not seem to get over the conflict.'

As 1937 ended, Freud got several offers to publish a book on the psychoanalysis of the Bible. He rejected them all. Before anything else, he had to finish *Moses*, with whom he had identified for so long. But he had not dared to do so yet and now the barbarians were at the gates.

CHAPTER 8

World History in a Teacup:
The Anschluss

In *Mein Kampf*, Hitler wrote: 'reunion [of Austria to Germany, the Anschluss] must be regarded as the supreme task of our lives, and one to be achieved by any means possible. People of one blood should belong to one Reich.'

On 17 November 1937 a group of Austrian politicians visited Hermann Goering. He asked Count Peter Reverta, the Director of Security along the Upper Austrian Border, 'Do you really think that, if the Führer wanted to force the Anschluss, Austria would be able to defend herself?' Austria was not making any defensive preparations, Reverta started to say, but Goering interrupted: 'I may as well tell you that this union will be carried out no matter what happens, for the Führer is determined at all costs to settle the question.'

Goering specialised in bombast, but there were no specific plans to invade. Hitler did write a document in June 1937. Called Operation Otto because of Otto von Habsburg, it assumed that the Emperor would be only too happy to be set back on his throne by Nazi forces. But Otto resisted the temptation. So Hitler had to improvise and create some plausible reason to justify an invasion. By November 1937 Nazi leaders were hinting at the exact time when they would order troops across the border, knowing that neither Britain nor France would lift a finger, or half a battalion, to stop them. Hitler dreamed of returning in triumph to the land of his birth. Stanley Baldwin, the previous British Prime Minister, had said he 'knew little of Europe and disliked what he knew'. His successor, Neville Chamberlain, felt he had a special mission 'to come to friendly terms with the dictators of Italy and Germany'.

On 20 December 1937 Freud wrote to Stefan Zweig, 'The government here is different but the people are the same as their brethren in the Reich. Our throat is being squeezed ever more tightly although for the time being we are not choked completely.' Some of the Nazi 'rules' amazed Freud, particularly the one which banned German Jews giving their children German names. In return, Freud suggested, Jews should ban Germans from using Jewish names like Joseph.

Freud had already told Zweig ruefully that he felt his work was behind him and that no one could know how the future would judge it. 'I am not so certain myself,' he said, and then admitted, 'I have surely not discovered more than a small fragment of truth. The immediate future looks grim for psychoanalysis as well. In any case I am not likely to experience anything enjoyable during the weeks and months I may still have to live.'

Max Schur noted that 1938 started badly in terms of his patient's health. Freud had an ulcer, so Hans Pichler had to operate inside the oral nasal cavity. There were clear signs that the cancer had become more threatening. Freud took the news stoically, as he had done two years earlier.

Strangely, Hitler hesitated to invade Austria, but the Austrian Chancellor, Kurt von Schuschnigg, played his hand poorly. For six weeks he delayed meeting the Führer, so that when he did finally go to visit him in Berteschgarten in January, it looked as if he had been forced to do so. Hitler refused to let him smoke and yelled constantly at him. Schuschnigg had, in fact, prepared a list of concessions before going to Berteschgarten. He would let members of the Austrian branch of the Nazis take part in student and athletic associations. The concessions merely whetted Hitler's appetite. The Chancellor was forced to do more than let Nazi athletes compete; he had to offer the Austrian Nazi leader a seat in his Cabinet. Schuschnigg admitted later that he did not dare contradict Hitler when they were face to face.

'I was sure of one thing. Never again war against Germany', Schuschnigg wrote in his memoirs. But he still had some pride:

I am neither capable nor desirous of playing the puppet's role. I carry the political responsibility...I cannot be expected to look on while the country is being wrecked by violence. I am in the fortunate position of being able to call up the whole world as a witness of who is right and who is seeking for peace. I am absolutely resolved to do this at the time I think necessary.

In February 1938, writing to Eitingon, Freud praised the 'brave and in some ways decent government' of Schuschnigg, which was trying to find the means of holding out against the Nazis. The letter also had a sentence of wry despair: 'One cannot avoid occasionally thinking of Meister Anton's closing words in one of Hebbel's dramas, "I no longer understand this world."'

On 9 March Schuschnigg finally announced that he would hold a plebiscite four days later on whether to unite with Germany. Organising a national election in four days was, of course, desperate as well as bizarre.

The announcement triggered panic in Berlin; even after five years in power, Hitler did not feel in complete control. A trial was about to start which might reveal how the Gestapo had plotted against a German First World War hero, General Frisch. Hitler was terrified that when news of this plot got out, there would be moves to remove him as Chancellor. He needed to distract attention; he ranted and raged, and rage made him decisive.

Some 17 hours after Schuschnigg announced the plebiscite, the German border was closed. Trains were stopped. German troops moved to the Austrian frontier. At 9.30a.m. German and Austrian representatives met for two hours. A defiant Schuschnigg refused to accept new Nazi demands, but the Austrian President, Wilhelm Miklas, panicked and insisted his Chancellor resign. Schuschnigg had no option. The plebiscite was called off. Hitler had been right. After that, no one paid much attention to the trial involving the heroic General Frisch any more.

Jews in Vienna were terrified. The large number of secret Nazis and Nazi sympathisers were jubilant. But they were sure many Jews would try to escape and hide their assets before they took over. In *The Royal Game*, Stefan Zweig's character Dr B, the doctor who seems to have been an odd mix of a younger Freud and his son Martin, explains:

I was able to burn the most important documents the moment I heard President Schuschnigg's resignation speech. The rest of the papers along with the essential certificates for the securities held abroad...I sent literally at the last minute just before those fellows [the SS] smashed my door in – to my uncle, hiding them in a laundry basket carried by my elderly and reliable housekeeper...They suspected – and in fact rightly so – that of the money which had passed through our hands substantial amounts were still hidden and out of their reach. People like me from whom important information might be extracted were not bundled into concentration camps but were reserved for special treatment.

Martin Freud behaved in an almost identical manner, which is why it seems likely that Zweig wrote *The Royal Game* after talking to him, his sister and their father. Freud himself had a tense conversation with Paula Fichtl and told her that tomorrow the Nazis would be coming. 'That is bad,' he said. The next morning Paula served breakfast as usual, while Freud fed some of his soft boiled egg to Jofi. We owe to Fichtl the nice detail that the telephone Freud hated was in the dining room. It would become a lifeline to the outside world in the next 11 weeks.

On 12 March 1938 German troops marched across the border and met no opposition. A young American who was living in Vienna, George Clare, watched lorries packed with screaming men drive into the city, each vehicle draped with a huge swastika flag. The men shouted, '*Ein Volk, Ein Reich, ein Führer*' – 'One people, one land, one leader' – as well as '*Juda verrecke*' – 'Perish, Judah'. Clare was shocked by the 'full fury of their hate. It is a sound one can never forget.' Squadron after squadron of Luftwaffe bombers flew over the city. *The Times* headline called Vienna a 'City of Frenzy and Fear'.

Paula Fichtl still wanted to go shopping, however. Freud warned her to be careful and he was right. When she walked down the street, neighbours who knew she worked for a Jewish family screamed, 'You should be ashamed of working for Jews.' She ran back into the apartment.

Freud listened to the radio, which gave an hour-by-hour commentary. There was no resistance. 'I was able to listen first to our challenge and then to our surrender, to the rejoicing and then the counter-rejoicing,' he wrote to Arnold Zweig.

German troops were astonished by the warmth with which they were welcomed. Freud had assured Jones that the Austrians would not be as barbaric as the Germans, but now he wrote to Zweig, 'The people in their worship of anti-Semitism are entirely at one with their brothers in the Reich.' Freud and a writer for the official SS paper *Das Schwarze Korps* agreed. The paper noted, 'The Viennese have managed to do overnight what we have failed to achieve in the slow-moving ponderous north to this day. In Austria a boycott of the Jews does not have to be organised – the people themselves have initiated it.'

Respectable men and women went into Jewish-owned toy shops and sweet shops, allowed their children to take what they wanted and swaggered out without paying. Jews were grabbed and forced to their knees in the street; they were made to rub out slogans in favour of the Schuschnigg plebiscite with acid. Sometimes the Austrians made them do that without gloves so the acid burned their hands. 'At last the Jews are working,' people yelled. Within a month 90 per cent of Austrians wore the swastika. Many Jews fled to the border and some did manage to get out to Italy and Switzerland.

Hitler came to Vienna on 14 March and addressed cheering crowds in the Heldenplatz. Twenty-five years after he had left Vienna with no money and no prospects, he returned as the conquering hero who had united the *Volk*.

Freud had to cope with the Anschluss in terrible physical pain. According to Max Schur, three weeks earlier he had had an operation. On 21 March Freud wrote that he had 'to cancel my work for twelve days and I lay with pain and hot water bottles on the couch that is meant for others'. He seems to have found it hard to believe what was happening.

Before reading Anny Rosenberg Katan, I would have hesitated to suggest that Freud was in a state of denial, but this is precisely what she describes. And if so, he would hardly have been the only 'great' Jew to suffer from that.

On 1 March 1938 Louis Rothschild had returned to Vienna after a skiing holiday. Ten days later a telegram warned him a German invasion was imminent, but Rothschild ignored the warning. Finally, as German troops came over the border, he had himself driven to the airport. As he tried to get on his plane, he was recognised by an SS man and his passport was seized. Rothschild went back to his palace with his valet. In the evening, men with swastika armbands surrounded the palace.

The butler, who seems to have been an Austrian version of P.G. Wodehouse's Jeeves, informed 'the gentlemen of the SS' that it was not convenient for the Baron to be arrested. The Nazis had no way of dealing with this fusillade of etiquette and went away. But snobbery could not outface guns for ever. The SS came back with more men. The butler managed to stall them again: this time the Baron was at lunch and, if they wanted to arrest him, they would have to wait until he had finished his meal. Watched by six SS men, the Baron proceeded to act as if nothing out of the ordinary was happening. He finished his lunch with dried fruit, as usual, smoked a cigarette, as usual, took his heart medicine, as usual, and then kindly agreed to be arrested. The Nazis marched him off, one would like to imagine, in golden handcuffs.

When it became clear that the Baron was not coming home, his valet packed a small bag and took it to police HQ at the Hotel Metropole. He was sent away.

The Baron showed poise too. When he was asked the next day what his palace was worth, he answered, 'What is Vienna cathedral worth?'

'Insolence,' the Nazi interrogator replied.

For all his wealth, Rothschild was sent to a room in the cellar where the

Nazis thought it a nice joke to keep him locked up with the General Secretary of the Austrian Communist Party. Within days they would be joined by another prisoner, ex-Chancellor Karl von Schuschnigg himself.

The day after the Nazis marched into Vienna, Martin Freud went to his office at 7 Berggasse, which was also the office of the Internationaler Psychoanalytischer Verlag. As he later wrote:

> I knew I must destroy documents of great importance. I had in the course of my normal duties as a lawyer invested money of my clients in reputable and stable currency abroad, this having been perfectly legal under lenient Austrian laws, but I knew it would be a crime in the eyes of the dollar-hungry Nazis.

He had to protect his clients, 'including my father', by destroying any evidence of these transactions.

As he was pulling out files, Martin was interrupted by a nervous client who demanded to have all his documents now. Even with the Nazis threatening, it was important to remember one's manners. 'Natural Austrian courtesy made this man stay and chat,' Martin continued. By the time the man finally left, Martin had not destroyed any documents but, just as he was about to begin, a gang strutted into his office. Mobs were roaming the city and targeting Jews. Even the radio, which was now controlled by the Nazis, warned of the danger of thugs looting.

A haggard-looking man took out a pistol and pressed it against Martin's head. 'Why not shoot him and be finished with him?' he shouted.

Martin was terrified, but then he saw that someone was watching from across the road. When he realised who this neighbour was, he knew he would get no help from him. The man was a Nazi sympathiser.

The gang took their time, knowing they had no reason to be worried that the police might stop them. They opened the safe and took all the foreign money. After some hours, they got bored and the atmosphere became a little less tense. Martin asked if he might have a cup of tea. The gang put this to the vote and decided that he could as long as he washed the cup and saucer. Amazingly, Martin Freud rejected these conditions.

Ernest Jones then walked into the office. The gang did not allow him to speak to Martin. Jones, with his usual instinct for survival, told them he was British, not a Jew, and managed to persuade them to let him leave. He walked down the stairs and decided that the most sensible step was to get a Nazi of some seniority to come and deal with the situation. Jones also went to tell Anna Freud what was going on.

The gang drifted away, until only one of them was left. Martin started to bribe him – he must have had some money left on him – saying that he had to go to the toilet because the stress had brought on diarrhoea. On each trip Martin took some of the files and flushed the documents away.

But Martin did not flush unobserved. The Nazi sympathiser, watching from across the street, realised something funny was going on and called the Gestapo. So for the first – but not the last – time a Nazi came to the help of the Freuds.

Within minutes a young blond District Commissioner arrived. He sent his men to find the rest of the gang. This officer 'radiated an authority which had an immediate effect on the rabble which had been tormenting me for so long,' Martin noted. The District Commissioner was even polite to Martin and allowed his sister, Anna, to join him. She had been waiting outside.

The Commissioner told his men that this matter did not merit a formal report. He then gave Martin a *passierschein* (safe conduct) which would allow them to see him the next day. Martin does not say what happened when they went, but it seems likely that the District Commissioner realised documents had been destroyed and he could have arrested Freud. But he did not. This was not the only time Freud's son found himself at some risk after the Nazi takeover.

Anna and Martin went back to their parents' apartment to find there had also been an incident there. As Paula Fichtl described it, a number of Gestapo men turned up. Martha Freud was calm. She told them that in her house they did not let guests stand up while they waited, so would they please sit down. She then graciously told the Gestapo that they had some cash in the house.

'Help yourselves, gentlemen,' Martha said.

The cash came to the not inconsiderable sum of 6,000 schillings. Freud then walked into the room looking worried, but said nothing. The 'gentlemen of the SS' took the money and, bizarrely, provided a formal receipt.

Freud said to his wife as he saw the Nazis take the 6,000 schillings, 'Dear me, I have never taken so much for a single visit.'

Even more frightening, the Gestapo men took the passports of all the family, just as Baron Rothschild's passport had been confiscated. The Freud family now had no official papers in a city where anyone could be stopped at any time and asked to prove who they were. Many of those who could not produce papers were arrested.

Freud had powerful friends he could telephone and he did so. One was his ex-patient William Bullitt, who had been a member of the American delegation to the 1919 treaty discussions at Versailles. President Wilson sent Bullitt on a secret mission to Russia. Bullitt argued America should recognise Lenin's Bolshevik government. When his advice was rejected, Bullitt resigned. It was fitting that, in 1933, Roosevelt chose Bullitt to be the first American ambassador to the Soviet Union.

Bullitt was now the American ambassador in Paris and he went at once to see the German ambassador, Graf von Welczeck. Bullitt let him know what the world would think if Freud were ill-treated. Welczeck knew Freud's reputation and did not need any persuading. He promised to make the point to Berlin, but the ambassador was not much liked by the Nazis and had little influence.

Like many buildings, the block at 19 Berggasse was draped with a swastika flag. The Gestapo, well aware that Freud lived there, set up an observation post outside the main entrance. But the Freuds were able to call on a number of well-connected people in the building to help protect them. Dorothy Burlingham, Anna Freud's 'devoted friend', had an apartment above them.

Burlingham had installed an internal telephone between her apartment and that of the Freuds. If the Gestapo came again, Paula Fichtl was supposed to steal away and quietly call Burlingham on the house phone and Burlingham would then get help. She rang the American consul, John Wiley, who came to meet Freud. Bullitt told Wiley to visit the apartment frequently, so that the watching Gestapo would know they were being watched themselves. An official American Embassy car with the Stars and Stripes fluttering was usually parked outside.

Bullitt and Burlingham were not the only support Freud had. Princess Marie Bonaparte talked to friends she had in various embassies in Vienna. Diplomats were asked to inform the descendant of Napoleon of any threat to the Professor's safety. 'The Princess is of inestimable value to us,' Freud told Arnold Zweig.

From the windows of his apartment, Freud could see that the street outside was full of Nazi soldiers and sympathisers. Jews were being stopped, humiliated and beaten up. It had an immediate effect on him. Paula Fichtl saw that her master was no longer able to write. But he could not let his patients down. They continued to come and he continued to treat them.

On 13 March the Vienna Psychoanalytic Society met. Freud reached into his knowledge of Jewish history for the right story to keep up their morale. He told his friends, 'After the destruction of the temple in Jerusalem by Titus, Rabbi Jochanan ben Zakkai asked for permission to open a school at Jabneh for the study of the Torah. We are going to do the same. We are after all accustomed by our history and tradition, and some of us by our personal experience, to being persecuted.'

The Society voted to dissolve itself and recommended that all of its members flee. They would reconvene wherever Freud went to live, but he still hoped he would not have to leave Vienna. Anna Freud took the precaution of getting Pichler, her father's surgeon, to issue a certificate saying Freud was very ill. The fact that Pichler was not a Jew made it even more useful. Martin Freud added that the surgeon was, in fact, a 'prominent Nazi'.

Kommissar Sauerwald

The board of the Verlag met the next day at 7 Berggasse and Nazis were present. The sheer speed of these developments suggests that Austrian Nazis had long planned to target Freud. His books were among those burned when the Nazis had started to govern Germany. Now there was a 35-year-old stranger at the Verlag, Anton Sauerwald. His employee Emil Rothleitner had climbed in the ranks of the Nazi Party and by 1938 was a senior person in the running of the party in the 9th district of Vienna, which included the Berggasse. He was in a position to recommend who should be appointed to the new roles the new situation required.

The moment they took over, the Nazis decided to set up the same system of control they were using in Germany. Every Jewish business would have a Nazi appointed to run it. Sauerwald never explained whether he specifically asked to be appointed as Freud's *Kommissar*, or whether this was a decision made for him. Geoffrey Cocks suggests that the reason he was appointed was that Sauerwald was also a doctor, but there is no evidence that Sauerwald was a doctor of anything other than chemistry. It seems much more likely that Rothleitner recommended his boss for the job because, as an educated man, Sauerwald was less likely to be intimidated by Freud. Later, Sauerwald claimed that a lawyer called Dr Mann appointed him *Kommissar*.

Sauerwald had the confidence to be very hostile at that first meeting of the Verlag. He shouted at the two non-Jewish analysts, Richard Sterba and his wife, Editha Sterba-Radanowicz-Hartmann, and asked why they had become mixed up with 'Jewish pigs'. He told them that 'since the circumstances had changed', as the Nazis liked to put it, he now controlled the Verlag. He demanded to see all the records of the business. The board of the Verlag had no option but to comply.

Freud's friends abroad were desperately worried. Arnold Zweig wrote on 16 March to ask how he was. He and Eitingon wanted to know if the

Princess and Jones had come. They were worried, for 'without you we are like a flock without a shepherd, like children without a father to put it in Biblical terms'. Zweig added, 'The Berggasse dominates all our thoughts.' Freud said he had been recovering from his illness when 'these events occurred, world history in a teacup'.

To make sure they could squeeze the last asset out of the Jews, the Nazis sent one of their 'Jewish specialists' to Vienna, Adolf Eichmann. Sauerwald would have been very conscious of his presence; the Vienna police now reported directly to Berlin. Sauerwald was told to do the same and it would complicate matters.

In 1937 Eichmann and his superior, Herbert Hagen, went to the Middle East. Their orders were to see whether Jews could be sent to Palestine, which was then under the British Mandate. The two men landed in Haifa and hoped to meet Jewish leaders like David Ben Gurion. The last thing the British wanted, however, was to have more Jews come to Palestine, as that would increase tensions with the indigenous Arabs.

Eichmann and Hagen were given only transit visas and had to take the train from Haifa to Cairo (in those days there were regular services from Beirut to Cairo via Tel Aviv). There they met Feival Polkes, an agent of the Haganah, the Jewish resistance. Polkes was keen to get their cooperation in facilitating Jewish emigration from Europe. But Eichmann and Hagen realised the British would never allow hundreds of thousands of Jews into Palestine, so a plan which could have saved millions of lives was not even considered.

In Vienna, Eichmann was often in the Hotel Metropole, where Louis Rothschild was being held while the Nazis tried to work out just how large a ransom they could extract for him. Berlin also sent economists and accountants to Vienna to estimate the wealth of the Jews. This was not the first 'Terror' to spawn a terrifying but at times ludicrous bureaucracy. A secret Vienna instruction, for example, told the police how to handle Jews of good standing. Healthy men should be arrested. Their property could be destroyed without interference from the local police. But that had to be done carefully. If officers needed to use fire to destroy property they should take care not to start 'a general conflagration'.

We are now so appalled by the extermination of 6 million Jews it is easy to forget that, before the Wannsee Conference settled on the Final Solution, the Nazi project aimed to terrorise Jews, rob them of their assets and throw them out of Europe.

According to Paula Fichtl, if the Gestapo came to 19 Berggasse again, they would have to swarm past a film-star-like apparition on the stairs leading up to the apartment. Princess Marie Bonaparte had arrived and she took up sentry duties, ready to repel the Nazis with style. She wore full regalia – a blue mink stole wrapped around her shoulders – and was enveloped in 'clouds of stephanotis', a fashionable perfume of the time. White leather gloves and a brown crocodile handbag completed her outfit. Fichtl brought her tea and chocolate regularly, a kindness the Princess did not forget.

To be able to enlist the help of the President of the United States as well as that of a descendant of Napoleon was not given to many Jews. William Bullitt knew President Roosevelt well. There would have been no problem in getting visas to go to America; Roosevelt would probably have signed one personally for Freud and every member of his family. The President was also persuaded to telegram Hitler to say it was unthinkable that Freud should be harmed. Hitler does not seem to have replied.

But going to America was never an option for Freud. He called it a 'gigantic mistake' with only one redeeming feature, and that was 'tobacco... the only excuse I know for Columbus's misdeed'. He might have told Max Eastman that he did not hate the country but he had bad memories of his visit to Clark University. Jung had been temperamental, the food was too rich and there were not enough toilets. We owe to Clement Freud the detail that Freud had to ask Jung to walk very close to him while he urinated down his trouser leg. No wonder Freud hated both America – and Jung. On the subject of America, Freud was not rational. England was the only option, but the British authorities did not want to let many refugees in.

Some well-meaning friends had no concept of the new realities Jews faced. Six days after the Nazis marched into Vienna, Binswanger wrote from Zurich, 'You would be welcome here at any time as soon as you feel the need for a change of air.' He evidently imagined that Freud could just hop on a train to Switzerland; he had no sense of the paperwork Jews needed to leave Vienna.

The Nazis wanted to know about everything Jews owned. Freud's assets were valued at just over 125,000 Reichsmarks. He would have to pay a 'flight tax' of 25 per cent. The valuation of Freud's assets was based on his books, art works, furniture and other goods, as well as cash. He did not have 31,250 Reichsmarks in money in Vienna. If he did not pay the flight tax, however, he and his family would not be allowed to leave. And he did not dare draw on any accounts abroad. Martin Freud was right in saying that the 'dollar-hungry' Nazis would make it a crime for Jews to have sent money out of Austria. Evidence of the now illegal bank accounts would let them make life completely hellish for Freud. Goebbels and Himmler wanted all psychoanalysts jailed. Some in Berlin wanted to put Freud on trial. He and his family were suddenly 'in a very dangerous situation', as Anna Freud wrote.

Freud was lucky that he had friends who could help, especially Marie Bonaparte, for whom money was no object. But William Bullitt was concerned that it might cost him more than $10,000 to help get the Freud family out of Vienna. This was a fabulous sum, of course. Bullitt wrote to the American consul, Wiley, to instruct him not to get into a situation where more cash might be demanded of him.

The Nazis had other foes to face. The second time the Gestapo arrived at 19 Berggasse, Paula Fichtl even tried to stop them getting into the flat by pushing all of her 54 kilos against the door.

'Shameless hussy,' a Gestapo man yelled as they swept past the housekeeper.

Freud told her his fate did not matter much as far as he was concerned, saying, 'I am almost dead.'

The Nazis behaved like perfect gangsters. Paula overheard one of them say, 'Nothing will happen to the Professor if he does what we want.'

I suspect, though she does not name him, that the man who said that was Anton Sauerwald. His career at Vienna University had left him with a certain respect for intellectuals. In the next few months the student who had liked 'Professor Herzig' often referred to Freud as 'Herr Professor'.

CHAPTER 9

The Worst Day of Freud's Life

As the *Treuehandler*, Sauerwald's task was to find Jews guilty of something so that more pressure could be put on them to hand over more money. We have seen that the Nazis protested against the Swiss banking laws in 1933. They believed, not entirely wrongly, that sensible Jews who had any money had opened at least one secret bank account.

Nothing in Sauerwald's history up to 1938 suggests that he was particularly moral, let alone that he had any sympathy for Jews, but he did know how to work and pay attention to details. Sauerwald examined the records of the Freud family and of the Verlag; he read the letters people had sent to all members of the family, including those where Sam thanked Freud for money received. It did not take him long to realise that Freud had been sending money out of the country for years. Martin had not succeeded in destroying every record. Sauerwald also discovered that Freud's publishing house owed money to its suppliers. Jews were not allowed to leave Austria until they and the companies they owned had paid all their debts. Freud would need to find considerable sums of money to pay what the Verlag owed as well as the flight tax for himself and his family.

Sauerwald had to deal with three organisations in Berlin with very definite views on what should happen to the Verlag. The Gestapo, the Ministry of Health and the Presspolizei demanded an immediate liquidation of all its assets. Sauerwald did not try to argue with them, but he went to see two of the non-Jewish analysts, August Aichhorn and Editha Sterba-Radanowicz-Hartmann. Sauerwald wanted them to become joint liquidators of the Verlag. They both refused.

The puzzle remains Sauerwald. He had been abusive at the first meetings of the Verlag, but he then became far less hostile. No one could understand why. After the war Sauerwald explained his first impressions of Freud. It was clear to him that Freud was in an 'emotionally fragile condition', a very sick old man. Sauerwald insisted that he tried to be 'sympathetic to his condition' and, perhaps with a trace of vanity, that he behaved to him like a good doctor would. 'I tried to find the necessary calming words for him and his family,' Sauerwald claimed. 'I decided I would make sure he did not suffer any more shocks.'

We do not have to rely exclusively on what Sauerwald said, which could have been tailored to show him in a good light. Anna Freud, Freud's lawyer, Alfred Indra, and Marie Bonaparte supported his version of events, as did Max Schur.

Martin Freud saw, during one of the Gestapo's many visits to 19 Berggasse, an SS man push Sauerwald aside as Sauerwald was politely knocking at Freud's door to ask if he could come in.

'We do not knock at doors,' the SS man shouted.

'What can you expect of Prussians?' Sauerwald said, not to the SS man but later to Schur. Prussians had no manners. Schur kept a note of this unexpected exchange.

After the war, Sauerwald emphasised his own decency. He felt it would have been inhuman to treat an old man with no respect.

But there may have been a more academic reason for Sauerwald becoming less hostile. He had always been quite conscientious and it was now his job to administer the Verlag. The first sensible thing to do was to read the books it had published.

The books had an extraordinary impact on him, an impact Sauerwald knew he must not let his Nazi superiors suspect. Freud loved Conan Doyle, who had made his detective Sherlock Holmes say that, when you have eliminated the impossible, the improbable must explain what happened. It was improbable that Sauerwald would help Freud. It is improbable that the only reason Sauerwald's attitude changed was reading Freud. It is, however, probable that Sauerwald decided Freud was worth helping, for at least two reasons: he was a world figure and he was a friend of Sauerwald's revered professor, Josef Herzig. But it was also clear that Freud had money abroad, as did his influential friends. There is a note appended to the court proceedings after the war that Sauerwald had estimated Freud's worth at between 2 and 3 million schillings, a considerable fortune. In *Why War?*, Freud had noted how mixed people's motives were in times of crisis – greed, idealism, fear and humanity all combined. Sauerwald tried to suggest that he had acted just out of humanity. If that were so, he would have been a saint and he does not seem to have been that.

Oskar Schindler's motives for helping Jews were also mixed. He needed good workers for his factories and could see no sense in killing Jews; it was only gradually that he became outraged by the Nazis. Even those he had helped admitted he was a flawed hero.

Some psychologists who have studied how individuals respond in dictatorships say there is a pattern of rebellion, of crossing the line, that starts with small transgressions. After having read Freud's books, Sauerwald did not disclose to his superiors that Freud had many secret bank accounts abroad. Instead, he took the evidence back to his own apartment, where he had a *Panzerkassette*, a locked box for important documents. Taking documents home was not specifically against orders and he could explain. If the Gestapo found out, Sauerwald could say that he had brought the documents back to study them. He was looking at the line but he had not crossed it yet.

Father and Daughter

On Tuesday 22 March the Gestapo marched into 19 Berggasse again. Ernest Jones had left Vienna on the same day and so was in no position to help. The Gestapo men said they had come to arrest Anna Freud. They were confronted not just by the family but by Princess Marie Bonaparte. Her husband was worried about what the Nazis might do to her and had made her promise to stay at the Greek Embassy. Marie ignored him, as she often did, and spent her time at 19 Berggasse – and not just on the stairs in her mink.

When the SS men said they were arresting Anna, the Princess tried to insist that she should also be arrested. She told Martin Freud that the idea of marching a Princess into their cells terrified the Nazis. Martin had returned to the apartment too late to see this confrontation, but he was just in time to rush to the window and see his sister being bundled into an open car by four heavily armed SS men. Anna appeared quite calm.

Inside, the remaining SS men ransacked everything. One burly man pulled on the handles of a cupboard and finally yanked it open. He found himself looking not at secret documents or gold, but at piles of beautifully laundered linen tied together with coloured ribbons. He had opened Martha's laundry cupboard. He started to pull the contents out, only to be met with splendid disdain. 'Without showing the slightest fear mother joined the fellow and in highly indignant tones told him precisely what she thought about his shocking behaviour,' Martin Freud records. The SS man looked terrified at her outburst and so Martha saved her linen – and her dignity.

When he heard that Anna had been taken away, Schur came at once. He knew Freud would be distraught and he was right. Freud was terrified that he would never see her again. The usually calm therapist showed all his feelings, raw. He paced up and down and smoked one cigar after another.

When the Nazis arrested her, Anna Freud was 42 years old. Photos taken just a few years earlier show her as an intense, attractive and very Jewish-looking woman; she liked to wear a beret which gave her a gamine look. She was the only one of Freud's children who had made a success of a career by then. She was recognised as a brilliant child therapist. She had managed this both because of her relationship with her father and despite it. They loved, respected and depended on each other. Freud had some reasons to feel guilty towards her. He knew, even if he did not say it, that she had never married partly at least because of her devotion to him.

When she was 18 years old, Anna had gone to England to improve her English. Freud had asked Ernest Jones to look after her, but Jones did rather more; he began to court Anna. Freud was not happy about that, for both good and bad reasons. Jones had lost two hospital jobs because of complaints women patients had made about his behaviour. The randy 'Welsh Wizard' had had a number of mistresses and was not likely to make an ideal husband, but Freud would probably not have been happy if his beloved Shakespeare himself had wooed his daughter. He told Jones that she was 'still far away from sexual longings'. Freud was usually alive to irony, but he was too close to Anna to see any irony in that. The pioneer who had seen that children were sexual was protesting that his 18-year-old daughter had no sexual feelings. Father and daughter had agreed 'that she should not consider marriage or the preliminaries before she gets 2 or 3 years older,' he told Jones, and added he did not expect her to 'break the treaty'.

For once Jones did not meekly accept what Freud said. He shot back that Anna 'will surely be a remarkable woman later on, provided that her sexual repression does not injure her. She is of course tremendously bound to you.' Anna stayed cool towards Jones, though whether this was because she did not find him attractive or because of her relationship with her father we do not know.

When Anna was 23 years old, her father started analysing her. Today that would be thought totally unethical. The usual defence is that in those early days the rules were less fixed. If so, one wonders why the fact he was analysing Anna was 'a jealously kept secret'. Father and daughter agreed Anna needed help because she suffered from depression, insomnia and daydreams linked to masturbation. She expressed some of these conflicts in many poems and stories she wrote, but none of them were published in her lifetime. Small extracts were quoted in her authorised biography. For four years, Anna lay on her father's couch like any other patient. He always saw her at 10p.m. just before bedtime.

Freud did not hide how much he depended on Anna. In a letter to Lou Andreas-Salomé written in 1922, he had said, 'I have felt sorry for her for quite some time now, because she is still living at home with us old folks but yet, on the other hand, if she really had left us, I would have felt diminished, like what is happening to me now, for example, almost as if I had to give up smoking.' We have seen that Freud compared the pleasure Anna gave him to smoking a good cigar.

Father and daughter do not seem to have agreed on how successful the analysis was. In a letter to Lou, also in 1922, Anna said, 'With me, everything became so problematic because of two basic faults: from a discontent or insatiability with myself that makes me look for affection from others, and then from actually sticking with the others once I have found them. [The first] is just what you and Papa cannot understand.'

Freud believed, however, that he had understood his daughter perfectly. In 1935 the Italian analyst Eduardo Weiss asked Freud whether or not he should analyse his own son; Freud said that his analysis of Anna 'had gone well'. Paul Roazen, the distinguished historian of analysis, suggested there were unspoken conflicts between Anna and her father. 'Anna may have been more afraid of her father than either of them knew,' he wrote. While her father's motives may have been 'the very best', 'medically and humanly the situation was bizarre'.

In analysis the patient usually works through problems with their parents through their relationship with the analyst. The analyst represents the parent, so the patient/child can work through childhood issues again. But how could that happen if the analyst was one of the patient's parents?

Freud would have been 'invading the privacy of her soul; he added new transference emotions to their relationship, without the possibility of ever really dissolving them. Taking his daughter into analysis undoubtedly gratified an Oedipal tie on his part,' Roazen judged. The psychoanalytic movement might benefit as Anna became an analyst, but for her 'the analysis helped to limit the possibilities for personal gratification, although she had a role in her father's life as well as her eventual leadership of the movement, which constituted a rich exchange'. Then Roazen softened; he was, after all, talking about the father of psychoanalysis: 'Perhaps only by normal standards was her relationship to such a father a tragic one.'

One sign of that 'Oedipal tie' was that, even in her late twenties, Anna could get jealous of both her mother and her Aunt Minna. They fought over who should accompany him on trips, as well as sometimes over who should fit his prosthesis. Anna shared his thinking more than anyone else.

Anna became director of the Vienna Psychoanalytic Training Institute and in 1937 she started a nursery school for poor children. The money came mainly from Dorothy Burlingham and Edith Jackson. The nursery was experimental. Children were allowed freedom in choosing their own food and organising their own play. Though some of the children's parents had been reduced to begging, Anna and Dorothy were very struck 'by the fact that they brought the children to us, not because we fed and clothed them and kept them for the length of the day, but because "they learned so much", i.e. they learned to move freely, to eat independently, to speak, to express their preferences. To our own surprise the parents valued this beyond everything.' As soon as the Nazis took over, the nursery had to be closed down, of course.

On 22 March Anna did not go unprepared to meet the Gestapo. Not unreasonably, she was frightened she would be tortured and persuaded Max Schur to give her two tablets of Veronal to swallow as a last resort. But she had a plan. She felt that it was dangerous to be kept waiting too long in the corridors of the Hotel Metropole. People could vanish into the cellar without anyone noticing. Martin Freud added mysteriously that, 'through the influence of some friends', Anna was allowed to leave the corridor and was taken to a room where other Jews were being questioned. No one objected.

In *The Royal Game*, Stefan Zweig described the interrogations at the Hotel Metropole. Reading his text, it is hard to believe his descriptions are not based on real experiences that had been recounted to him, as I argued in comparing his fiction and Martin's factual account of burning documents. Zweig's 'fictional' Dr B hated waiting: 'I had to wait in the ante room of the chief interrogator. You always had to wait before every session. Making you wait was also part of the technique.' The aim was to produce tension which would reduce 'your will to resist', so the Nazis 'made you wait pointlessly, pointlessly waiting, one hour, two hours before the interrogation to exhaust your body and break down your spirit'. Dr B continued:

Then at last the interrogation begins. They sent for you and you were taken along a corridor or two. You didn't know where you were going. You waited somewhere and you didn't know where you were. Then abruptly you were standing in front of a table with a few people in uniform sitting at it. On the table was a pile of papers; documents whose contents you knew nothing about. Then the questions started, genuine and fake, straightforward and crafty, superficial questions and catch questions.

In the apartment at Berggasse, Schur did not manage to calm his patient. Freud continued to pace up and down, lighting one cigar after another, smoking, smoking and smoking. Paula Fichtl and Dorothy Burlingham both wrote that it was obviously the worst day of his life.

In the Hotel Metropole, Anna had to wait and wait. When it was finally her turn, the Gestapo men put a clever question to ruffle her. She was asked what it meant to be a member of an international organisation. The Gestapo told her they had information about a conspiracy of Jewish ex-soldiers who were about to terrorise Vienna. It was too dangerous to laugh at the idea. Anna explained the only international organisation she belonged to was the International Psychoanalytic Association. Analysts might be a 'gang', as her father had said to Binswanger, but they had not yet resorted to bombing each other with anything more than words and emotional threats. The International Psychoanalytic Association did not have concealed guns. But it was hard for her to stay calm. Like Dr B, Anna had a secret, the secret her brother Martin had protected when he flushed documents about his father's secret bank accounts down the toilet at 7 Berggasse.

Dr B described very clearly the anxieties that being questioned provoked: 'Gradually I could feel how my nerves were beginning to break up and…recognising the dangers I braced myself to my nerve ends. The same thought came flickering in and out. What do they know? And when they found out, how would they use the information?'

Anna thought she had one advantage, however, as she faced her interrogators. Müller-Braunschweig might be working for Matthias Goering at the Institute now, but he was still devoted to her father. There are two accounts of what happened next. According to one, Anna produced a 'letter of homage' Müller-Braunschweig had written to her about her father. She wanted to let the Gestapo know that the Freuds had friends in high places. Martin Freud said that this only angered the Nazis. It was again a matter of etiquette, which could be so treacherous. The letter began very correctly with *'Sehr geehrtes gnädiges Fräulein'*, a gracious form of address Jews were now not entitled to. The second version of this story suggests that Anna Freud did not show the Gestapo the letter but that it had been intercepted by them.

The Gestapo were very interested in the attitude of non-Jewish therapists to Freud. Matthias Goering was in an excellent position to ask the Gestapo to keep track of the letters written by analysts so that he could be certain who was loyal to him and the Nazi cause, and who still hankered after the old master. Goering had his moments of paranoia, which was why he had banned Boehm from teaching and would take revenge on Müller-Braunschweig. The latter claimed he paid a heavy price for writing the letter of homage. He was accused of being a Jew lover and never allowed to publish and teach again at the Institute.

The interrogators did not put Anna in the prison cells that had been set up in the basement. She was allowed to leave the Hotel Metropole by the end of the evening. Freud was relieved beyond words when she finally returned home safely late on 22 March. Max Schur said that for once Freud showed his true feelings. The frail old man wept. He had been frightened he would never again see his Antigone, as he called Anna.

Anna's arrest terrified Freud and was the turning point. After years of hesitation, he knew he had no choice, even if he did not have long to live. In the next few days, he prepared a list for the British consul in Vienna of those he wanted to accompany him to England. Schur reproduced the list in full:

- Sigmund Freud – aged 82.
- Martha Freud – aged 77.
- Minna Bernays, sister-in-law, aged 73.
- Anna Freud – daughter, aged 42.
- Martin Freud – son, aged 48.
- Esti Freud - wife of Martin, aged 41.
- Walter Freud – son of Martin, aged 16.
- Sophie Freud – daughter of Martin, aged 14.
- Enkel Ernst Halberstadt – grandson, aged 24.
- Mathilde – daughter, aged 50.
- Robert Hollitscher – husband of Mathilde, aged 62.
- Max Schur – Freud's personal doctor, aged 39.
- Schur's wife, Helen, aged 26.
- Schur's two small children.
- Paula Fichtl – housekeeper, aged 36.
- Mitzi, the other maid to the Freud household, aged around 30.

Jones claims that it was he who persuaded Freud that he had to leave, but Freud at first countered that it would be like a soldier deserting the army. Then the Welsh Wizard waxed lyrical. He reminded Freud of what had happened when the *Titanic* hit the iceberg. The captain had gone down with the ship, a heroic but useless sacrifice. The second in command had been more sensible, making sure the passengers got into the lifeboats and then accompanying them to help them survive. Jones perhaps overstated his own part in persuading Freud that he had to do everything possible in order to leave, but Jones certainly worked tirelessly over the next three months to effect the escape.

As soon as he got back to London, Jones went to see his cousin Wilfred Trotter, a well-known doctor. Trotter gave him a letter of introduction to Sir William Bragg, the President of the Royal Society, which had been set up in 1662 to promote scientific research (Isaac Newton was one of its founders). The most famous physicist in the world, Einstein, might have condemned the Nazis, but Bragg still asked Jones, 'Do you really think the Germans are so unkind to the Jews?'

Jones could assure him of their 'unkindness'. Jews were being beaten up in the streets by mobs, he told Bragg. At his best, Jones was a terrier and he did not leave the offices of the Royal Society until he got a letter from Bragg inviting Freud to Britain. Jones then walked across St James's Park to the Home Office to see a man with whom he had an unlikely bond, the Home Secretary, Sir Samuel Hoare. The two men had gone figure skating together; it should be remembered that before he wrote his biography of Freud, Jones's most successful book was *The Elements of Figure Skating*.

Samuel Hoare had had to resign as Foreign Secretary after Mussolini invaded Ethiopia and he felt he needed to be careful because there was a lot of opposition to letting too many Jews come to Britain. Jones again insisted. He finally got Hoare to issue an entry visa immediately for all the Freud family, as well as for Fichtl and the maid, Mitzi. It was Jones's finest hour. It is hard to believe that he could not have persuaded Hoare to also issue visits for Freud's four sisters, who were living in Vienna. But they were not on the list.

It was, of course, no good Freud being allowed into England if he could not get out of Vienna. The uncertainties depressed him. On 17 April Paula Fichtl reported that Freud could not hear anything. This was something new: there had never before been any problem with Freud's hearing. Sauerwald described Freud as being very anxious.

Then Anna Freud had a conversation with her father when they seemed to have no chance of escape.

'Wouldn't it be better if we all killed ourselves?' she asked her beloved Papa.

Freud was adamant. 'Why? Because they would like us to,' Freud replied. He had no intention of giving them the pleasure.

Anna only allowed Schur to report this dialogue in *Freud: Living and Dying* 34 years after it occurred. Her father's attitude and her own reticence make complete sense if one remembers how many of Freud's relatives had killed themselves.

In March and April 1938 in Vienna, the suicide rate among Jews soared. Rumours had it that 500 Jews had killed themselves 'since the circumstances changed', as the Nazis liked to put it. Even Berlin was embarrassed by the rumour that so many Jews had committed suicide. Towards the end of April official statistics were issued saying that only 96 Jews had in fact done so. Ironically, just at this moment, Dororthy Burlingham's Christian husband, Robert, whom Freud had treated, killed himself too.

On 13 April Jones had a letter published in *The Times* in which he assured the world that Freud 'was not a dying man who has been denied his liberty'. Freud was in good health for his age and was still at work. For reasons of diplomacy, Jones also said that Freud was free. There was no point in aggravating the Nazis.

For the only time in their relationship, Freud wrote more letters to Jones than Jones wrote to him. On 23 April he asked Jones to try also to arrange entry for Dr Maxim Steiner, a dermatologist who had been one of the original members of the Vienna Psychoanalytic Society.

Writing could sometimes distract Freud from the uncertainties. 'I also work for an hour a day at my *Moses*, which torments me like a ghost not laid. I wonder if I shall ever complete the third part despite all the outer and inner difficulties,' he told Jones. Freud needed to work more than ever and started to translate a chapter on Samuel Butler for Isaiah Berlin's book *The Unconscious*.

On 12 May Freud wrote to his son Ernst, 'Two prospects keep me going in these grim times – to rejoin you all and to die in freedom.' But it would take a lot of negotiations before he could die in freedom and it was vital not to upset Sauerwald. He had abused Richard and his wife Editha for working with Jews. There is nothing before his encounter with the Freuds to suggest that he would take risks for Jews.

Vienna was a small place and Sauerwald had been a student at the university. Anna and Alfred Indra now asked discreetly what people knew about him. The answers they received were alarming. Sauerwald was not merely a well-qualified chemist; he had been a member of the Nazi Party for years and had made bombs during the disturbances of 1933 and 1934. Their fate was in the hands of a man who was both a sincere Nazi and a terrorist.

CHAPTER 10

Anton Sauerwald

On 5 May Sauerwald summoned another meeting of the Vienna Psychoanalytic Society and of the Verlag. Ernest Jones returned from London, as did Marie Bonaparte from Paris. Despite having written his letter of homage, Müller-Braunschweig was not frozen out and he attended, as well as Professor Goering, as Sauerwald called Matthias. The meeting took place at 7 Berggasse, so Freud did not go himself.

Sauerwald was brisk. The financial situation of the Verlag was not good. Its total assets were no more than 30,000 Reichsmarks because it was *passiv*. It was not trading and owed far more than that. Its debts would have to be settled before Freud could leave Vienna.

The meeting then considered how to move the business to London. Seven weeks had now passed since the Anschluss when Germany annexed Austria without any opposition. Sauerwald was at least disposed to try to be helpful, though he would have to clear matters with Berlin. Then there was a clinical problem. Freud and his colleagues had been treating a number of patients who were not Jewish. As they were now forbidden to carry on practising, there were a number of Aryans who needed therapy. The meeting tried to find new therapists for these patients, but there were not enough non-Jewish therapists left in Vienna. The meeting agreed that it was not possible to refer these to ordinary psychiatrists.

The same day Sauerwald signed the exit visa for Minna, something dear to Freud's heart. She had been recuperating in a sanatorium for a few months and was too ill to travel on her own, so Dorothy Burlingham came back to take her to London.

The next day, 6 May, was Freud's 82nd birthday. He had now lived longer than his father and his brother. There were no celebrations, but there was another meeting at Freud's apartment, which Sauerwald himself attended. Freud and Anna signed in the presence of their lawyer, Alfred Indra, a *Gedenkprotokoll*, which translates as a 'deed of intention'. It promised that the Freuds would pay all the taxes the Nazis demanded.

Sauerwald was in a strange position. He knew that Freud had money abroad but not much in Vienna. The Gestapo had not returned the 6,000 schillings they had taken. Freud had had to pay the exit tax for Minna. What Sauerwald did not know, however, was that when the Gestapo searched the apartment, they had not found some gold Freud owned. He gave the gold to Marie Bonaparte, who took it to the Greek Embassy. Was this failure a miracle or the result of some aristocratic bribery? I have not been able to establish that, but it is known that the gold was smuggled out in a diplomatic pouch. It was worth $4,824, about £1,000 at the rate of exchange then. Since the price of gold was $38 an ounce, Freud's gold must have weighed about 125 ounces – in other words, this was not a small amount of gold to have managed to conceal and smuggle out.

Martin Freud was the next person to leave, but he never mentions having to pay an exit tax and he wrote about the event a little mysteriously: 'Finally I was ordered out of Vienna, a measure which could have possibly been inspired by friends who did not think my temperament sufficiently equable to be trusted.' Under pressure, he might have betrayed secrets.

What Martin was unwilling to admit – and what is clear from an affidavit of Alfred Indra's after the war – is that Martin had been making some provocative remarks about the Nazis which could have ended with him being sent to the *kazzette*, a form of internment. Indra went on to give a remarkable piece of information. The person who usually helped keep Martin Freud out of trouble was Sauerwald. He intervened on a number of occasions when Martin was in danger of being arrested. There is no reason why Indra should lie about that. Furthermore, as the lawyer of the Freud family, he would have been involved in any legal problems Martin faced. And Indra's is not the only evidence.

The story Martin Freud tells about his escape does not seem totally frank, a suspicion confirmed by a letter Anna wrote (years later) to her cousin Harry.

About Sauerwald I do not know what Martin ever told you about him.

I suppose you know that Martin who was quite beside himself at that time had kept some very incriminating papers about our affairs in

Switzerland in his desk. They were found there but Sauerwald kept them safely locked up until we were gone [...] Martin will never forgive the position that he was suddenly powerless while Sauerwald had all the power. But he did not misuse his power and very few people are able to withstand such a temptation.

Martin wrote that he managed to get out thanks to his cook. The vice-president of the Vienna police was a friend of hers and so, through this contact, Martin was able to leave and also to buy back documents which had been seized. His version ignores the question of whether he obtained an exit visa. It seems likely that he bribed the vice-president of the Vienna police to make his escape easier, at the very least. It was best to have both a proper visa and a crooked policeman.

It would be dangerous to be found on the train with a lot of money on him, Martin knew. He took the risk of sending some banknotes by post to Paris and kept only a quantity of coins. He did not want to waste these, though, so he went to the restaurant car and ordered a whole roast chicken. He asked the dining-car attendant to keep the chicken in the train fridge till they got to Paris. The man became suspicious; there must be something bizarre about a Jew who wanted a chicken kept on ice. Martin claims the attendant threatened to report him for breach of regulations, so Martin took the chicken to his compartment, where he 'devoured it without pleasure'. He reached Paris safely and rather full.

On 24 May Mathilde Freud left Vienna with her husband and reached London with fewer complications. But Sauerwald would still not sign an exit visa for Freud, Martha and Anna. One reason was that there were difficulties with the liquidation of the Verlag. A few days after the 5 May meeting a Dr Ehrlich stormed in from Germany. He said that Berlin did not want the Verlag to transfer its operations to London. Sauerwald discussed the problem privately with Marie Bonaparte and they came to an arrangement. She agreed to buy the Verlag and pay all its debts in Austria and Germany. But Sauerwald again had to clear this with Berlin. Fearing that he might not get approval, he appealed to Matthias Goering, who asked his cousin Hermann for help. It says something about the weird politics of the Reich that even though Hermann Goering, Hitler's deputy, intervened, Berlin would still not allow the Verlag to be sold to the Princess of Greece.

Sauerwald was in a quandary. Three organisations in Berlin were demanding reports, and the records of Freud's secret bank accounts were in his locked box at home. He began to feel that he was taking a risk in hiding documents about Freud's banking operations. I have pointed to research which suggests that in dictatorships dissidents often start with small transgressions, which then set them on the path. Sauerwald went much further now. He began to disobey direct orders from Berlin. Again, the first actual disobedience was modest. He checked which books did not belong to the Verlag but to foreigners. The regime had no right to seize those; many of the foreigners were not even Jews, but it was assumed they could be part of the loot. Sauerwald packed these books and returned them to their original owners.

It was the next step Sauerwald took that completely crossed the line and would put him at great risk if anyone ever found out. Sauerwald did not want to see the books of the Verlag destroyed. They were the root documents of psychoanalysis. He got in touch with the director of the Austrian National Library, who also knew the Gestapo wanted all the stock of Verlag books destroyed as they were 'Jewish filth'. He persuaded the director, Dr Paul Heigl, to work with him. At the dead of night, Sauerwald and Marie Bonaparte packed books in the Verlag offices and transported them to the Austrian National Library. Heigl made sure that only reliable helpers were on hand to take them in and lock them away. The books were still there when the war ended.

It is a pity that the People's Court did not commission a psychological assessment of Sauerwald when he was tried after the war. He had abandoned a promising research career. He had walked out of his job at a time of great economic uncertainty. He had persuaded his parents to put up the money for his commercial chemical laboratory, which he claimed was a completely reputable business but in fact made bombs. And he fooled the Vienna police into hiring him as a forensic expert, persuading them he was a sound professional man.

After the war, Sauerwald made much of the fact that in 1937 he acquired a rifle to go hunting with and also a pistol. He would not have been allowed to get permits for them if the authorities had believed he was a threat to public order or an illegal Nazi. All scientific activities were strictly controlled by the authorities, he said. He insisted that his lab was respectable over and over again.

Max Schur said that no one could understand why Sauerwald had saved the Freuds and thought that reading Freud's books had changed Sauerwald's attitude. Schur eventually gave a more rounded explanation. Freud's brother Alexander met with Sauerwald and asked him directly what his motives had been. It is impossible to be sure whether the speech Schur said Sauerwald then made is accurate word for word, but he reports that Sauerwald told Alexander Freud:

The Führer of course knows best and realises that the Fatherland is in a state of siege. The Jews, due to their internationalist leanings and their tendency towards individualistic behaviour, cannot form a reliable element of the population. Thus they have to be eliminated. This might be deplorable but the end justifies the means. This does not mean, however, that an individual should not be permitted to alleviate individual hardship in selected cases.

What is odd is that Schur dates this speech to 1939. At that time not even Hitler had suggested in public that Jews should be 'eliminated', as the mentally ill should be. Eichmann's memo set out that the policy then was to rob rich Jews and expel poor ones. It is hard to believe that Sauerwald would have spoken of 'elimination' so early. But the rest of the explanation attributed to him by Schur makes sense. Schur went on to argue that the *Kommissar* 'gradually developed some guilt feelings and tried to come to terms with his conscience whenever circumstances permitted'.

As he wondered whether or not to sign the papers for Freud's exit visa, Sauerwald got a new order from Berlin. The Freuds were to be moved out of their apartment and the premises used to house a new 'Race Institute'; it would study why the Aryan race was superior. That was an insult too far and it seems to have tilted the balance. Sauerwald finally signed the papers saying that there was no impediment to Freud leaving. But that was far from the only paperwork Freud needed to get out.

Last-minute Panic, Last-minute Packing

It was a huge wrench for Freud to leave Vienna. He had books, he had an art collection, he had medical records, he had letters. He complained about the amount of work involved in packing, doing accounts and giving final presents. He wrote to Ernst on 12 May that he feared he would lose most of his art collection, apart from two small pieces Marie Bonaparte had already taken back to Paris and a few others which she had bought in Athens and was keeping for him in Paris. How much of his collection could travel from Vienna was 'very uncertain. The whole thing reminds me of a man trying to recue a bird cage from the burning house.'

The next day Freud wrote to Jones that he had had no wish to celebrate his birthday on the 6th and that he was sitting in his study 'with nothing whatever to do and generally useless'. He was finding it hard to write because he knew his letters were seen by a censor. Once, Freud reminded Jones, he had traced back the 'so called physiological feeble mindedness of women' to the fact that women were forbidden to think about sex. Women had acquired a dislike for thinking as a result and Freud now compared his lot to theirs: 'Imagine how such a censorship must affect me who have always been in the habit of expressing freely what I believe.'

Despite the censorship, it is possible to follow the many twists and turns of the next month, because once Minna reached London she and Freud exchanged letters. These show how his moods changed as he tried to master his anxieties. He was an old man in fear for his life. On 14 May Freud wrote that they were now in possession of the French and English passes they needed. But an obsessional bureaucracy ruled and these passes were only valid for 14 days.

Even leading Nazis felt there was too much bureaucracy. A memo sent to the Security Head Office in Berlin on 22 August by Adolf Eichmann complains:

> there were more and more instances in Vienna where Jews, eager to emigrate, had to stand in line for days and weeks to arrange the necessary paperwork for their emigration. Over that time there were many failures because of lack of organisation and unqualified officials. This damages our interest in forcing the Jews to emigrate from Austria...
>
> One of the problems with the emigration of Jews from Vienna is created by the activity of lawyers. Because of the complicated system, obtaining the necessary paperwork for a passport can take up to two or three months. For example, a certificate confirming that one does not have a criminal record may take 6–8 weeks to obtain. Rich Jews therefore employ Aryan lawyers to get the papers.
>
> These lawyers manage to obtain favourable treatment by the authorities. They or their workers will come to an office with 20–30 applications and take up a great deal of the clerk's time, while poor Jews are standing in the street in a line that hardly moves for days. This has caused only problems. First, it has enabled the rich Jews to leave the country without problem, while the poor Jews stay behind – this is contrary to our interest. Furthermore, it is already being said abroad that obtaining a passport in Vienna costs RM 1,000. The lawyers take enormous sums for each passport, and the rich Jews pay willingly. Since obtaining a passport by the Central Office for Emigration takes only up to 8 days (we get the certificate from the police within 48 hours),

lawyers have already approached some of the government and party offices.

They have lost good business since the creation of the Central Office.

Furthermore, the Central Office has not arranged separate hours for these lawyers – a fact which increases their bitterness. The aim of the Central Office for Emigration is to force the poor Jews to emigrate and to make the rich ones pay.

Anna had to cope with this bureaucracy. One of the new Nazi rules was that Jews who had permission to leave Vienna had to report to the police every day. Anna had to comply once Sauerwald had signed the exit visa. When she first told her father she had to do this, he replied, 'You have of course refused to obey so humiliating an order.' Martin said this showed his father's 'defiant spirit', but given the way Anna's friend Anny Rosenberg Katan described Freud, it seems another instance of denial. Anna was by now well aware of the risks run by anyone who refused to obey a Gestapo order. Defiance was a luxury Jews could not afford, even if they were world-famous.

Freud still did not have a paper called *Der Steuer*. 'Everything depends on this,' he wrote to Minna, as 'without that we are not certain to get across the border. We await this paper with anxiety.' It was not the only document he discovered he would need. The Nazis had a genius for obstructive bureaucracy. To leave, Jews also needed a *bedenklichkeitserklaerung*. This paper confirmed that the police had no reasons for detaining the Jew because he or she had completed the necessary formalities, had left no debts to Aryans and had paid the exit tax.

Freud was also worried about the logistics of the trip. He fussed to Minna that he needed one night in a decent bed between the two nights he would spend in sleeping cars. He would have to take the night train across the Channel. Anna had to cope with too much, but 'she looked after everything'.

If the Gestapo were brutal, that was not true of Sauerwald, as Freud told Minna. The *Kommissar* had promised that within a week the fate of the antiques collection would be clear. Freud ended by saying that Minna and Dorothy should 'be joyful that you are outside'. He hoped that they would meet in Paris again.

Freud was not sure what to do about those of his personal books that had not been removed to the National Library. He chose the ones that he wanted to take with him to London and disposed of the rest. He sold some to a Jewish bookseller called Sonnenfeld who had a shop on the Berggasse. But

Sonnenfeld himself was soon arrested and robbed of the collection. Other books went to a more substantial dealer. Within weeks, they were offered for sale for 1,850 Reichsmarks as 'a special collection on neurology and psychiatry of a Viennese scientist'. The scientist was not named, but some people at least knew who he was.

A sharp New York librarian, Dr Jacob Shatsky, heard the collection was for sale and bought it for the New York State Psychiatric Institute. He had been tipped off that the scientist was Freud. The ease with which this sale was achieved suggests Sauerwald helped and perhaps he even received money for that piece of inside information. Freud's collection contained some rarities, including *Artine* by the French poet René Char with an original engraving by Salvador Dalí, a man who had been inspired by Freud. Dalí first read Freud in a Spanish translation. Char had sent the book as a present and offered it 'with deep admiration and the greatest respect'. Char became a hero of the French Resistance later.

When he wrote to Minna on 20 May Freud could not help saying, 'You have so often wanted to come to England and now you are there.' He had cleared his writing desk but they were still not allowed to leave and Anna was striving with 'much intelligence and good humour to work us free'. But money continued to be a big problem, even though the exit taxes had been paid. 'We don't know with what means we shall pay our bills,' he confessed to Minna. 'Hopefully we shall sort out the money problems for the tickets.' He wanted to take his leave of some of his favourite places, but this was a risk, as he might be recognised, and recognised as a Jew. The neighbours had mistaken one elderly man for Freud and beaten him up. He did manage to get out twice, he told Minna, but he never revisited 'the garden of our childhood', which probably meant the Prater.

We are lucky to have a detailed visual record of the apartment at 19 Berggasse as it was in April 1938. One of the non-Jewish analysts who had refused to help liquidate the Verlag, August Aichhorn, had written a minor classic, *Wayward Youth*, on young criminals. He was very fat, rather eccentric – he always wore black – and had something of a crush on Anna Freud. Aichhorn often had coffee at the Café Museum with a young Jewish photographer, Edmund Engelman.

A few weeks after the Nazis took over, Aichhorn told Engelman, 'A museum can be created once the storm is over.' But a museum had to have exhibits. Engelman agreed to take photographs of the apartment. He would have to do so without using any flashlights because the apartment was being watched by the Gestapo. They wanted to make sure that the Freud family did not smuggle any of their valuables out, especially after the suspicions Martin's behaviour had aroused.

Engelman recalled that, on his first visit to the apartment, he 'was amazed by the unbelievable number of fine artistic objects'. The photographs give a beautiful record of Freud's home. Some tables are laden with ten or more statuettes, many of which Hilda Doolittle had described. The photographs included one of a chair Anna Freud had had specially designed for her father so that he could sit comfortably while writing. Behind Freud's specially designed analytic chair in the consulting room were four original paintings by Wilhelm Busch: an ass looking at a painter who is working, a fish spitting at a fly, a rhinoceros looking at a black man and a chicken struggling to spit out a fly.

After Engelman had spent some days in the apartment, Freud walked in on him. 'We stared at each other,' Engelman wrote. The young photographer said that he felt 'flustered and embarrassed' in the presence of the great man, whom Aichhorn had insisted he must not stress. Freud 'looked concerned' but stayed calm and 'matter of fact'. Aichhorn explained who Engelman was and, very luckily, the young man had some of his photographs with him. He presented these to Freud, explaining they were a souvenir that he had been meaning to give him.

Freud looked at Aichhorn and Engelman and then broke into a smile. He was very pleased and thanked the photographer. This record of his apartment would mean a great deal to him when he was in London. Engelman then asked Freud if he would allow him to take photographs of himself. Freud agreed and so we have pictures of himself, Anna and his wife just before they left Vienna.

Engelman learned a few days later that the Gestapo were searching for him, so he gave the photographs to Aichhorn. The young photographer was desperate to leave the city quickly and felt it was much too dangerous to try to carry the negatives with him.

Since the Nazis had taken over, Freud stayed in his apartment nearly all the time, a prisoner in his own home. Pichler came to see him quite often and Schur visited every day. Freud's physical condition was not bad and there were no new lesions, but, according to Schur, 'the crust formations were bothersome and needed constant attention'. He was referring to crusts high up in the nasal cavity.

In his next letter to Minna, written on 23 May, Freud complained that it was raining and his study was darker than usual. But he had one piece of good news. He had arranged with the help of 'unser Kommissar' Sauerwald for some of his antiquities to be sold for 30,000 Reichsmarks. That 'would nearly secure the border fees,' Freud wrote. But he was not telling his sister-in-law the whole truth. Marie Bonaparte knew that Freud was short of money and paid the exit taxes for all the family. Alfred Indra, Freud's lawyer, explained that the Princess had sent him the funds that were needed, which he duly handed over to the tax authorities.

But money was still a problem, because not all the family were going. Freud and his brother Alexander wanted to leave as much as they could for their four sisters, who were staying behind. Freud had to contemplate selling more of his books, part of the stock he wanted to ship to London. The idea did not please him, but he had to do it. When he wrote to Minna, he quoted Lord Byron, who had had to sell his library, and said, 'I won't be plucked of my feathers.'

On 26 May Freud wrote to Minna, 'The situation has stayed the same. Once a day we speak with London, twice a day with Paris.' He had been telephoned by an English journalist who wanted to confirm the rumour that Freud was coming to London. Freud was careful with him. But in the midst of all the anxieties, some routines persisted. Freud had started playing a card game called Tarok in the 1890s and once a week he held Tarok parties in his house – the women were, of course, excluded. Paula Fichtl served coffee and dry cakes. Anxiety about leaving was no reason not to continue playing Tarok, so he had a *Tarokpartie* with August Aichhorn and other friends.

Again Freud complained of the 'ghastly weather' which meant that he could not go out. Marie Bonaparte had decided to 'visit us once more in Vienna and to accompany us over the border', he had written in an earlier letter, but now it seemed the Princess had to stay in France for a wedding. Freud was bitterly disappointed.

Two days later, Freud's first sentence in his letter to Minna again reveals his anxiety: 'From Headquarters' there was no news 'naturally'. 'The way they treat us,' he added, 'showed no urgency at all'.

Still, Freud was now more hopeful, though he was frightened of being too optimistic. It could yet go wrong so easily. He was also careful in his letters, because they might be being intercepted by the Gestapo. Stefan Zweig thought so, because he wrote to Freud after he had left Vienna, 'Your handwriting revealed what your words had to conceal.'

At a number of points I have suggested that the Nazis were made anxious by having to deal with people who in normal times would have been seen as their social betters. Anna Freud had spent weeks being charming to Sauerwald. The Princess and Dorothy Burlingham were also utterly sweet to him. The deal that Marie Bonaparte and Sauerwald discussed would allow

Freud to take his library, his sculpture collection and much furniture, including the famous couch, to London. Sauerwald said that he supervised the packing of 1,000 pieces of art, as well as the books. That was not all. The man who accused the Jews of not being a reliable element of the population had to help pack a large quantity of their clothes and bedlinen.

Though all the taxes had been paid and all the documents agreed, Freud was still afraid to believe that he would be allowed to leave. On 1 June he took a walk to the Türkenschanzpark in the 18th district with Anna and Martha. The effort 'showed me once again how little I can trust myself to do'. Martha had to stop all the time because she got so tired.

In the evening Freud started a letter to Minna, but he did not have the energy to finish it, though not because he was too tired. He felt too anxious in case there was some unexpected hitch, some new bureaucratic obstacle, some new demand for money, papers or permits. They were also in danger of running out of suitcases. Martha, Anna and Paula Fichtl had already packed 20.

The next day Freud started the letter to Minna again. This time he did finish it, writing, 'Today I can see more clearly and try again.' He felt more certain now that they would leave, but his mood was still sombre: 'I was not prepared for how dark it was on my dining table. I tried to use the electrical light but then shadows fell across my hand.' So Freud preferred to write half in the dark. He was still oppressed by all the details that had to be finalised and by the failure of 'Headquarters' to move more quickly. 'We still have xyz formalities' to get through, he told Minna.

Freud talked again of '*unser Kommissar*' and of Indra, the lawyer. Both were very friendly and 'we believe we will be able to travel tomorrow'. Anna went to Thomas Cook to buy tickets and to get whatever foreign currency they could extract from the bank. The queues were long. But they were not yet able to make sleeping-car reservations. In this frenzy of last-minute activity, a tiny detail is particularly moving. One of Freud's sisters came, bringing a small amount of foreign change she had kept from a trip abroad. Her brother would need every sou when he got out, she thought.

'You cannot imagine what the small things are,' Freud added, and Anna had to deal with them all. The Berggasse tenants included couples Freud had known for years; people still tried to observe the decencies. The Freuds wanted to say a proper goodbye to their neighbours and even to leave them some small gifts, which they did.

Freud hoped that his physician would travel with him, but Max Schur came down with acute appendicitis. 'I was desperate and tried to wait for a few hours, but eventually had to be operated on,' Schur said. Five days after the operation, he tried to get up to visit his patient, but he collapsed on the way to 19 Berggasse.

Anna came to tell Schur they couldn't wait for him; the situation was getting too dangerous. Freud was not strong enough to travel without a physician, so they had to find a last-minute replacement. A friend of Anna's, Dr Josephine Stross, agreed to travel with Freud as his doctor. Sauerwald claimed that it had not been easy to arrange this. He must have worked bureaucratic wonders to get Dr Stross a quick exit visa and Jones must have performed equal miracles to get her an entry visa to France and Britain in such a short time.

Hans Pichler came on 2 June to give his famous patient a final check. The examination revealed nothing suspicious. He and Freud imagined they would never see each other again.

Stress and Leaving

There was a final bureaucratic hitch, precisely as Freud had dreaded. The Gestapo insisted on a reference, as they did not want to be accused of brutality towards a famous man. They asked Freud to confirm that he had been treated properly. They did not see, or pretended not to see, the irony of his reply. 'I most warmly recommend the Gestapo to everybody,' he wrote.

The news that the Freuds were leaving even reached Palestine. Eitingon in Jerusalem phoned Arnold Zweig in Tel Aviv who wrote at once to Freud: 'Although I still cannot quite believe that everything will go according to plan I want to think that after all the frightful things that have happened this little favour of fortune will at last come off.' Athena, he said, had to smile on them.

The best account of the day they left comes from Paula Fichtl, who noted small, ordinary details. She took the precaution of sewing some gold coins into the lining of her coat. Breakfast was served as normal. Freud had his usual soft-boiled egg and Anna suggested he sip a vermouth, one of his favourite drinks. No one talked much.

At midday, Paula ordered two taxis to take them and the 20 suitcases to the Westbahnhof. As she was about to leave the apartment she loved for the last time, she saw some dust on the sofa and whisked it off. New tenants would be coming and she did not want anyone to complain it had been left dirty. The taxis came at 2p.m. Freud kept his new chow, Lun, on his lap as they drove to the station.

Freud, Martha, Anna, Josephine Stross, Paula Fichtl and the maid were to join the Orient Express, which was coming from Istanbul. So many others had left or died, Freud observed, that they needed only two compartments. The last word Freud wrote in Vienna is now in the collection at Manchester University. He scribbled a postcard to Sam saying they were leaving and that he hoped finally to meet his nephew after a gap of 30 years.

They had reservations in the new steel S-class sleeping cars, which were painted blue with gold lining and lettering. At 3.25 the train pulled out of the Westbahnhof. The first stop was Salzburg, where Paula Fichtl's relatives lived. All her family came to the station to say goodbye to her and one of her brothers gave her a bouquet of edelweiss, Austria's national flower. The train crossed into Germany and stopped in Munich, from where it travelled close to Dachau.

Although Freud did not know it, the group was not alone. Wilhelm Bullitt had insisted that the American Consulate in Vienna send a man to watch over Freud and his family; he was under strict instructions to intervene if there were any problems. Bullitt told them this later.

At 2.45a.m. on 4 June the Orient Express reached the border between Germany and France. All Jews who were getting out feared trouble at the last minute. As William Reich had observed, the Nazis created fear brilliantly. Freud and Martha were very tired. Anna had to handle the officials. They looked at the passports and the exit visas in complete silence and then walked out of the compartment. After the Nazis had marched down the corridor to the next carriage, the conductor came to see the Freuds. 'I wish I could come with you,' Paula Fichtl remembers him saying.

As they crossed the Rhine, the relief was huge. Freud wrote in his diary, 'After the Rhine Bridge we were free.' Anna brought out the vermouth and they toasted their escape.

Stefan Zweig wrote to Freud, 'But whatever may have been lost, whatever must be built anew, the main thing is you are out and you look back on the smoking ruins like people fleeing from Sodom.'

In Vienna, Schur, who had been too sick to travel because of his ruptured appendix, said he felt 'lonely and abandoned as never before'. Sauerwald had a problem too. He had agreed to get 1,000 items out of Vienna. To do that would mean squaring things with the Gestapo and dealing with customs and the police, after already having dealt with the 20 suitcases the Freud family had taken on the Orient Express.

The moment Freud crossed the border, the change in him was remarkable. He shook off the stress of the previous three months and was ready to concentrate on work. Though this is an area that has been rather overlooked, the productivity of the last 15 months of his life would turn out to be remarkable.

CHAPTER 11

Freedom

On the morning of 4 June Freud, Martha, Anna, Paula Fichtl and Mitzi arrived at the Gare de l'Est. William Bullitt, Marie Bonaparte, Ernest Jones and Martin Freud were there to meet them. Minna was too sick to come from London. The family was settled in the Bonaparte Bentley and the Bonaparte Rolls, and the Princess took them to her house in Saint-Cloud. They would sit in the garden where Topsy had scrapped with the chow mongrel.

The pictures which show Freud lying down on a chaise longue wearing a cap suggest it was just a day of rest. It was not, though. First, the Princess offered them a fine lunch to celebrate. Paula Fichtl was amazed to be asked to sit at the table with all the other guests. She had never been waited on before.

Freud's first task was to discuss an unfinished project he had started long ago with William Bullitt: their work on Woodrow Wilson. Bullitt was very opinionated, and far less deferential to Freud than most of his patients and ex-patients, so the collaboration was not easy. Bullitt objected to some passages Freud had inserted. In 1932 Bullitt had returned to the United States to work on Roosevelt's campaign and believed he would never again find time to work on the manuscript. Freud was annoyed by Bullitt's tendency to secretiveness. But they were determined to finish their book, because Hitler's rise to power had made their thesis astonishingly relevant.

The book is a neglected source of information on both Wilson and Freud's thinking. It is neither pure biography nor pure psychoanalysis but rather a long *J'Accuse*. Freud and Bullitt find the President guilty as a man, a politician, a university president, a writer and even as a patient (because he irritated his doctor).

Freud hardly went into the project without prejudice, as back in 1926 he had told Max Eastman, 'You should not have gone into the war at all!' adding, 'Your Woodrow Wilson was the silliest fool of the century, if not of all centuries.'

It took Bullitt and Freud seven years to achieve a first draft, because Freud insisted that they find out as much as possible about Woodrow Wilson's childhood and his private life. Bullitt knew many of the late President's friends and wrote to them all. Few were reticent. The book does not acknowledge, however, that Freud's nephew Edward Bernays had also known Wilson well. Freud and Bullitt had access to many intimate details; the book was history written by formidably privileged insiders.

Woodrow Wilson was a man in the grip of powerful unconscious forces, Freud and Bullitt claimed. He would not have agreed to the French and British demands at Versailles if he had been analysed. His father was a Presbyterian minister who had high ambitions for his son even when Woodrow was just four months old and, presumably, in nappies. 'That baby is dignified enough to be Moderator of the General Assembly,' his father wrote proudly. Wilson's father was physically very affectionate. He liked to chase his son in the garden, catch him and give him a great hug. Even as adults, the two men kissed emotionally whenever they met.

But the relationship was inevitably unequal, the son being the passive one, and that passivity would come to haunt him. Freud and Bullitt had no doubt that Woodrow's love for his father went too far: 'He not only expresses his love and admiration for his father but also removes his father by incorporating his father in himself as if by an act of cannibalism. Thenceforth he is himself the great admired father.' American presidents have been accused of many things, but only Wilson has been accused of cannibalism, I think.

Woodrow Wilson rebelled against his father only once. He did not go into the ministry but into academia. In 1895 Wilson's father came to live with him. The result: Wilson broke down completely. The reasons were as purely Oedipal as you could get, Freud and Bullitt said. Wilson could not allow himself to express any hostility to his father, but in his unexplored unconscious he was a boy with an unresolved Oedipal complex who wanted to 'annihilate the Reverend Joseph Ruggles Wilson'.

Wilson became the president of Princeton in June 1902. Three months later, his father died. 'After his father's death his [Woodrow's] addiction to speech making which was already excessive grew to fantastic proportions.'

One of the pleasures of the book is its bitchy tone: 'The Reverend Joseph Ruggles Wilson, who incidentally is not to be recommended as a model for fathers, had made his son love him so deeply and submissively that the flood of passivity he had aroused could be satisfied by no other man or activity.'

The turning point for Wilson came when he met Colonel George Harvey, who admired his speeches and decided Wilson could be nominated to run for President of the United States. Everything then happened very quickly. Wilson was elected Governor of New Jersey and two years later, in 1912, elected President. 'Thenceforth there was a somewhat unusual amount of deity in the character of Woodrow Wilson,' sniped Bullitt and Freud. Wilson was now inclined to see himself as God's instrument on earth. Freud had more sympathy with patients who thought rats were gnawing at their buttocks. The book declared that someone who was so sure he had 'a special personal intimacy with the Almighty is unfitted for relations with the children of men'.

When the First World War broke out, Wilson proclaimed the neutrality of the United States. His adviser, Colonel House, wrote on 10 November 1915 that Wilson must use all his skills and the resources of America on 'behalf of some plan by which the peace of the world may be maintained'. House went on to say, 'This is the part I think that you are destined to play in this world tragedy and it is the noblest part that has ever come to a son of man.'

Freud and Bullitt commented, 'Woodrow Wilson who in his unconscious was God and Christ could not resist such words.' He longed to be the bringer of peace on earth, not just because that was a noble ideal but because he identified with God and his feminine side identified with Christ.

Ten months before the war ended, Wilson set out 14 basic points for a just peace, but his failure to deal with his inner conflicts with his father crippled him. The world was paying the price, according to Freud and Bullitt.

When the President came to Paris in March 1919, huge crowds lined the avenues to cheer him. Wilson was seen as a saviour, but he did not know how to turn this to his political advantage. He wilted when faced by Clemenceau and Lloyd George. Once confronted by strong men, 'the deep underlying femininity of his nature began to control him and he discovered he did not want to fight them with force. He wanted to preach sermons to them.'

Clemenceau and Lloyd George sensed the President's vulnerability. On 27 March Clemenceau demanded a 30-year occupation of the Rhineland and an annexation of the Saar.

When Wilson said this had never been part of the war aims, Clemenceau exploded, 'You are pro-German. You are seeking to destroy France.'

Wilson then sulked that perhaps Clemenceau wanted him to go home.

'I do not wish you to go home, but I intend to do so myself,' Clemenceau replied, and with that put on his hat and walked out.

Deeply offended, Wilson went for a long drive in the Bois de Boulogne and missed lunch. When he got back, he stood up and made an appeal. His speech even impressed Clemenceau, who shook the President's hand, saying, 'You are a good man, Mr President, and you are a great man.'

Clemenceau might flatter, but he did not change his position. Wilson told his aides the problem was that Clemenceau had 'a feminine mind'. In fact, nothing 'less feminine than Clemenceau's refusal to be swept off his feet by Wilson's oratory could be imagined', claimed Freud and Bullitt. They identified a textbook case of projection: Wilson, the man with the feminine mind, claimed Clemenceau was too feminine, meanwhile refusing to use 'the masculine weapons in his hands'. Instead Wilson merely repeated his peace plan.

Not surprisingly, this failure of nerve triggered another 'nervous' collapse. On 9 April Wilson compromised on the Saar and 'never again did he threaten to fight for the peace he had set out to give the world'. The world was suffering the consequences at the end of the 1930s. Freud then referred to his beloved Shakespeare, judging that Lloyd George, the 'Welsh Shylock', was 'unwilling to abandon one molecule of the British pound of flesh'.

The Treaty of Versailles was delivered to the Germans on 7 May. The German President called it a document 'dictated by hate' and reminded Wilson that it broke many promises he had made to him.

The writing of the psycho-biography has verve, wit and urgency. Agreeing on the final text gave Freud great pleasure, as everything else did during his brief stay in Paris. He told Marie that her home 'had restored our dignity and morale. After having been wrapped in love for 12 hours, we left proud and rich under the protection of Athena.' She had given him a little antique statue of the goddess with the following note:

> Athena
> Peace and Reason
> Greets those who have fled
> From the mad inferno.

It was an inferno whose causes Freud and Bullitt had now explained.

At the end of the Freuds' stay, Marie's magnificent vehicles drove them to the Gare du Nord, which has, appropriately, classical Greek figures decorating its front entrance. This time there was no reason to be anxious about crossing the frontier. Jones had obtained documents from Sir Samuel Hoare, so Freud and his family would be treated as if they belonged to a diplomatic mission.

As he crossed the Channel, Freud dreamed that he was landing not at Dover but at Pevensey, where William the Conqueror had come ashore in 1066. This was hardly the dream of a dispossessed or depressed man but more that of a conquistador.

Freud was now an old man in a hurry. With the final text of the Wilson book agreed, he had two other books to finish, *Moses and Monotheism* and *An Outline of Psychoanalysis*. Four years earlier Freud had written, 'I do not only think but I *know* [his italics] that I shall let myself be deterred by this second obstacle, by external danger, from publishing the last portion of my study on Moses.' In Britain, he would be free of external dangers and finally able to write in safety. He would also have the chance to see Sam at last.

London Life

When Freud, Martha and Anna arrived at Victoria station, it was what we would now call a media event. Newsreels recorded him getting off the train; the papers put the story on their front pages. The *British Medical Journal* noted that doctors would feel proud that their country had offered Freud asylum.

One immediate problem was Freud's dog. Even at his most energetic, Jones could not manage to circumvent the quarantine regulations designed to stop rabies coming into Britain. Lun was taken to what Fichtl called 'the animal asylum' in South Kensington. Freud missed his chow dreadfully.

He also realised that in letters to his colleagues he had said very little of his fears during the last 11 weeks. He wrote to Eitingon:

It is hardly an accident that I have remained so matter of fact up to now. The emotional climate of these days is hard to grasp, almost indescribable. The feeling of triumph on being liberated is too strongly mixed with sorrow for in spite of everything I greatly loved the prison from which I have been released.

He wondered, 'How long will a fatigued heart be able to accomplish any work'? He very much wanted to see Minna but had not managed to do that yet.

Freud had other reasons for being depressed. The *New York Times* reported on 4 June 1938 that Freud's Verlag and 'all his money' had been confiscated. Freud told reporters, 'All my money and property in Vienna is gone.' He was not being totally truthful, but the *New York Times* did not get to see his bank records. An account card shows that three accounts were still active: the guilder account in Holland was closed on 30 June 1938; Freud's other two accounts that we have records of were closed on 31 July and 19 September 1938. It seems inevitable that there were more accounts, because Freud's letters to Sam in the 1920s show money being sent from at least five banks.

Stefan Zweig, who had moved to central London, wrote to Freud on 6 June from his Hallam Street address. He did not want to disturb him yet, but they must meet once Freud had recovered from his 'bitter journey'. Zweig gave Freud his ex-directory number: Langham 3993.

On 8 June Freud wrote to Marie Bonaparte that they had been flooded with flowers. There had been only three autograph collectors and a woman painter who wanted him to sit for a portrait. He also received a letter from a woman whose mother had been diagnosed as incurable but surely the great therapist could cure her. There was a letter from 'an enterprising delicatessen' as well – presumably a Jewish one. There were other offers, including 'a rambling four page telegram from Cleveland Ohio' inviting Freud to make his home there. He told Marie that he would write back saying it was not possible as they had already unpacked. He could hardly bear to pack 20 suitcases again. Finally he thanked Marie for her cigars, which had been stripped of nicotine and were rather tasteless (Freud did not like these unmanly cigars any more than he liked contraception). 'He soon found some tasty ones,' Schur noted.

On 9 June Sam came down from Manchester and the two men finally met. Sadly, there is no record of what they said to each other.

News of Freud's triumphant arrival had repercussions in Vienna. The Gestapo made enquiries at the hospital where Max Schur had been operated on; they wanted to satisfy themselves that he had had appendicitis and did not have some sinister reason for not leaving Vienna. Schur's wife, Helen, was summoned to the exit-tax office to satisfy them about some new detail. If she could not do that, they would revoke the permission to leave. Luckily she succeeded.

Schur finally left Vienna on 10 June 1938 with his family and reached London five days later. He found that Freud had had some cardiac problems during the trip and had an irritable bladder, but otherwise was in rather good health. Schur did not seem to realise that escaping Vienna was better than the best therapy for Freud. He was free and free to work. The liberation meant he could consider another potential triumph, the Nobel Prize again, with some detachment. This time Einstein would not be arguing against Freud getting the award.

Chaim Weizmann, the Zionist leader who later became President of Israel, came to visit and told Freud that on 17 June a resolution had been passed at the Sociological Institute welcoming him. H.G. Wells visited two days later. Three secretaries of the Royal Society came to see Freud on 23 June so that he could sign its charter of Fellows. He had been made a 'foreign' Fellow of the Society. That was a rare honour and new Fellows always signed the charter at the Society's offices. Freud pleaded infirmity for not doing so and did not admit he had been well enough to visit Lun at the 'animal asylum'.

London had never had very much significance for Freud before, but he had written about the city when describing neurotics and their fixations. He had drawn a poetic comparison between memorials and the mind: 'If you walk through London you will find before one of the greatest railway stations of the city a richly decorated Gothic pillar – Charing Cross.' The pillar commemorated the grief of Henry II when his wife, Eleanor of Aquitaine, died. Her coffin was taken to Westminster and the King had Gothic crosses erected at each of the places where the coffin was set down. Charing Cross was the last of them. Jones had told Freud that the word Charing was derived from *chère reine*. Then there was the Monument. After the Great Fire of London in 1666, the citizens of London built a tall pillar in the City. 'These monuments are memory symbols like the hysterical symptoms,' Freud wrote. In his diary, he likened Londoners to hysterics and neurotics:

> not only in that they remember the painful experiences of the distant past, but because they are still strongly affected by them. They cannot escape from the past and neglect present reality in its favour.

But Freud *had* escaped, if not his past then at least the city of his past. He was delighted he had met 'with the friendliest reception in lovely, free magnanimous England'. He could have stayed depressed, as every day there was 'distressing news from Vienna and the continuous appeals for help which serve only to remind one of one's helplessness'. Instead, he felt a wonderful sense of liberation and it flowed into his pen, which no longer slipped from his grasp. 'I am once more able to speak and write – I had almost said "and think" – as I wish or I must,' he told Stefan Zweig. He sat down every day at his writing desk to finish *Moses* at last.

On 12 July Freud recorded a two-minute speech for the BBC. It is the best recording of his voice we have – and sounds disconcertingly squeaky. Freud explained he had started his career as a neurologist, briefly outlined the nature of analysis and thanked England for the wonderful welcome it had afforded him and his family.

Freud had not totally escaped the Nazis, however, because they continued to 'bleed' him, as he put it. On 18 July the Nazi foreign currency office ordered Freud to turn over a Swiss bank account denominated in Dutch guilders. He complied because he was afraid that his four sisters in Vienna would suffer if he did not. This was the account that was finally closed on 31 July, so the Nazis got yet more money out of him; it was, as usual, transferred to them by the lawyer, Dr Indra. But there was still some money left in at least one account that he had managed to keep secret with Sauerwald's help, as well as the gold smuggled out through the Greek Embassy. There had to be some funds because Freud arranged to buy a house at 20 Maresfield Gardens for £6,000. He did not borrow the money from Marie. Sauerwald's estimate that Freud was worth over 2 million schillings was a good one. Local estate agents who have some sense of the history of London property prices believe Freud paid far too much for his new house. Even more remarkably, Freud managed to get a mortgage from Barclays Bank – some achievement for a man of 82 in those conservative days.

Freud received so many letters that the post office said they knew where to deliver a letter that was just addressed 'Freud – London'. He got 'with a frequency surprising to a foreigner communications which were concerned with the state of my soul and which pointed out how much Christ had to offer…The good people' wanted to make him a Christian, at the end of his life.

Marie Bonaparte came to London for three days on 23 June. Freud had asked for her help in getting his four sisters out of Vienna and she promised she would try. But even with her connections, she could not get permission from the French authorities to allow the sisters to go to Paris. They needed, as Freud did, both exit visas from the Nazis and entry visas to the new country. Neither were forthcoming. The evidence suggests that Marie really tried hard only for Rosa, who, she suggested, should be awarded Greek citizenship. Celia Bertin, in her thorough biography of the Princess, says very little about Marie Bonaparte's attempts. Yet there were powerful allies Marie could have enlisted. Bullitt was the American ambassador in Paris and could have asked the French government to do him a favour. Jones had not lost his contacts in Whitehall. But the sisters remained in Nazi Vienna as the plight of Jews there got worse.

On 24 June Arnold Zweig wrote that he was delighted Freud's name was being considered again by the Nobel Committee. Freud refused to get too excited, saying analysis had 'several good enemies' among the grandees who decided who would receive the award, 'so though the money would be very welcome after the way the Nazis bled me in Vienna and since neither my son nor my son in law is a rich man, Anna and I have agreed that one is not bound to have everything'. Freud ended with some irony, saying that he and his inseparable daughter had decided that he would renounce the Prize and she would renounce the journey to Stockholm to collect it.

Surrealist Surprise

As he settled in, Freud received many visitors, perhaps the most interesting being Salvador Dalí, the Surrealist painter. He first read Freud's *The Interpretation of Dreams* in a Spanish translation in 1925 and his book *The Tragic Myth of Millet's Angelus* is written rather like a Freudian case history. In 1956 Dalí was asked if he had ever undergone psychoanalysis and replied that he had met Freud two years before Freud died. 'My first period is influenced by Freud completely,' Dalí said, but insisted he had never needed psychoanalysis 'because I am not crazy. You see my kind of craziness is a craziness of precision and clarity, to the contrary of a psychopathological's craziness.'

Some people doubt the meeting ever took place. Dalí himself was to blame. In his autobiography, he said he tried to visit Freud three times and found the great man out of town each time. But in fact there was a very reliable witness. Stefan Zweig took Dalí and a would-be analyst Edward James to see Freud on 19 July 1938. The three of them were together when Dalí drew his famous sketch of Freud, one of his most evocative and moving likenesses.

Freud wrote to Zweig the next day, thanking him for bringing the visitors. He commented, 'I had been inclined till then to take the surrealists who seem to have chosen me as their patron saint as absolutely mad – 95% mad let's say as if we were discussing alcohol.' But Dalí, with his 'fanatical eyes and his undoubted technical mastery', would make an interesting subject for an analytic study. How did he come to create his works? This letter completely contradicts some accounts that claim the meeting was not a success and that Dalí bored Freud.

Freud did not stay long in the rented house at 39 Elsworthy Road. In late August he and his family moved into the Esplanade Hotel in Warrington Crescent, Maida Vale. The hotel is now called the Colonnades and has a Freud suite. There is a telling photograph of Freud outside the hotel at the bottom of two sets of two steps. He is not even using his cane, so he must have been well enough to walk up them. Freud would stay there until September.

Medical Matters

One of Max Schur's first tasks was to make sure that Freud could get proper medical help if an emergency arose. Hans Pichler had referred Freud to a Dr George Exner, who had been his pupil, but Pichler was not sure Exner could cope with the complexities of Freud's nose and mouth. The lesions could easily turn malignant again and they were hard to operate on, being high up the nasal cavity. Quite exceptionally, the Home Office gave Schur permission to act as Freud's doctor before he had passed the examinations he needed to practise in Britain.

Being a young-ish doctor in a foreign country had its problems. Schur had to struggle to learn how to work with Exner. Medical vanities were the problem. Exner would defer to Pichler, his old teacher, but not to Schur. Early in August, Schur found a small lesion in front of the area where the last operation had been performed. This was worrying, but Exner 'listened with a mixture of disbelief and annoyance to the statements of a foreigner'. Very concerned, Schur wrote to Pichler to ask if he would come from Vienna. Pichler must have told Freud how worried Schur was, because Freud became angry and accused Schur of being alarmist.

But Freud himself told Marie Bonaparte the bad medical news. On 18 August she wrote to Freud, saying that Professor Rigaud of the Marie Curie Institute advocated more electro-coagulation. During the next few days, Schur had found a large area had lesions behind the place of the last operation; he thought this was ominous. Schur now asked Pichler to come to London urgently.

Freud had every reason to live, because finally, in August, his book on Moses would be published in German, 37 years after he had first stood in front of Michelangelo's great statue.

CHAPTER 12

Moses and Monotheism

On 14 November 1986 Professor Yosef Hayim Yerushalmi gave the Lionel Trilling Lecture at Columbia University. He revealed he had obtained from the Library of Congress a hitherto unknown version of Freud's *Moses and Monotheism* and that this original draft was 'different in significant ways from the published version'. Freud, it was clear, had been too anxious to state his views on anti-Semitism while he was in Vienna.

In his 1937 article in *Imago*, Freud wrote, 'To deprive a people of the man whom they take pride in as the greatest of their sons is not a thing to be gladly or carelessly undertaken – especially when one himself belongs to that people.' There was no mention of the present dilemmas Jews faced. But Freud wanted to write something far more direct, Yerushalmi argued, because the unpublished version read, 'My immediate purpose was to gain knowledge of the person Moses, my more distant goal to contribute thereby to the solution of a problem, still current today.'

Freud explained that his book had been written twice, 'the first time a few years ago in Vienna where I did not think it would be possible to publish it. I determined to give it up but it tormented me like an unlaid ghost.' Ironically, the Nazi invasion which forced Freud to leave 'freed me from any anxiety'. In England he was able to say what he thought without fearing that the authorities, Father Schmidt or the Pope would take revenge on psychoanalysis. The moment he crossed the Channel, Freud admitted, 'I found the temptation irresistible to make the knowledge I held accessible to the world'. He began to revise the work with fervour. Freud sometimes joked that he had Hitler to thank for forcing him to go to London: 'Thank the Führer' was the quip he often used.

Moses and Monotheism is a mixture of psychoanalysis, biblical criticism and analysis of anti-Semitism. It is an examination by a Jew of why Jews have been hated through the ages. In the book, Freud explored three different threads. First, he believed that Exodus got it completely wrong: Moses was not a Jew but an Egyptian. Pharaoh's daughter did not find the baby floating in a basket amid the bulrushes and take him to Pharaoh's palace. That kind of fable was typical of many stories of the origins of heroes. In reality, the prophet was an Egyptian and probably a member of Pharaoh's Court. There was a rumour that Moses might even have been a general who led Egyptian forces in Ethiopia, the Jewish historian Josephus claimed.

Second, the very name Moses was suggestive. Freud acknowledged his debt to a 19th-century English historian, James Henry Breasted, who pointed out that Moses was a noun in Egyptian; *mose* meant 'child'. Little Egyptians had names like Amen-mose, meaning 'Amen-a-child' or Ptah-mose, meaning 'Ptah-a-child'. Moses was not a Jewish name at all. No author, Freud said, had even considered the obvious, that a child born in Egypt who had an Egyptian name might be Egyptian – and not Jewish at all. If Moses was not Jewish, just what religion did he belong to or believe in? Freud knew his answer would outrage Jews and Christians alike.

The third theme centred on the birth of monotheism. Ancient Egypt rejoiced in nearly as many gods as palm trees. There were gods of the moon, the sun, the earth and stars; there were gods of abstractions, such as truth and justice; and then there were animal gods – cats and crocodiles were favourites.

Around 1370 BC the Egyptians were becoming sceptical about their all too obvious gods. The school of priests in the sun temple at Heliopolis had been developing the idea of a universal god who, unlike the dog, cat and fish deities, was a very ethical being. These reforming priests found a new Pharaoh sympathetic to their 'heresy'. Akhenaten's father allowed them to worship the sun god and spread the solar gospel. His son was even more of an enthusiastic sun-worshipper, but he was spiritually subtle too. The sun was not just the brightest object in the sky but a symbol of the divine being whose energy was manifested in its rays.

Freud quoted a German historian, Adolf Erman, who wrote *Die ägyptische religion* in 1905: 'There are...words which are meant to express in an abstract form the fact that not the star itself was worshipped, but the Being that manifested itself in it.' The significant advance was that Akhenaten's god was exclusive, not one god among many. One of his hymns, from 1370 BC, praised him with the words: 'O Thou only God, there is no other God than Thou.' There was not one god greater than other gods but just one God.

Six years into his reign, Akhenaten left Thebes and built a new capital lower down the Nile at Tell el-Amarna to mark the change. The site now is a desolate spot in the desert about three hours from Cairo.

Freud argued that Moses was an important official, perhaps even a priest at the time of Akhenaten, able, ambitious and a devout believer in the new religion. When Akhenaten died, vicious religious disputes started. The traditional priests tried to bring back the old gods and outlaw the new monotheism.

Moses faced a clear choice, according to Freud: either to abandon his new faith or to do something dramatic. Here Freud offered a daring hypothesis. Moses decided that if his country was turning its back on the new – and true – religion, he would found a new empire with a new people who believed in a new religion: that of the one and only God. A new religion needed believers. Moses did not have to seek far, as Egypt was full of Jews who were flattered that a noble Egyptian took an interest in them. They listened and accepted Moses, who 'placed himself at their head'. (Freud assumed that generations of slavery had made the Jews unusually placid intellectually and that no iconoclast asked Moses, 'What makes you think you are a prophet?')

For his part, Moses insisted that the Jews adopt some Egyptian ways. The Greek historian Herodotus had noticed a telling thing on a visit to Egypt in 450 BC: the Egyptians had a horror of pigs. Freud therefore argued that making pork totally forbidden – as it is under kosher laws – was in fact an ancient Egyptian custom. Freud then suggested that it was Moses who insisted on Jewish boys being circumcised. Forget the covenant with Abraham as recorded in Genesis; it was Moses the Egyptian who made the Jews snip their foreskins. For Freud, this was highly significant, as he had always believed that Jews were persecuted because they were circumcised and, therefore, reminded men of their fears of castration.

Freud felt that the Book of Exodus was partly right. Somehow Moses persuaded the Pharaoh to let his people go. But the 40 years of wandering in the desert did not proceed as told in the Bible. There was no parting of the Red Sea. Moses simply waved goodbye to the Pyramids and marched his followers into Sinai. The new Pharaoh who had succeeded Akhenaten did not even bother to pursue them. According to Freud, written and archaeological evidence suggested that the Exodus from Egypt took place between 1358 and 1350 BC, soon after the death of Akhenaten.

But the wanderings of the Jews did not end in the Sinai desert, as Exodus claimed. They went to Meribah Kadesh – Kadesh means 'holy' and Meribah a 'place of the waters'. There they made an alliance with a tribe from the land of Midian. Freud suggested that the priests of each tribe first praised the superior qualities of their own god and then reached a compromise. The Jews embraced the Midianite god, Jahve, who was a volcano god. As there were volcanoes in western Arabia, it would have been sensible, Freud argued, to worship and appease a volcanic deity. This god was rather primitive, belching flames and inclined to violence, but was just what the Jews needed to stiffen their resolve, as they intended to conquer Canaan. In return, the Midianites accepted some Jewish practices, though it is unclear what these might have been. This compromise did not please Moses, whose faith was not in a god who was volcanic or even tribal.

How were the Jews to make Moses accept the compromise when he was so opposed to it? The truth for Freud had been provided in the work of a German biblical scholar, Ernst Sellin, who claimed that Moses never made it to the Promised Land because he was murdered by the unruly Jews for rejecting the deal at Meribah Kadesh. Sellin had based his sensational theory on a reading of the Book of Hosea, but Freud could now explain what Sellin had been unable to.

Moses would not compromise with the volcano god, so the Jews killed their 'father' Moses, just as the Stone Age sons had killed their father in *Totem and Taboo*. But they could not escape the guilt feelings either. After the Neanderthal sons murdered their father, they stuck him on a totem; the Jews, being more advanced, proclaimed Moses the real father of their new religion.

Freud then made an extraordinary leap of the imagination. In the section of *Moses and Monotheism* called 'The Analogy', he argued that there was a long gap between the Jews beginning to worship the volcano god and the emergence of monotheistic Judaism as we know it – about eight centuries, Freud reckoned. It was not just human children who had a latency period – this was Freud's 'leap' – Judaism had one too. He quoted the biblical scholar Paul Volz, who wrote in 1907, 'the exalted work of Moses was understood and carried through to begin with only feebly and scantily till, in the course of centuries, it penetrated more and more and at length in the great prophets it met with like spirits who continued the lonely man's work'.

The different identities of the Egyptian one god and the volcano god have affected the Chosen People ever since: 'Jews are riven by an oscillation between Akhenaten's "Universal" God and Yahweh/Jehovah the Tribal God.' Suffering in biblical days meant 'their God became hard, relentless, and, as it were, wrapped in gloom. But the Jews had the consolation of knowing they were His chosen people.' Though he was somewhat vague in describing the process, Freud claimed that over 800 years the Jewish God came to resemble the Mosaic Egyptian god. But traces of the conflict between the tribal god and the advanced ethical deity could be found in the Second Commandment: it does not say there are no other gods, but 'Thou shalt have no other gods before me', the implication being that there are minor gods behind Yahweh.

Freud then provided one of those case histories that he could make so riveting. It concerned a little boy who as so often happened 'in middle class families shared his parents' bedroom during the first years of his life'. The child had often observed sexual acts between his parents – seeing some things and hearing still more. He was very sensitive to noises and once he had woken up could not get to sleep again. The child became aggressively masculine and 'began to excite his little penis with his hand and to attempt various sexual attacks on his mother'. The mother then forbade him to touch his penis. (Marthe Robert, in fact, argues that one reason Freud developed his ideas about Moses is that at the end of his life he was trying once again to distance himself from his own father and so was finishing off Jacob – symbolically at least.)

In the third part of the book, with considerable passion, Freud tried to understand why Jews had been hated and why so many Christians had been willing to persecute them for centuries. He pointed out that 'the poor Jewish people, who with its usual stiff-necked obduracy continued to deny the murder of their father', were endlessly accused of killing the Christian God. And, being arrogant and stiff-necked, Jews denied it was their fault. 'You won't admit that you murdered God,' screeched the anti-Semites. Then the ones who were more honest said, 'It is true, we did the same thing, but we admitted it, and since then we have been purified.'

Freud believed that this story had had a deep impact on Jews, arguing that it was a characteristic of Jews

> that they have a very good opinion of themselves, think themselves nobler, on a higher level, superior to the others, from whom they are also separated by many of their customs. With this they are animated by a special trust in life, such as is bestowed by the secret possession of a precious gift; it is a kind of optimism. Religious people would call it trust in God.

As the Chosen People, Jews felt especially close to God. Freud said they shared 'in the grandeur of God', which made them proud and confident. This new one God had blessed them above all other peoples. Moreover, Jews were forced to become more intellectual because they worshipped a God who could not be seen. As a result, Freud claimed, Jews were less slaves to their instincts than other groups. It is hard not to see in this an attack on the Nazis, who were certainly slaves to their instincts. The world condemned the insufferable arrogance of Jews and made them suffer for it, however.

With *Moses and Monotheism* Freud had managed the remarkable feat of writing a book which praised Jews and the Jewish heritage while at the same time outraging the rabbis – and not just the rabbis.

In it he also claimed that 'the Christian religion did not maintain the high levels in things of the mind to which Judaism soared'. Christianity was not up to the challenge of monotheism and so it brought back many lesser gods 'lightly veiled' and in subordinate positions. In addition, it restored the great Mother Goddess to her pedestal. Freud argued that the triumph of Christianity was a fresh victory for the priests of Amun over Akhenaten's superior god after an interval of 1,500 years. It's hardly surprising that Freud's argument was likely to upset just about everyone.

A number of rabbis learned what Freud was writing about and begged him to stop. Wasn't Hitler making enough trouble for Jews? Did Freud have to add to their misery by denying the truths of the Torah? Many Christian theologians were not keen on the Akhenaten thesis either, since the Gospels speak of a direct line of descent – 14 generations from Moses to David and 14 generations from David to Jesus. But those who urged him to keep quiet did not know Freud, a man who had never considered keeping his ideas to himself to spare others. There is no way of knowing whether Freud was right or not about Moses, but there is now a consensus that the Pharaoh Akhenaten 'invented' monotheism. So Freud was right about that, and well ahead of specialist scholars.

Freud published *Moses and Monotheism* in Amsterdam. It was, as he expected, very controversial and received with outrage. It had been a long while since one of his works was so harshly criticised. Even many of his fellow analysts hated it. In London the *News Chronicle* called for Freud to be sent back to Germany – the paper forgot he had actually come from Austria. There is no sign that Freud minded the row. The book sold 1,800 copies in two months and he was very happy with that. He wanted the book to be translated quickly, but hesitated about who should do it. Ernest Jones insisted that he could produce an English version quickly with help from his wife.

While Freud was following how people reacted to his work on Moses, the cancer came back. And so did Pichler, who flew to London on 7 September having been summoned by Schur. There was no doubt, it was a race against time; immediate surgery was needed and it would have to be radical. Pichler needed to cut in through the cheek and lips. He asked Schur if Freud's heart could take the strain of an operation and Schur said he thought Freud would cope.

The two Austrian doctors arrived at the London Clinic on 8 September. Neither was entitled to operate in Britain, but Pichler had a European reputation and the British surgeon, Exner, had been his pupil. Pichler took control in the operating theatre. He split Freud's lip, carried the incision up the nose and managed to excise a great deal of pathological tissue. Under the microscope the tissue did not seem to be cancerous. Pichler then performed another electro-coagulation.

Schur had been right about Freud coping. The evening after the operation, Freud was feeling well enough to read, Pichler wrote in his notes. Anna wrote to Marie Bonaparte that Pichler had behaved 'exceedingly well', a phrase which makes complete sense when one realises that Pichler was a member of the Nazi Party. Freud then had a good night's sleep. After visiting his patient in the morning, Pichler flew back to Vienna.

On 27 September 1938 Freud moved into the house at 20 Maresfield Gardens. Paula Fichtl unrolled the Persian carpet which had come from Vienna and then she and Anna arranged the art objects exactly as they had been in the Berggasse. Sauerwald had managed to get the 1,000 antiquities out of Austria. He claimed that he had had to pay for three carriages in a freight train to load all the Freuds' goods. Neither Jones nor Marie Bonaparte says a word about what was an astonishing feat of transportation across hostile frontiers. Sauerwald had obviously crossed another line.

By making Maresfield Gardens seem as much like 19 Berggasse as possible, Anna, Martha and Paula were trying to comfort Freud, and he needed comforting as the latest operation had drained him. He complained to Marie, 'I am abominably tired and weak in my movements although I began yesterday with three patients but it is not going easily.'

Clearly, Freud's health was getting worse. He had managed the steps going up to the Esplanade Hotel, but now Minna was confined to a bedroom on the first floor and Freud could not visit her because he could not climb the stairs. Soon after that Minna had to be sent to a nursing home.

There were also problems with the English translation of *Moses and Monotheism*. Jones was slow, did not turn up to discuss progress and then excused himself, saying that he had a cold. He warned Freud that he might not finish the translation till February or March. Freud was ironic: Jones had insisted on taking 'this burden on yourself. I know that you have many things to do which are at least as important as this', but he did not want to die before the book appeared in English.

There was some light relief in the shape of his all too eager disciple, A.A. Roback, who had hoped to organise a Festschrift for Freud's 80th birthday. Roback sent some cuttings to Freud in October 1938. A poem about his escape to London had appeared in the Yiddish press in New York, a Mr Twersky was bringing out a book called *The Young Freud* and the enclosed cuttings purported to tell the story of his escape. Freud replied that he was glad to forget the Nazi invasion and commented on a newspaper piece Roback had sent. The story claimed that Freud had been 'ransomed'. He shot back that it was 'fabrication and lies. I often wonder about the mentality of American journalists who can get pleasure out of such performances.' He asked Roback if he had seen people collecting funds in Boston to ransom him. 'Probably no more than I have.' The idiots of the press would distort his book on Moses and claim he was writing 'The Psychoanalysis of the Bible', Freud added.

Hilda Doolittle came to visit Freud, but she was frustrated because she could get no time with him alone. It was quite different talking to him with others around. Marie Bonaparte came back on 29 October and stayed for five days. She had no positive news about making arrangements for Freud's four sisters to leave Vienna.

That same day Freud wrote a fulsome letter to a woman he did not know, Rachel Berdach. He had received a copy of her book, *The Emperor, the Sages and Death*, which told the story of the Holy Roman Emperor Frederick II and Rabbi Jacob Charif Ben Aron. Frederick was a collector just like Freud, but he had the power to collect more than objets d'art. He collected wise men – Arabs, Jews and Greeks – and their wisdom, encouraging them to exchange views on science, medicine, astronomy and astrology. Berdach's book has a gripping debate between an Arab healer and a bishop in which the Arab explains why he finds the story of the resurrection of Lazarus absurd and revolting. Lazarus suffered a vile ordeal: he died, was brought back to life just to make the point that Christ was a great healer and, that done, expired again.

In the book, Rabbi Ben Aron slowly becomes the dominant figure. He has a student who follows him to Frederick's Court. The student dies, leaving behind writings which ask profound questions. Do animals have any sense of when they are close to death or are humans the only species to be cursed with such awareness? Why did God inflict this insight on us? After his student dies, the rabbi becomes depressed. He wakes up one night and the silence seems uncanny. He runs through the town; it is empty. He goes into the countryside. Nothing is left alive. The Angel of Death has swooped over the world but somehow forgotten the rabbi. He then does die, having begged the angel to return to take him away.

Freud wrote to Berdach that he had not read anything so 'substantial and poetically accomplished for a long time'. Its excellence made him wonder why she had written him such a diffident letter and he asked if 'the priority you grant to death' meant that she was very young. To the end he was something of a flirt, on paper at least, as a great many therapists seem to have been.

Years later Max Schur met Berdach, who had been in analysis with Theodor Reik. With her permission, Reik told Schur that she had lost someone very dear to her when she was very young.

In November 1938 Poppy Hartwig wrote to tell Freud that her brother Morris had died. Morris had sent Freud a letter out of the blue and he had replied to it. Freud now learned that 62-year-old Morris had died in a motor car crash near Port Elizabeth, South Africa – yet another accident in the family. Poppy and Morris both gave some family history but none of the Manchester letters ever speak of the disappeared John Freud, the nephew Freud had played with when they were both toddlers.

On 28 November Freud wrote to Hilda Doolittle with a small mystery. A gift of gardenias 'by chance or intention, they are my favourite flowers', had been delivered to Maresfield Gardens. He noted that these were the flowers that ancient Greeks used to mark the return of the gods – 'or goods', he punned. He suspected she was responsible and thanked her for 'so charming a gesture'.

On 18 December Freud wrote to Arnold Zweig, whose son had been in a car crash. He was relieved the boy was well and ended that life 'would be quite comfortable if weren't for this and that and a lot of other things too'. He was waiting for a second bone splinter to detach itself which would make his mouth less painful. Schur felt this stubborn chip should come out and eventually managed to perform a small operation himself. 'I shall not easily forget Freud's reaction of gratitude. Which needed no words but was expressed by the look on his face and an especially warm handshake,' he later recalled.

After the operation, Freud wrote sadly to Eitingon, 'I am waiting like a hungry dog for a bone which has been promised to me only it is supposed to be one of my own.' He was finding it hard to work more than four hours a day.

Poppy sent her famous uncle presents for Christmas. Freud was embarrassed that they had sent her none, and when he wrote to thank her, he apologised. He would make up for it, he promised; Poppy would get a good reception when she came to visit them again.

Two days after Christmas, Freud was well enough to write a long letter to Marie Bonaparte. They had been freezing in London; his garden was covered with snow, which looked beautiful, but 'we dare not imagine what London will look like when all the snow turns to water'. There was no end to 'the usual news of death and suicide from Vienna'. Evidently there was no news about his four sisters there.

Schur said that Freud was now too tired to do creative work but he was still tinkering with *An Outline of Psychoanalysis*, his final thoughts on his life's work. Those who came to visit, such as Leonard and Virginia Woolf, did sense that Freud was not the force he had once been.

The Woolfs had been publishing English translations of Freud's works since 1924, when a discreet advertisement told the reading public that they could buy *Collected Papers* by Sigmund Freud, MD, Vols 1 and 2, and that the complete set, including three more volumes, would cost 4 guineas. The Woolfs paid Freud £50 as an advance on each volume, but they had never met their author before.

Freud was, Leonard Woolf noted, not just a genius but also, 'as unlike many geniuses, an extraordinarily nice man'. He had an 'extraordinarily civilised temperament...which made every kind of relationship with him so pleasant'.

Soon after Freud settled, Woolf had made 'discreet inquiries as to whether he would like Virginia and me to come and see him. The answer was yes and in the afternoon of January 28 1939 we went and had tea with him. I feel no call to praise the famous men I have known' – and Woolf had known more than a few, his acquaintances including Bertrand Russell, the poets W.B. Yeats and T.S. Eliot, Nehru and John Maynard Keynes, none of whom had left him agog with admiration. 'Nearly all famous men are disappointing or bores or both. Freud was neither; he had an aura not of fame but of greatness. The terrible cancer of the mouth...had already attacked him.'

He then added, 'Freud was extraordinarily courteous in a formal old fashioned way – for instance he almost ceremoniously presented Virginia with a flower.' It was a narcissus. 'There was something about him of the half extinct volcano, something sombre, suppressed, reserved. He gave me a feeling which only very few people whom I have met gave me, a feeling of great gentleness, but behind the great gentleness, great strength.'

Freud was 'a screwed up shrunken very old man with a monkey's light eyes paralysed spasmodic movements inarticulate; but alert. Difficult talk. Immense potential, an old fire now flickering,' Woolf recorded.

Perhaps the most intriguing remark is one that Virginia Woolf noted, according to her husband. Freud said to them, 'It would have been worse if you had not won the war. I said we often felt guilty – if we had failed, Hitler would not have been. No, he said with great emphasis, he would have been infinitely worse.' Unfortunately Freud did not elaborate on this statement and Virginia Woolf made no attempt to explain it.

They also had some fun. Leonard Woolf said that a few days before they went to visit he had read the report of a case in which a man had stolen books from the famous bookshop Foyles on Charing Cross Road. Some of the books were Freud's. Leonard noted, 'The magistrate fines him [the thief] and said that he wished he could sentence him to read all Freud's books as a punishment. I told Freud about this and he was amused and, in a queer way, also deprecatory about it. His books he said had made him infamous, not famous. A formidable man.'

In January the persistent A.A. Roback wrote to say that he had been in touch with Jung. Freud warned him that 'you would not heighten Jung's esteem for yourself through politeness'. Roback also asked Freud if he had really said, when the Gestapo took his money, that he had never charged as much. On 9 February Freud replied, 'I actually did make the remark you mentioned when the Nazis confiscated from me 6,000 schillings – not 8,000. It was something like "I never walked off with that much after a visit".'

Then came the most unexpected visitor of all.

Sauerwald in London

Anton Sauerwald suddenly turned up to see Freud in the spring of 1939. At his trial, Sauerwald claimed that Freud had written and invited him. The reason was purely business. Now that the antiquities had reached London, they devised a plan for getting Marie Bonaparte to buy the stock of books the Verlag still had in Germany. Sauerwald said Freud also wanted to discuss his bank accounts. But it was not only books and banks that the two men discussed.

Though Schur gave many details of Freud's illness and did mention Sauerwald, his account is vague after March 1939. The reason is simple. Schur had obtained a visa to go to America, but he felt he could not leave when his patient was so ill. However, American visas had time limits. If Schur did not arrive by 21 April, he would forfeit the precious right to live there. Freud understood and gave his doctor his blessing to sail for New York.

In a letter to Marie written in April, Freud said that his handwriting was poor and that his pen 'has left me like my physician'. He added that things were 'not going well with me'. He had the impression that he was being deceived about the true state of the cancer. There was an attempt by Exner to operate but it seems to have been botched.

Freud was now dreadfully weak and, more humiliating, he smelled disgusting. When his beloved dog came out of quarantine, Lun refused to come near him because he stank so vilely. Freud never ate in front of other people, because the botched operation had made it impossible for him to eat without dribbling and making a mess. Paula had to clean food off his trousers, his jacket and the floor. For a fastidious man like Freud, these were terrible humiliations.

As Sauerwald was in London, Freud seized the opportunity. He asked his old *Kommissar* to see if he could persuade Pichler to come to London again. Freud had faith that his Viennese surgeon could perform another operation that would buy him some more time.

Sauerwald promised to do his best and the moment he got back to Vienna he went to see Pichler and explained the situation. Pichler was not Jewish, so there were no complicated formalities. As it was so urgent, Sauerwald drove Pichler to the Channel and from Dover, all the way to Hampstead, where Pichler examined his patient. Freud's instinct had been right. It was a matter of life and death. Pichler again managed to persuade colleagues at the London Clinic to allow him to operate.

Sauerwald said, as Freud had done years earlier, that Pichler charged high fees and, at his trial, he produced Pichler's bill, which said that it had been paid by Sauerwald. This raises another intriguing question. Sauerwald insisted that he was a poor man and was getting a salary of 500 Reichsmarks a month. So how would he have had the money to pay Pichler? He claimed that he justified paying for Pichler's fees as 'moving expenses' and got the money from the Gestapo, but this sounds a little far-fetched. It seems much more likely either that Marie Bonaparte paid or, if I am right and Sauerwald had received cash for his help, that he now used some of that to settle the fee for the operation. Pichler certainly got paid, as his receipt is in the Vienna city archives.

Later Sauerwald described himself as something of a saviour, but that was not the way one member of Freud's family remembered it. His nephew Harry wrote, 'The Gestapo had graciously left him in possession of a sufficient sum of money to tide him over the first days of his exile. Shall we call it naivete or shamelessness when a Nazi official visited him in London a long time afterward and demanded this amount back?' Paula had said long ago that Harry was the only member of the family who was not that bright. She felt she was his intellectual equal. There is no evidence that any Nazi other than Sauerwald came to see Freud in London. Harry's mistakes would cost the *Kommissar* dear.

Pichler had done his best, but the greatest doctors in the world could not reverse the mouth cancer now. It was inoperable. Freud would have to live with it – and die with it. Freud would never see his last book published, but he was determined to make it part of his legacy. He had said his final word on Moses. It was now time to return to his ideas about sexuality and analysis one last time.

CHAPTER 13

Last Words, Last Battles

Though he was ill, Freud managed to finish *An Outline of Psychoanalysis*. It is a short book but not one for beginners, as it makes many assumptions about the knowledge readers already have. At the start of Chapter 5, 'Explanatory Notes on the Interpretation of Dreams', Freud writes a sentence which reflects much of his beliefs and character: 'States of conflict and turbulence alone can further our knowledge.'

For a large part of the book, Freud used military metaphors. The task of therapy was to strengthen the ego, which has been weakened by conflict and 'we have to come to its aid'. He compared the situation to being 'in a civil war which has to be decided by the assistance of an ally from the outside'. The ego could only accept help if it still had some 'degree of coherence'. The ego of neurotics often did still have that, which is why many of them managed to function in the real world; the psychotic ego was just too chaotic to do that. So with the neurotics 'we make a deal', Freud said. They had to speak with total honesty and the analyst would guarantee complete discretion.

As he summed up his life's work, Freud highlighted successes, failures and worries about the future of the discipline he had founded. No philosopher or psychologist could begin to explain consciousness or how mind and body are linked, but he could still provide 'a first report on the facts that we have observed'. Psychoanalysis had 'proved fruitful after all', as it had found that the laws by which the unconscious worked differed from those of the conscious mind. He had not wasted his time.

Freud repeated one of his long-held beliefs: that where the id and the superego are, the ego will be. It's not hard to unpick this sharp phrase. If we recognise the forces in our unconscious, we are less at their mercy. If we know ourselves, we can control, at least to some extent, our chaotic, aggressive and destructive impulses. Self-knowledge is power.

Next Freud returned to the sexuality of children. He recognised it was 'understandable' that psychoanalysis caused some shock when it pointed to how sexual children could be, but he was dismayed that so many intelligent, even artistic, people still refused to admit the existence of the Oedipus Complex. When he had suggested that Hamlet was an Oedipal drama, the 'lack of understanding from the literary world demonstrated the huge extent to which the mass of humans were prepared to cling to their infantile repressions'.

Freud then turned his attention to the tricks patients used in order to hide what they could not face. Patients had to reveal not just the intimacies they knew they hid from others, but also those they were not aware of hiding – their unknown unknowns, to use a modern phrase. This was why, Freud stressed, patients had to 'tell us everything', even if it seemed trivial, stupid or bizarre. Analysis had to create a space where patients were not civilised, not inhibited and self-critical. Only then would the analyst get truly valuable material.

To describe the role of the analyst, Freud used a striking image: the analyst was offering to act as a guide on a particularly difficult mountain. But patients wanted more than a mere guide; this role was too unemotional. This led Freud on to the question of transference, that very powerful process. The analyst had to be aware that patients wanted his approval and even love. Freud, we should remember, was writing this almost certainly with the assistance of Anna, whom he had analysed. He may in fact have been dictating to her, as he was now so weak.

If transference worked, patients found that their ego got stronger and the analyst could re-educate them, but Freud warned against 'misusing our influence'. However much the analyst may be tempted to become a teacher and a role model, 'to create humans in his own image', he must resist it. That is not his task; the last thing patients needed was to be turned into dependent children again.

The simplest cures happened, Freud claimed, when there was strong positive transference which let the analyst use his power to show patients what caused their problems and persuaded them to be healed. But if negative transference became more powerful, the insights would be 'blown away like chaff in the wind'. The analyst found that painful, seeing months, even years, of work turn into hostility.

The analyst had to make the patient see both how real and how unreal transference was. It was best, Freud said, if neither the love nor the hostility became too extreme. 'If we succeed as we mostly do,' Freud added, 'in making the patient see the nature of transference, then it gives him more power to feed to the ego.' A strong ego can wallop the resistances into submission. The only evidence Freud had for this was his own assessment of how well his patients had fared and his fellow analysts' assessments of their patients, all very subjective sources. He never allowed any objective test of how well analysis succeeded – the legacy of Uncle Josef.

The ideal way for a patient to behave was to carry on as normal outside the analytic hour, but to let everything out within the hour. Analysis is a Wendy house for grown-ups, if you like. (In my research on children's play I observed the most remarkable sexual goings-on in a Wendy house in a Montessori nursery, including a scene where little boys ironed each other's penises. No harm was done. It was a toy iron!)

Freud stressed the importance of timing. A good analyst had to keep distinct 'our knowledge and his knowledge'; the analyst might have deduced things very early on but patients might not yet be ready for the revelations. The analyst had to judge very carefully when to reveal his insights and deductions.

Under pressure the ego became defensive, which was no help. What we want, Freud – ever the armchair general – said, is for 'the ego emboldened by the security our help affords it, to venture to attack to recapture what it has lost'. But the ego is often a bit of a coward and needs the analyst to arm it. With its loins girded and its ammunition provided by the analyst, the ego is now ready to advance. It has an unlikely ally, the id. 'The battle that now develops if we achieve what we intend to achieve – namely to incite the ego to overcome its resistances – is carried out under our direction.' Field Marshal Freud commanded the forces of the ego, ordering them to outflank the superego and the id, and wrote that the mark of victory was as if 'a constant danger has been eliminated'.

Sometimes real life did the trick. He had noticed occasionally an extraordinary transformation in a patient after a real calamity. It was as if the catastrophe had made them suffer enough, so they could at least send their neurotic symptoms packing. This led to the issue of suicide, which, I have argued, blighted the Freud family.

Two other themes are striking. Despite his dealings with Marie Bonaparte, Hilda Doolittle and Karen Horney, Freud held to his belief that girls suffered from penis envy. They were wounded when they realised they did not have a penis but a clitoris instead. The clitoris was so much more discreet and girls certainly could not wave it around. This lack had 'permanent consequences for her character development', Freud added. Many girls rejected sexual life as a consequence, he said.

Then, in a more diffident tone than that used in the rest of the book, Freud claimed that suicide occurred when the self-preservation drive has undergone 'a reversal'. Suicidal patients could not endure being 'restored to health by our treatment and resist it with every means at their disposal'. Freud was sophisticated philosophically and would have known that what he was writing here was completely circular. He was saying that individuals killed themselves because their will to live was reversed. It is impossible not to conclude that discussing suicide reminded him of his failure to help those members of his family who had killed themselves.

But the future was bright. Chemicals might provide cures. For the moment, however, Freud said, analysis offered the best hope for those who were in distress. Every day now, he was in great physical distress himself. It was clear to Schur that the cancer was inoperable and incurable, so all he could do was to alleviate Freud's pain. He had an obstinate patient, though, because Freud hated taking anything stronger than aspirin.

The End of Age

In a newspaper interview in May 1939 Matthias Goering argued that, as a Jew, Freud could not understand that the unconscious is not a domain of repressed sexual activity, but the 'foundation of life', the source of creativity. The 'new German psychotherapy' aimed to 'strengthen belief in the meaning of life and reinforce the link with the higher world of values; it was to convey to the patient the consciousness of being bound and incorporated into the common destiny of the German people'. Freud would have known what Goering said. He and Anna were still getting letters from Germany.

That month Alfred Indra, the lawyer, called on Freud on his way back to Vienna from America. Freud was in a flippant mood and said, 'So you are going back to – I can't recall the name of the city.'

According to Ernest Jones, Indra thought this showed Freud was losing his memory, but Jones was, for once, sharper when he said it was a deliberate mistake. Freud also replied to his sister Anna when she wrote to wish him a happy 83rd birthday. He was grateful, but it was really not such good fortune to live to be so old. It seems to have been his last letter to her. Neither of them said a word about their four sisters left in Vienna.

Over the summer, H.G. Wells tried to get British citizenship for Freud, with the help of an MP, Oliver Locker-Lampson. But his proposal in Parliament was rejected, a sign of the anti-Semitism that still prevailed and in fact got worse as an estimated 60,000 refugees arrived from Europe. *Moses and Monotheism* had also not endeared Freud to the British.

One of the last substantial letters Freud wrote was to A.A. Roback, who bizarrely sent him a dollar bill in the post. On 10 July Freud returned it, saying he had always been able to take care of his correspondence and a dollar was too small a sum to be distributed to refugees. Roback had asked how the American criticism of *Moses and Monotheism* had affected him. Freud assured him it would hardly affect his 'frame of mind'.

A month later, Roback sent him reviews of a play then on in Warsaw which was based on *The Interpretation of Dreams*. Freud does not seem to have replied. The pain was getting worse. Schur offered him stronger and stronger sedatives, but Freud still refused to take anything more than aspirin. He would rather think in torment than not think at all, he said.

At one point, Jones told Freud there had been some discussion of not telling him how bad his condition was. 'By what right,' Freud demanded, as he had done in 1923. But there would be no reprieve now.

Marie Bonaparte came to Maresfield Gardens on 6 August. Freud was still concerned about the fate of his sisters in Vienna, but she could do nothing. Dolfi, Mitzi, Rosa and Pauli would not get out now.

Soon after Bonaparte returned to Paris, Max Schur, who had returned from America, moved into Maresfield Gardens so that he could be with his patient all the time. This allowed him to see how Freud behaved in the shadow of death. Schur was full of admiration, because he never heard Freud direct an 'angry or impatient word' at anyone. Schur would now have to deliver on the bargain they had made back in 1928, when he first became Freud's physician.

On 3 September Britain declared war on Germany. The next three weeks saw Freud's condition deteriorate. He was in more and more pain and now he could not think well any more, which he found utterly distressing. The suffering made no sense to him if his brain was not functioning normally.

In his last letter to Freud, dated 14 September 1939, nine days before Freud's death, Stefan Zweig wrote, 'I hope that you are suffering only from the era, as we all do, and not also from physical pain. We must stand firm now – it would be absurd to die without having first seen the criminals sent to hell.' He does not seem to have realised how sick Freud was.

Maresfield Gardens was now a house in which a much loved man was dying. He was tended by his wife, Martha, his daughters, Anna and Mathilde, and Paula Fichtl. Minna was in a nursing home. As before, it was Fichtl who spoke of the ordinary details, of the meals they tried to get him to eat, of the three sad women at his bedside. Freud did not write another word, it seems.

On 21 September, in severe pain, Freud asked Schur to administer a dose of morphine large enough to ease him out of life. The suffering did not make sense any more. Freud said goodbye to his wife, to his daughter Mathilde, to his sons and, finally, to Anna, who did not want him to do this. But Freud saw no point in prolonging his existence now and prepared himself lucidly. Schur gave him several large injections of morphine over the course of the next 48 hours. It was what we now call an assisted suicide.

Freud died towards midnight on 23 September 1939. He died in Hampstead, in freedom, but as a stateless refugee, not the Englishman of his 'intense wish phantasy'. He was cremated three days later, on 26 September, at the Golders Green Crematorium. The family had asked Ernest Jones to give the funeral oration and he rose to the occasion.

Jones said that it had been hard to wish Freud to live a day longer when he was suffering so much. He said that he thought of friends who were far away, such as Brill, Sachs and Eitingon, as well as of Ferenczi and Abraham, who had died. He paid respect to 'what in others expresses itself as religious feeling' but in Freud was expressed 'as a transcendental belief in the value of life and in the value of love'. Jones recalled Freud's vivid personality and 'instinctive love of truth'. He added that he felt no one could ever have lied to Freud. 'One can say of him that as never a man loved life more, so never man feared death less.'

Jones made the point that Freud had died in a country which had given him 'more courtesy, more esteem and more honour than his own or any other land'. He finished in some style: 'So we take our leave of a man whose like we shall not know again. From our hearts we thank him for having lived; for having done; for having loved.' Stefan Zweig then gave a speech in which he recalled their long friendship and Freud's courage and humanity.

Martha wrote to Jones to thank him and added that all the sympathy she had received made her forget she was among strangers in Britain.

There were many obituaries. The most original perhaps was a fine poem which was written by W.H. Auden in memory of the man he called 'an important Jew' who

> went his way down among the lost people like Dante,
> down to the stinking fosse where the injured
> lead the ugly life of the rejected.

The authoritative scientific journal *Nature* asked Cyril Burt, a psychologist who had made his name with studies of intelligence, for an obituary. On 28 October he wrote, '[Freud's] bold speculations and even bolder expressions of them aroused initial opposition', but the traumas of the First World War 'quickly convinced workers like Rivers, Myers and MacDougall that there was a most important foundation of truth in the novel doctrines that Freud had advanced'.

Thomas Mann declared, 'Freudian theory is one of the most important foundation stones for an edifice to be built by future generations, the dwelling of a freer and wiser humanity.'

Freud had made a will in London and he left an estate of over £22,000 – a large sum at the time.

Sauerwald Again

As Freud was laid to rest, his unlikely helper Sauerwald was called up by the Wehrmacht. With his academic qualifications, Sauerwald was drafted into the Luftwaffe and got a commission. In the summer of 1940 he became involved with the Nazi commune. Everyone involved with the commune was also a member of the party.

Members picked lots to decide who could build a house on what spot. There were strict rules about how large a plot was needed for each house, but the war made it impossible for tenants to build houses, as building materials were needed for the war effort. The 29 families in the commune made the best of it and decided instead to lay out allotment gardens on the ground they owned. Sauerwald was responsible for landscaping. The 29 families dwindled to 15 over the next three years.

The death of Freud did not mean the end of Sauerwald's involvement with the family or the business. He still had to settle the affairs of the Verlag and finally achieved that in 1941.

The war changed the lives of many psychoanalysts and psychotherapists. Matthias Goering joined the Luftwaffe as Sauerwald had done. The 1914–18 war had made his cousin Hermann very aware of the pressures pilots faced in combat. He encouraged Matthias to build links between the Goering Institute and the Luftwaffe. Many officers attended seminars at the Institute to learn how to handle their men better.

During the Battle of Britain, Goering even persuaded the Luftwaffe to set up mental health stations at aerodromes so pilots who survived dangerous missions could get immediate help in dealing with their anxieties. This was a perfect use for the short-term therapy Goering favoured. In dealing with stress, the Royal Air Force deployed the stiff-upper-lip approach, while the Luftwaffe deployed therapists who asked pilots how they felt after being shot at by Spitfires. We know which side won.

As Goering was working for the Luftwaffe, he could not maintain day-to-day control of the Institute. The few Freudians still there exploited his absence and managed to continue training psychotherapists and even to stay in charge of the polyclinic. Some of these were partially Jewish, in fact, according to Geoffrey Cocks. The Freudians even dared to make their patients lie down on the analytic couch to which Goering objected so much. But there were limits. The Freudians had to compromise and use euphemisms, talking of 'depth psychotherapy' instead of 'psychoanalysis'.

In these bizarre conditions Working Group A, as the Freudians were called, trained 34 analysts between 1938 and 1945. The psychoanalyst Gerard Chrzanowski interviewed some of them and then wrote:

> Neither the people inside the Institute nor organised German psychiatry outside of the Institute believed that psychoanalysis had been extinguished. Not one person interviewed by us expressed the slightest doubt that he had continued to function as a psychoanalyst throughout the Hitler years. We have no doubt as to their sincerity.

Both patients and analysts feared that what they said in treatment might be betrayed to the Gestapo or to the police. However, 'whether one likes what it became or not', psychoanalysis was going on, albeit 'in a most peculiar way', the analyst Jon Rittmeister reported in 1939. He was later executed by the Nazis. The behaviour of the analysts at the Institute revealed 'a degree of social blindness, moral cowardice and self-seeking', according to Geoffrey Cocks. Freud had said in *Analysis Terminable and Interminable* that many analysts had psychological problems. This was shocking confirmation of that.

None of the analysts protested as the Goering Institute became involved with and justified Hitler's 'euthanasia' programme. Leading members of the Institute, including Boehm, came to accept euthanasia as a solution for the 'untreatable' patient. Europe could rid itself not just of Jews but of all so-called defectives.

Death in the Camps

After Freud and Martha left their apartment at Berggasse, it was taken over by Nazi officials, but the Race Institute did not move in, as Berlin had wanted.

This book would not be complete without saying something briefly of the lives and deaths of Freud's four sisters in Vienna. Their position soon became increasingly desperate. By late 1939, they were moved out of their homes. Nazi policy was to hand good housing over to good Austrians and put the Jewish families into special – and very cramped – apartments. Once-well-off families were forced to share bedrooms and toilets with many others. The sisters soon spent the 160,000 schillings that Freud and their other brother, Alexander, had left them. From America, Harry Freud organized $200 a month which was sent to the aunts through a man called Kafka. Harry's father believed that the aunts would be safe as long as they were getting money from abroad as the Nazis were desperate for dollars. On 14 June 1941 he wrote to his son about them saying that 'the head must not abandon hope'. But it was impossible to get news. A few months later Alexander suggested to Harry that there had to be a way of contacting Sauerwald but, by 1942, the United States was at war with Germany. There was no way of learning anything about the aunts.

As late as 8 June 1943, Anna wrote to Harry that she had 'the feeling' the aunts were still alive. But she was wrong.

There are conflicting accounts of the fate of the sisters. Harry left details in his family history, which include many corrections that he scribbled over. Sir Martin Gilbert, the distinguished biographer of Churchill, in his account of the Holocaust, offers one set of accounts. Harald Leupold-Löewenthal, the Freud scholar, studied the fate of the sisters in detail and often differs from Gilbert.

We perhaps know most about the fate of Regina Deborah Graf-Freud (Rosa), who was 79 when the war started. Freud liked her more than the other girls because he felt that she had, like himself, 'a nicely developed tendency towards neurasthenia', as he had written back in 1910. Rosa did not have a happy life. After a traumatic love affair, she married a doctor, Heinrich Graf, who died in 1908, when he was 56 years old. Their son, Hermann Adolf, died in action during the First World War and their daughter, Cäcilie, committed suicide.

The last document from Rosa was a letter the International Red Cross sent to Maresfield Gardens. She was allowed to send only 25 words; they were addressed to her sister-in-law, starting, 'Dear Martha! Greetings with heartfelt emotion. Wondering about the state of your Alexander's family. Four alone. Sad. Painful. Health. Yours warmly'. Rosa ended with four sad words that revealed a total denial of the realities: 'Best furnishings in storage.'

Gilbert suggests Rosa died in Auschwitz as does Harry Freud. On the other hand, Leupold-Löewenthal claims she was deported to Theresienstadt on 28 August 1942. The transcript of the 1946 Nuremberg Trials includes a statement from a witness which describes the arrival of one of Freud's sisters at a camp – and it may have been Rosa. She introduced herself to the commandant as Sigmund Freud's sister. He examined her papers and

> said that there was probably some mistake and showed her the railroad signs, telling her that there would be a train to take her back to Vienna in two hours. She could leave her belongings, go into the showers and, after bathing, her documents and her ticket to Vienna would be ready... Of course, the woman went to the bath-house and never returned.

It is a sign of the confusion that Gilbert cites an account in which it is claimed Rosa asked to be given 'lighter walk' where it seems likely that the right phrase is 'lighter work'. The commandant of Theresienstadt camp was Siegfried Seidel; after the war, he was charged with having been personally responsible for 16 executions. Seidel was found guilty by the same court that tried Sauerwald and was hanged.

The next sister, Maria Moritz-Freud (Mitzi), was 78 at the start of the war. She had a tragic life before her tragic death. She worked as a governess and, in 1887, married her Romanian cousin Moritz Freud, who I argued committed suicide in 1920 as a result of financial problems. One of their four children, Lilly Marlé-Freud, became a famous actress and inspired the song 'Lili Marlene'. After Mitzi's youngest child, Theodor (Teddy), drowned in 1923 in Berlin, she came back to Vienna to live with her sisters. It was not the end of the tragedies she had to deal with, as both Mitzi's son-in-law and daughter killed themselves. According to Leupold-Löewenthal, Mitzi was deported first to Theresienstadt on 29 June 1942, then to Maly Trostinec, where she disappeared. She would almost certainly have been gassed. Harry Freud's notes initially claimed she died at Treblinka but then he scribbled that out and wrote in 'Auschwitz'.

Esther Adolfine (Dolfi), who was a year younger than Mitzi, never married and looked after first her father when he fell ill, then her mother. Her nephew Martin Freud thought that would have been very hard. Dolfi 'was not clever or in any way remarkable, and it might be true to say that constant attendance on Amalie had suppressed her personality into a condition of dependence from which she never recovered,' he noted. She was deported to Theresienstadt on 28 August 1942, where she was said to have died from 'internal haemorrhages' on 5 February 1943. It seems likely that she died of malnutrition. There is unanimity on her fate.

The youngest sister, Pauline Regine Winternitz-Freud (Pauli), was 75 in 1939. She had married Valentin Winternitz and emigrated to the United States, where their daughter, Rose Beatrice, was born on 18 March 1896. After her husband's death in 1900, Pauli returned to Berlin. Her daughter suffered a severe nervous breakdown. Gilbert argues Pauli was taken to Treblinka on 23 September 1942 and Harry concurs. However, Leopold-Löewenthal claims that, in June, Pauli was taken to Theresienstadt, then to Maly Trostinec where she was murdered.

In 1945, in some despair Anna Freud wrote to Harry, wondering if they would ever learn what had happened to the sisters. Harry received a letter in 1946 from a bureau that was trying to discover the fate of those taken to the camps. It said no trace of the four sisters could be found.

Freud had been lucky to die in his own bed at a time of his own choosing. Minna Bernays died in London in 1941 after a long illness.

Stefan Zweig managed to achieve what Freud had not and became a British citizen in 1940, but he left England soon after. He moved to New York and then settled in Brazil. In 1941 he and his wife committed suicide, taking poison. The Europe he had loved had destroyed itself and he refused to be a witness to the destruction.

In 1942 the musicologist Max Graf surprised analysts by revealing that in 1906, perhaps to thank him for reports on Little Hans, Freud had given him an unpublished paper. The subject reflected Freud's interest in the stage and was called *Psychopathic Characters on the Stage*. The text was never published in German, but Graf now had an English translation, which was published in 1942.

CHAPTER 14

After the War: Psychoanalysis in Germany and Austria, 1940–50

At the start of my research, I got talking to a young Austrian woman on the number 15 bus, which goes between Paddington station and the Blackwall Tunnel in London. I explained I was writing about how Freud had escaped Vienna. She smiled and said, 'You know, I went to the Sigmund Freud High School, but I have no idea if the school had any connection with Freud at all.' The school had never bothered to explain to its pupils why it was named after the founder of analysis.

Such reticence is very Austrian. The young woman told me, 'In Austria they still don't talk about the war', as if she were not really an Austrian herself. She added, 'It is a pity, as those who know about it are getting old. My grandparents were part of it, but they never say anything about it.'

In trying to finish this story, I encountered a degree of reticence which I found astonishing more than 60 years after the war. But it has to be remembered that only 20 years ago Austria had a president, Kurt Waldheim, who was an ex-Nazi, and I have already mentioned how its revamped Nazi Party, which was led by Jorg Haider until his death, still consistently gets between 15 and 20 per cent of the votes in elections.

In 1945, after Sauerwald was released from the prisoner of war camp at Bad Heilbrunn, he went back to Vienna, which had been divided into British, French, Russian and American zones. Much of the city had been destroyed, so obviously conditions were grim. Sauerwald could not find his wife. Marianne had worked in a factory towards the end of the war but by now she had left Vienna and her apartment. Sauerwald could not get back into his own home and the new tenant had stolen many of his possessions.

Eventually, Sauerwald discovered that Marianne had gone to Brixlegg, in the Tyrol, and he followed her. Brixlegg might also give him a chance to find work, since for 500 years it had been an important mining area and there was a copper refinery there. He knew the place because he had been hunting in the Tyrol (this was why he had acquired a hunting rifle in 1937) and Brixlegg afforded good sport.

It also had an exotic history. The local castle had been restored by Fanny Reid Grohman, an Irish woman who claimed to be a relative of the Duke of Wellington. Her son became a celebrity; one of his books, published in 1878, has the irresistible title *Gaddings with a Primitive People* and explains the customs of the Tyrol before it became a tourist destination. Grohman also produced the authoritative edition of the *The Master of Game*, the second-oldest English book on hunting. He got his friend Teddy Roosevelt, who was an avid hunter, to write a foreword to it.

In the autumn of 1945 Sauerwald was reunited with Marianne and registered as a resident in Brixlegg. This change of address meant that he was hard to find, but Harry Freud tracked him down and had him arrested.

Freud's *Kommissar* was sent for trial in the People's Court, the *Volksgericht*, which was set up in the summer of 1945 by two laws. The first, the Nazi Prohibition Act, was passed by the Austrian Provisional Government on 8 May 1945, a few hours before Germany surrendered. The second, passed on 26 June 1945, was the War Criminals Act. The intention was to try Nazis and collaborators for:

- war crimes in a restricted sense and crimes against humanity.
- torture and acts of cruelty.
- violation of human dignity.
- expropriation, expulsion and resettlement.

Two professional judges and three lay assessors presided over the cases. There was a severe shortage of judges, as so many Austrian lawyers had worked for the Nazis. But the courts also had to deal with a question that had never arisen in Germany – the guilt of those who had joined the Nazi Party after the Austrian Chancellor Dollfuss had banned it in 1934 – the so-called 'illegals'. It became an act of treason to belong to the clandestine Nazi Party. The laws passed after the war also made it an offence to have lied about one's role in the Nazi Party.

The People's Court launched preliminary proceedings in 137,000 cases and the records of these proceedings were kept secret for nearly 50 years, the Austrian Research Centre for Post War Trials complained. I was told that I was very lucky I managed to see Sauerwald's file. The librarian at the Vienna city archives told me that if anyone else had been charged with Sauerwald that would never have been allowed.

The Research Centre analysed the cases brought against 40,000 individuals. In nearly a third of the cases the accused were charged with murder, war crimes and crimes of violence. There were proceedings against 11,500 defendants. Twenty-eight individuals were sentenced to death and 21 to life imprisonment. Around 6,000 defendants were found guilty in all.

Sauerwald was accused of war crimes, of having been an illegal member of the Nazi Party and of having profited by the 'Aryanisation' of Jewish property. The police interviewed a number of witnesses to decide whether or not he had been an active Nazi. Some of the questions asked were almost silly: for example, had Sauerwald hosted rowdy parties at his apartment? The witnesses disagreed on the extent of his Nazi activities, however. Anna Talg, his mother-in-law, insisted she had had no idea that he was a member of the party. Another neighbour contradicted that; Sauerwald had started to wear the uniform of a political leader after the Anschluss. One neighbour insisted she had seen Sauerwald's devoted wife, Marianne, wearing party insignia. This evidence makes his behaviour towards the Freuds all the more remarkable.

The behaviour of the Freud family towards him is also hard to explain. On 22 October 1945 Anna clearly knew of the plight of Sauerwald and wrote to Harry that:

> [the] truth is that we really owe our lives and our freedom to [Sauerwald] since he used his position as *Kommissar* to protect our personal safety. Without him we would never have got away. It was he who saw to our safe travel, who got Dr Stross her permit at the last moment so that Papa would not travel without a doctor. But much more than that. I suppose you know that Martin who was quite beside himself at that time had kept some very incriminating papers about our affairs in Switzerland in his desk. They were found there but Sauerwald kept them safely locked up until we were gone.

Having explained that Martin could not bear to deal with Sauerwald because Martin could not stand being powerless, Anna added that Sauerwald:

> was really my only friend and stand by after Martin and all our Jewish friends had left. The Princess always knew and thought the same about

him...so nothing should happen to Sauerwald. Or if he is arrested all these things should speak in his favour. Papa always said that perhaps some day we should repay our debt to him. Even more; after we had left he used to visit the aunts and sit with them very much as you used to do on a Sunday. They were only without protection after he had gone into the army.

Harry did not act on this letter. Once he had returned to the United States there is no evidence that he did anything to help Sauerwald. Nor did Anna, it must be said, even though she visited Vienna which she found rather upsetting. There is no obvious explanation for Harry's failure to act with a modicum of decency or justice.

Political influences undermined the work of the People's Court from the start. Half a million former members of the Nazi Party were a significant constituency. In 1945 the Nazis had lost their right to vote, but they got this back before the elections of 1949. Austrian politicians began to compete for their support and were keen to show they had the interests of the 'soldiers' generation' at heart. Typically there were long delays in settling claims for Jewish compensation. A British historian, Robert Knight, found a revealing sentence in the minutes of the government. The minister responsible for the settlement of Jewish claims for compensation stated: *'Ich bin dafür die Sache in die Länge zu ziehen'* – 'I suggest we drag out that issue.'

This makes what happened to Sauerwald all the more bizarre. No one ever accused him of violence against any Jew. Yet he spent some of the period between late 1945 and 1947 in jail, even though he was ill with tuberculosis. On 28 June 1947 he was so ill he was taken to stay in hospital for a month.

The Vienna police sent out a questionnaire as part of their investigation into Sauerwald's Nazi past. Questions focused on these issues:

- Did the accused call himself an illegal Nazi?
- Did he take an active part in Nazi activities and political acts and commit actions against Jews?
- Did he denounce people for political reasons?
- Did he play an active role in the Nazi Party either while it was banned or after the Anschluss?
- Did he give money to Nazi Party funds?

Sauerwald told the court a complicated tale about his membership of the Nazi Party. He had become a member but had never done anything much for the party. There had been a period in 1938 when Emil Rothleitner tried to train him to become a propaganda leader, but after two months that petered out. The only work he did for the Nazis, Sauerwald claimed, was once or twice distributing cinema tickets for propaganda newsreels.

Sauerwald kept insisting that he had worked ceaselessly for Freud. No one took much notice. The long periods in jail, the separation from his wife and the tuberculosis all took their toll on him. Losing the war did not seem to make the slightest difference to the way Vienna lawyers worked, ways Eichmann had criticised sharply in 1938. Sauerwald felt frustrated by the law's delays and his own illness. The truth was so simple. He had helped Freud and his family when they were desperately vulnerable.

The crucial evidence finally came from Anna Freud, 18 months after she knew Sauerwald was in trouble. She had replied to Marianne's desperate letter, but her reply did not get through. There was some confusion because Marianne could no longer get into her old flat to pick up mail and I have not been able to find out how Anna Freud's letter was finally delivered, but one way or another it was. Sauerwald was in jail at the time.

Anna Freud's letter was written on 22 July 1947 and is worth quoting in full. She told Marianne:

> My parents and I have in no way forgotten that we have every reason to be grateful to your husband in a number of regards.
>
> We were in a very precarious situation at that time and there was not any doubt that your husband used his office as our appointed commissar in such a manner as to protect my father. In his dealings with him he always showed great consideration and respect and did his utmost to prevent other functionaries of the regime bothering him. I well know that he kept documents which could have endangered our lives hidden in his desk for quite some time.

Anna knew perfectly well which documents Sauerwald had kept hidden in his desk: they were papers and statements relating to the secret bank accounts. The letter was also careful not to mention the fact that Sauerwald had probably managed to transport some of the 1,000 antiquities by less than legal means.

After the letter was admitted in evidence, Sauerwald was allowed out of jail, but he was not exonerated. He remained accused, in a sort of limbo, for a further 18 months. The court justified this on the grounds that it was not satisfied as to Sauerwald's frankness about his work for the Nazis.

Post-war Matters

At the Nuremberg trials, Hermann Goering was found guilty of crimes against humanity and sentenced to death. Shortly before he died, his brother Albert promised to take care of Hermann's wife, Emmy, and their daughter, Edda. On 15 October 1946, two hours before his execution, Hermann Goering committed suicide in his cell; he had managed to acquire some poison. Despite his many acts of kindness, Albert Goering was also imprisoned after the war. His name was enough, but those he had helped did not forget what he had done and they in turn helped him survive years of unemployment which embittered him. He died in 1966.

Felix Boehm and Carl Müller-Braunschweig bounced back after the war, though one report said of Müller-Braunschweig, 'I believe his personality has deteriorated during the Nazi regime...and I think he is "dark grey"' – Boehm was seen as possibly 'black', meaning completely corrupted.

On 16 October 1945 Müller-Braunschweig was asked to reconstruct the German Psychoanalytic Society and was appointed its president. The past might never have happened and the man whose 1933 paper had hailed the new true Nazi psychotherapy became the official representative of orthodox psychoanalysis, the once vilified Jewish science. He taught psychoanalysis at the Berlin Free University.

Müller-Braunschweig Boehm successor, did not have it much harder. In 1950 he became president of the reconstituted German Psychoanalytic Society and was upset that it was refused admission to the International Psychoanalytic Association. Boehm did not lack insight, so he cannot have really been surprised by the refusal.

After reaching Bolivia, the photographer Edmund Engelman, who took the last photographs of 19 Berggasse, managed to make it to New York. He had a hard time trying to establish himself there, but once the war was over he went to Vienna to find August Aichhorn, the man who had asked him to take the photographs. Aichhorn was no longer at the same address and no one seemed to know where he lived. Vienna was chaotic and devastated, Engelman noted. He was overjoyed to learn, when he eventually tracked down a secretary, Miss Regale, that Aichhorn had somehow got the negatives to Anna Freud. Engelman went on to have a successful career, not as a photographer but as an engineer. Years later, he managed to visit 19 Berggasse and was appalled by the state of the building. It was empty, dirty, sad. He called the place an 'abused premises'. He noticed, however, that the outline of the analytic couch was still marked on the floor.

At the start of 1949 Sauerwald was declared innocent of all charges apart from that of having been an illegal Nazi. The court said it had been impossible to judge on that, which explained why the case had dragged on for three years. But Sauerwald was free. He moved to Innsbruck in the next few years and seems to have had no further contact with the Freuds.

The firm of Freud and Co. traded at 61 Bloom Street in Manchester until 1942, when it moved to 2 and 4 Beever Street. Sam Freud died in 1945 at 35 Lansdowne Road, West Didsbury.

Martha Freud died in Hampstead in 1951, at the age of 90, surrounded by her children and grandchildren. Of John Freud, her husband's playmate in childhood, no one has ever found a trace.

On 20 December 1955 the People's Court was dissolved by a constitutional law. The prosecution of Nazi criminals had ceased some years earlier. The Austrians were not alone in wanting to forget. The Americans pardoned a great number of German war criminals convicted by Allied courts. Once the Cold War started, Germany was needed as an ally. Simon Wiesenthal, the famous 'Nazi hunter', said there was only one real winner of the Cold War, namely the old Nazis.

Anna Freud became a formidable psychoanalyst. With Dorothy Burlingham, she ran the Hampstead Nurseries. Gina Bon, who was Anna's secretary from 1970 to 1982, described their work in *Memories of Anna Freud and of Dorothy Burlingham*. According to Bon, Anna Freud stayed witty and wise for the rest of her life. Bon remembered a woman whose strength of mind and 'bright and undiminished spirit' was undimmed until the last.

Like her father, Anna had battles with fellow analysts and faced a serious attack on her father's reputation when, privately at first, Jeffrey Masson accused Freud of having suppressed evidence which proved that Viennese parents abused their children. Freud had first argued this was true, but then changed his mind and said these were just fantasies children had.

Leslie Sohn, who is possibly the oldest working analyst in Britain – he was 88 years old when I met him in 2008 – had been taught by her. He told me she was 'an intimidating presence'. Anna Freud died in 1982 in London.

Paula Fichtl was awarded a medal by the Austrian government in 1980.

Anton Sauerwald died in 1970 in Innsbruck.

It is ironic that it took longer to conclude the matter of the secret bank accounts than it took to conclude either world war or the Cold War.

CHAPTER 15

The Secret Bank Accounts

A fter the war, the World Jewish Congress claimed that Swiss banks had deliberately muddled the question of deposits made by Jews in the 1930s. For 60 years the gnomes of Zurich, as the British Prime Minister Harold Wilson called them, played their old games of protecting bank secrecy. Some Holocaust survivors even alleged that, when they asked about accounts set up by their long-dead relatives, officials told them to produce death certificates. Prove your families were gassed or you will not get a Swiss centime!

The World Jewish Congress was not going to accept interminable delays. It lobbied and harried; it persuaded American pension funds to threaten economic sanctions against the Swiss. But the Swiss are masters of protecting the franc. They set up an independent panel, under Paul Volcker, the former head of the American Federal Reserve, to resolve the issues concerning these accounts. Volcker would have access to all documents.

The World Jewish Congress started proceedings against the banks in the United States, where there was hope of quicker action, and 53 years after the war ended both sides decided to try to settle these issues behind closed doors. The American judge, Edward Korman, had some imagination. He took all the interested parties out to dinner in a Brooklyn steak house and then locked them in his courtroom to hammer out a settlement. It took only two days for the lawyers to achieve that. Swiss banks would have to stump up $1.25 billion by way of compensation.

But the Swiss government objected to the deal. As well as the panel under Volcker, the Swiss also established a commission, chaired by Jean-François Bergier, to study these controversial matters. Commissions need time. The settlement in Brooklyn was too hurried, they felt, and not all the evidence had been assessed. Korman ignored these arguments and told the banks to start paying.

In fact, Bergier was to provide some of the most damning evidence against the big Swiss banks. He discovered that in 1954 they made a secret pact, agreeing with one another to refuse to divulge information about any transactions more than 10 years old. Anything that had happened during and before the war would be kept secret. 'The banks relied on a combination of discreetly playing down the problem and erecting barriers to investigation,' the Bergier report said. The secrecy laws, the laws the Nazis had railed against, were used against Jewish depositors by the banks 'to legitimise their reluctance to provide information while at the same time charging high search fees for conducting investigations'. As a result of these fees, 'unclaimed accounts, deposits and safe-deposit boxes could also disappear in the space of a few decades'. Bergier found that when an account had very little money in it, 'it could be cashed in', often by the bank itself. Some bank employees stole unclaimed assets. He concluded that 'legal principles were exploited for corporate objectives'.

Though a compromise to release $800 million was reached in Brooklyn in 1998, it still took years of complex legal argument before victims got any money. It took three years, for example, for the banks to publish a list of 21,000 'probable' victims who had lost their money through the delinquencies of the system.

It was another adminstrative nightmare. Many claimants were old, poor, sick and close to death. In 2000 Judge Korman decided that the banks had to put up cash for an immediate aid programme for needy and ageing Holocaust survivors. The funds would make most difference to survivors and their families in the former Soviet Union, who were the poorest of all the Jewish groups. That incensed many Jewish survivors in the United States.

Naturally the people with the strongest claims for compensation were those who could prove they or their families had had accounts and how much was in them. Korman decided they should be allocated the $800 million. Almost nobody who had been involved in the investigations, on either the Swiss or the Jewish sides, thought it would be possible to find claimants for anything like this amount of money.

One of the people who read the list of account holders the banks produced was Freud's grandson Anton Walter Freud. He saw that there was more information on Freud's accounts than on most others. When Anton Walter Freud came forward in 2001, no one was sure how much money Freud had. As Freud was famous, his accounts were eventually one of the 2,597 claims examined in detail by the tribunal set up by Judge Korner. The lawyers found a customer card which proved that Freud had held one custody account and two demand-deposit accounts, one of which was denominated in Dutch guilders. Given that some accounts were set up in 1914, it is likely that some records had been destroyed. The card did not reveal either how much was in the accounts or to whom any monies had been paid.

The average held in custody accounts in 1945 was 13,000 Swiss francs and in deposit accounts 2,140 Swiss francs (in British terms roughly £5,000 and £850). As there was no specific evidence about how much money was in Freud's accounts, they were assumed to have held the average: a total of 17,280 Swiss francs in the three accounts. The Brooklyn court established a formula for dealing with interest rates and inflation since 1945 and ruled Freud would have had 216,000 Swiss francs in the bank by 2005. His heirs were to be paid that amount. Like thousands of others, though, Anton Walter Freud never lived to see the stolen money repaid. He died, aged 82, a few months before the tribunal finished work on his lawsuit.

Paul Volcker's report, published more than a year after the settlement, refrained from estimating the amount of Nazi victims' money the Swiss were still holding. He carefully worded his conclusion to appease both Jewish and Swiss members of the committee. It absolved the banks of 'systemic disruption' and 'organised discrimination'.

In early 2004 Judge Korman held another public hearing. There was a risk that he would fail to find takers for all the $800 million earmarked for account-holder claimants and he wanted to consult about how any money which was left over should be distributed. Jewish community workers pleaded for the money to be disbursed immediately, so that aged Holocaust survivors could be given a little dignity.

Many survivors, however, were upset at the thought of the court distributing money before all claimants to Swiss accounts had come forward. 'At our age, it's not easy to wait such a long time,' said Alice Fischer, whose family had been killed in Auschwitz and Mauthausen. 'And now we are discussing what to do with leftovers? I did not see a penny of the money yet.' Camp survivor Greta Beer begged the judge not to disburse the $800 million until the search for true claimants was complete. '$800 million is a sacred amount of money, Judge Korman,' she said. 'It has survived the Holocaust. It has survived the bank manipulations and come here to this country. It belongs to souls who from their grave have made the money come here to the United States. And it has to be distributed among us.' Despite such pleas, Judge Korman allowed the emergency payments to go ahead.

The next twist came in 2007, when Hans Baer, head of Bank Julius Baer, published his memoirs. One of the few Jews still working in Swiss banking, he was angry at what he discovered about the way Swiss banks had handled the issue of the accounts set up by desperate Jews in the 1930s. 'All of us came too late to the conclusion that the real scandal was not the dormant assets but the closed accounts,' said Baer. 'It is true that nobody had organised any great plunder…It was a Swiss variation – unorganised theft.'

Baer was shocked to discover that his own bank had charged a $75 'search fee' to claimants who enquired about a relative's account. Other banks charged even more. 'I could not have imagined discovering such improprieties. There was never a Jewish conspiracy. We simply became victims of our own smugness,' Baer wrote. Smugness seems too soft a word. I rang Bank Julius Baer, which referred me to the Association of Swiss Bankers, where I was told that the matter was still controversial. No one wanted to comment.

Two Last Words

In 1960 another Matthias Goering, a 49-year-old physiotherapist, was seen wearing a Jewish skullcap and a Star of David. The *New York Times* reported that he had embraced Judaism. He was keeping kosher, observing the Shabbat and learning Hebrew.

In a Jewish restaurant in Basle, Goering enthused about Israel. 'It feels like home,' he said. 'The Israelis are so friendly.'

Even when they heard his name, the reporter asked.

'Yes, they say they're so thankful I've made contact.'

I cannot help but think that Freud would have put his head back and laughed. I imagine that he would also have enjoyed his grandson Clement Freud's ancedote about travelling to China as part of a parliamentary fact-finding mission during the Cultural Revolution. The young Freud, the Liberal MP for Ely, travelled with the young Winston Churchill, the Conservative MP for Stretford.

On the last day the Minister for Information asked if there was anything at all I would like to ask. I said, 'Yes. Everything you do, you do with extreme care and precision…Now I am in your country with a colleague, than whom I am older, have been in Parliament longer, have held higher positions in our respective political parties: we are both staying at the Peking Palace Hotel and his suite is bigger than mine. Why?'

The embarassed Minister replied, 'It is because Mr Churchill had a famous grandfather.'

'It is the only time that I have been out-grandfathered,' Clement Freud concluded.

The Cast List

Immediate family of Jacob, Freud's Father

Jacob Freud: born Galicia, part of the Austro-Hungarian Empire, 1815; died Vienna, 1896.

Sylvia Kanner, first wife of Jacob: born Galicia, 1829; died Freiberg, 1852.

Rebecca, second wife of Jacob: born *c*. 1832; married 1852; died (or disappeared) by 1855.

Amalie Freud, third wife of Jacob: born Galicia, 1835; married 29 July 1855; died Vienna, 1930.

Josef Freud, brother of Jacob: born Galicia, 1824; died Vienna, 1897.

Children of Jacob and Sylvia

Philipp Freud: born Tysmenitz, Galicia, 1831; emigrated to Manchester, 1860; died Chorlton, Manchester, August 1911.

Emanuel Freud: born Tysmenitz, Galicia, 1833; emigrated to Manchester, 1860; died at Parbold, near Southport, 17 October 1914.

Children of Jacob and Amalie

Sigmund Freud: born Freiberg, 6 May 1856; married Martha Bernays, 14 September 1886; died London, 23 September 1939.

Julius Freud: born Freiberg, October 1857; died April 1858.

Anna Bernays-Freud: born Freiberg, 31 December 1858; married Eli Bernays, 14 October 1883; died New York, 11 March 1955.

Regina Deborah Graf-Freud (Rosa): born Freiberg, 21 March 1860; married Heinrich Graf, 17 May 1896; died in a concentration camp, 1942.

Maria Moritz-Freud (Mitzi): born Vienna, 22 March 1861; married Moritz Freud, 22 February 1887; died in a concentration camp, 1942.

Esther Adolfine Freud (Dolfi): born Vienna, 23 July 1862; unmarried; died in a concentration camp, 1943.

Pauline Regine Winternitz-Freud (Pauli): born Vienna, 3 May 1864; married Valentin Winternitz; died in a concentration camp, 1942.

Alexander Gotthold Efraim Freud: born Vienna, 15 April 1866; died Canada, 1943.

Immediate family of Martha, Sigmund Freud's wife

Berman Bernays, father: born Wandsbek, Hamburg, 1826; died Vienna, 1879.

Emmeline Bernays (née Philipp), mother: born Hamburg, 13 May 1830; died Vienna, 1890.

Eli Bernays, brother: born Hamburg, 1860; died New York, 1921, of appendicitis.

Martha Bernays: born Hamburg, 26 July 1861; married Sigmund Freud, 14 September 1886; died London, 2 November 1951.

Minna Bernays, sister: born Hamburg, 1865; died London, 1941.

Children of Sigmund and Martha

Mathilde Freud: born Vienna, 1887; married Robert Hollitscher 1909; died London, 1978.

Jean-Martin Freud: born Vienna, 1889; lawyer and publisher; married Ernestine Drucker 1919; died London, 1967.

Oliver Freud: born Vienna, 1891 (named for Oliver Cromwell, one of his father's heroes); civil engineer; married Henny Fuchs 1920; died Williamsburg, MA, 1969.

Ernst Freud: born Vienna, 1892; architect; married Lucie Brusch 1920; died London, 1970.

Sophie Freud: born Vienna, 1893; married Max Halberstadt; died of pneumonia, 1920.

Anna Freud: born Vienna, 1895; psychoanalyst; died London, 1982.

Other Relatives

Johann (John) Freud, Emanuel's son, Sigmund's nephew: born Freiberg, 13 August 1855; when and where he died not known.

Pauline Freud, Sigmund's niece: born Freiberg, 20 November 1856; died Manchester, 1944.

Solomon Samuel (Sam) Freud, Emanuel's son, Sigmund's nephew: born Manchester, 28 June 1860; died Didsbury, Manchester, 1945.

Mary (Poppy), Sigmund's niece: born 23 October 1873; married Frederick Oswald Hartwig; died Manchester, 1951.

Morris Herbert Walter, Philipp's son, Sigmund's nephew: born Manchester, 2 April 1876; died Port Elizabeth, South Africa, 28 November 1938.

Edward Bernays, Sigmund's nephew: born Vienna, 1891; died New York, 1995.

Harry Freud, Alexander's son, Sigmund's nephew: born 1909; died Yonkers, USA, 1968.

Household

Paula Fichtl: born Salzburg, 1902; the Freuds' housekeeper; died Salzburg, 1987.

Early Group of Psychoanalysts

August Aichhorn: born Vienna, 1878, an authority on juvenile delinquency; died Vienna, 1949.

Otto Fenichel: born Vienna, 1897; organised contact between psycho-analysts by means of secret circular letters during the war; died Los Angeles, 1946.

Ernest Jones: born Gowerton, South Wales, 1879: Welsh doctor nicknamed the Welsh Wizard, authorised biographer of Freud; died London, 1958.

Carl Jung: born Keswill, Thurgau, Switzerland, 1875; son of a Swiss pastor, psychiatrist and analyst who founded his own school after a bitter quarrel with Freud – Freud had seen him as his successor but the two men never had any contact after 1914; died Kusnacht, Switzerland, 1961.

Wilhelm Reich: born Dobzau, Galicia, 1897; one of the most brilliant and provocative of Freud's disciples; found guilty of offences under the Food and Drugs Act, he committed suicide in Lewisberg Federal Penitentiary, Pennsylvania, 1957.

Freud's Patients during This Period

William Bullitt: born Philadelphia, 1891; American diplomat, co-author with Freud of a book on President Woodrow Wilson; died Paris, 1967.

Princess Marie Bonaparte: born Saint-Cloud, 1882; the great-granddaughter of Napoleon, an analyst and a dog lover, like Freud; died St Tropez, 1962.

Dorothy Burlingham: born New York, 1891; close friend of Anna Freud; died London, 1989.

Hilda Doolittle (H.D.): born Bethlehem, Pennsylvania, 1886; American poet, author of the best book on the experience of being in analysis with Freud; died Zurich, 1961.

Freud's Doctors

Hans Pichler: born Vienna, 1877; oral surgeon who handled Freud's cancer from 1923 onwards; died Vienna, 1949.

Max Schur: born Stanislaw, 1897, personal physician; died New York, 1977.

The Nazis

Dr Felix Boehm: born Riga, 1881; psychoanalyst; died Berlin, 1958.

Hermann Goering: born Rosenheim, southern Germany, 1893; Hitler's deputy and head of the Luftwaffe; committed suicide Nuremberg, 1946.

Dr Matthias Goering: born Düsseldorf, 1879; psychoanalyst, though not a Freudian, and cousin of Hermann; died Poznan, 1945.

Dr Carl Müller-Braunschweig: born Braunschweig, 1881; psychoanalyst; died Berlin, 1958.

Dr Anton Sauerwald: born Vienna, 1903; chemist; died Innsbruck, 1970.

APPENDIX 2

The Restricted Files

The following files are restricted in addition to those listed in Chapter 2:

- Until 2050, correspondence with Felix and Helene Deutsch. The couple were analysts and Felix Deutsch was also Freud's doctor until 1923 when he was dismissed.
- Until 2057, correspondence with Elsa Foges: she was a cousin of Dora, one of Freud's cases which has caused endless controversy. Foges was interviewed in 1979, when she was 97 years old, by Anthony Stadlen. He wrote, 'Dora had always got on particularly well with her and had shared all sorts of secrets with her.' Frau Foges told Stadlen that she asked Dora at the time of her analysis in 1900, 'Who is this Freud?' Dora replied, 'He asks me lots of questions and I want to make an end of it.' Elsa Foges was never a patient of Freud and the files may well contain material critical of him, as Dora was poorly treated.
- Until 2057, correspondence with Clarence Oberndorf: he was an American psychoanalyst Freud treated in 1923 and 1924. They quarrelled about the meaning of a dream. When Oberndorf dreamed of a black horse and a white horse, Freud argued that it showed he had inhibitions about wanting to marry a black or white woman. Freud eventually became annoyed with Oberndorf, who did not accept this interpretation.
- Until 2057, correspondence with Eduardo Weiss: he was the psychoanalyst who founded the *Italian Journal of Psychoanalysis*. Freud corresponded with him about his own analysis of his daughter, Anna Freud.

- Ernst Kris: a psychoanalyst who was part of the team that analysed the character of Hitler for the Office of Strategic Studies in 1943.
- Oscar Rie: a psychoanalyst who was the doctor of Freud's six children.

Disputes about Access

At the start of the book I explained how the historian of analysis Phyllis Grosskurth tangled with the Library of Congress over access to the Bonaparte files. Grosskurth also accused the Library of ignoring the wishes of some donors. When Diana Rivière, daughter of Joan Rivière, one of Freud's translators, sold correspondence between her mother and Freud to the Sigmund Freud Archives, Ms Rivière said this material should be made available to serious scholars. When Grosskurth mentioned this to Dr K.R. Eissler, secretary of the Sigmund Freud Archives, it did not help. Eissler replied that 'the Sigmund Freud Archives had acquired the letters through purchase, not donation'. As the Archives now owned them, the archives controlled them and 'had deposited them in the Library of Congress while restricting them until the year 2000'. Grosskurth was angry. Other scholars also complained that Dr Eissler allowed favoured individuals access to certain documents, while denying it to others. Eissler sometimes even refused to let donors themselves see their own material once they had given it to the archives. At the end of 2009 Freud will have been dead for 70 years and his works thus come out of copyright.

References

Works by Sigmund Freud

All references are to the Standard Edition, edited by James Strachey with the help of Anna Freud. It was published by the Hogarth Press of London, which was run by Leonard and Virginia Woolf. It is abbreviated to SE and the figure that follows details the volume. The dates of the works are those of the original publications in German.

The Interpretation of Dreams, SE 4–5, 1899
The Psychopathology of Everyday Life, SE 6, 1901
Jokes and Their Relation to the Unconscious, SE 8, 1903
Three Essays on the Theory of Sexuality, SE 7, 1905
Totem and Taboo, SE 13, 1913, 1–161
The Moses of Michelangelo, originally published in *Imago*, SE 13, 1914, 211–38
Beyond the Pleasure Principle, SE 18, 1920, 7–64
The Ego and the Id, SE 19, 1923, 3–66
Resistances to Psycho-Analysis, SE 19, 1925
An Autobiographical Study, SE 20, 1925, 3–70
The Future of an Illusion, SE 21, 1927, 3–56
preface to the Hebrew translation of *Totem and Taboo*, Hogarth Press, London, 1930
Why War?, pamphlet for the League of Nations, SE 22, 1932, 197–215
'Analysis Terminable and Interminable', SE 23, 1937, 209–53
translation of Marie Bonaparte's *Topsy*, Albert de Lange, Brussels, 1937

Moses and Monotheism, SE 23, 1938, 3–137
An Outline of Psychoanalysis, SE 23, 1940, 141–207
with William Bullitt, *Woodrow Wilson*, W.W. Norton, New York, 1967

Letters

Freud, Sigmund
— *Letters of Sigmund Freud 1873–1939*, edited by Ernst Freud, Hogarth Press, London, 1961
— *Letters of Sigmund Freud and Eduard Silberstein: 1871–1881*, Harvard University Press, Cambridge, MA, 1989
Freud, Sigmund, and Rolland, Romain, *Correspondence, 1923–1936*, edited by Henri and Madeleine Vermorel, Presses Universitaires de France, Paris, 1993
Freud, Sigmund, and Freud, Samuel, *Letters (1914–1938)*, MS collection in John Rylands Library, University of Manchester (includes letters from Poppy Hartwig and Anna Freud), published in French as *Lettres de Famille de Freud et des Freud de Manchester*, Presses Universitaires de France, 1996, Paris

Works by Relatives and Friends

Bernays, Edward, *Crystallizing Public Opinion*, University of Oklahoma Press, Norman, OK, 1955
— *Propaganda*, Ig Publishing, New York, 2004
Bernays, Jacob, *Ein Lebensbild in Briefen*, 1861; reprinted, edited by M. Fraenkel and H. Marcus, Breslau, 1932
Bernays-Freud, Anna, *Eine Wienerin in New York*, Aufbau Verlag, Berlin, 2005
— 'My Brother Sigmund Freud', *American Mercury*, November 1940, 335–42
Bernays-Heller, Judith, 'Freud's Mother and Father', in *Freud as We Knew Him*, edited by H.M. Ruitenbeck, Wayne State University Press, Detroit, 1973
Berthelsen, Detlef, *La famille Freud au jour le jour: souvenirs de Paula Fichtl*, Presses Universitaires de France, Paris, 1991
Doolittle, Hilda, *Tribute to Freud*, W.W. Norton, New York, 1984
Freud, Anna, Report on the 16th International Psycho-Analytical Congress,

Bulletin of the International Psychoanalytic Association, 30, 1949, 178–208

Freud, Harry, 'Notes Towards an Autobiography': unpublished: Library of Congress, Harry Freud collection, Box 9

Freud, Martin, *Sigmund Freud: Man and Father*, Vanguard Press, New York, 1958

Mann, Thomas, 'An Appeal to Reason' (*Deutsche Ansprache: Ein Appell an die Vernunft*), *Berliner Tageblatt*, 18 October 1930; translated by Helen T. Lowe-Porter in *Order of the Day: Political Essays and Speeches of Two Decades*, Alfred Knopf, New York, 1942

— 'Freud and the Future' (*Freud und die Zukunft*), *Imago*, 22, 1936; translated by Helen T. Lowe-Porter in *Essays by Thomas Mann*, Vintage, New York, 1957

Zweig, Arnold, *Education before Verdun*, Viking Press, New York, 1936

Zweig, Stefan, *Mental Healers*, Cassell and Co., London, 1933

— *The Royal Game and Other Stories*, Holmes and Meier, New York, 2000

Biographies and Aspects of Freud's Work

Bakan, D., *Sigmund Freud and the Jewish Mystical Tradition*, Free Association Books, London, 1990

Baur, E., *Freud's Wien*, C.H. Beck, Munich, 2005

Bertin, C., *Marie Bonaparte*, Yale University Press, New Haven, CT, 1987

Bettlelheim, B., *Freud and Man's Soul*, Alfred Knopf, New York, 1982

Cioffi, F. (ed.), *Freud: Modern Judgements*, Macmillan, London, 1973

Dilman, I., *Freud and the Mind*, Blackwell, Oxford, 1984

Edelson, M., *Hypothesis and Evidence in Psychoanalysis*, University of Chicago Press, Chicago, 1984

Edmundson, M., *The Death of Sigmund Freud*, Bloomsbury, London, 2006

Fancher, R., *Psychoanalytic Psychology: The Development of Freud's Thought*, W.W. Norton, New York, 1973

Farrell, B.A., *The Standing of Psychoanalysis*, Oxford University Press, Oxford, 1981

Ferris, P., *Dr Freud*, Sinclair Stevenson, London, 1997

Forrester, J., *Dispatches from the Freud Wars*, Harvard University Press, Cambridge, MA, 1998

Gay, P., *Freud: A Life for Our Time*, Dent, London, 1988

Gilman, S., *Freud, Race and Gender*, Princeton University Press, Princeton, NJ, 1993

Hayman, R., *A Life of Jung*, Bloomsbury, London, 1993

Hofstadter, G.B., *Jung's Struggle with Freud*, Chiron, Willmette, IL, 1994

Hook, S. (ed.), *Psychoanalysis, Scientific Method, and Philosophy*, New York University Press, New York, 1959

Jones, E.R., *Sigmund Freud*, 3 vols, Basic Books, New York, 1953–7

Malcolm, J., *In the Freud Archives*, Alfred Knopf, New York, 1985

Masson, J., *The Assault on Truth: Freud's Suppression of the Seduction Theory*, Faber & Faber, London, 1984

Rand, N., and Torok, M., *Questions for Freud*, Harvard University Press, Cambridge, MA, 1997

Ricoeur, P., *Freud and Philosophy: An Essay in Interpretation*, translated by D. Savage, Yale University Press, New Haven, CT, 1970

Roazen, Paul, *Freud and His Followers*, Alfred Knopf, New York, 1975

Robert, M., *From Oedipus to Moses*, translated by Ralph Manheim, Anchor Books, New York, 1976

Roith, E., *The Riddle of Freud*, Tavistock, London, 1987

Sharaf, M., *Fury on Earth: A Biography of Wilhelm Reich*, Hutchinson, London, 1983

Sulloway, F., *Freud: Biologist of the Mind*, Basic Books, New York, 1979

Timms, E. (ed.), *Freud in Exile*, Yale University Press, New Haven, CT, 1988

Whyte, L.L., *The Unconscious Before Freud*, Basic Books, New York, 1960

Wollheim, R., *Freud*, Fontana, London, 1971

Wollheim, R. (ed.), *Freud: A Collection of Critical Essays*, Anchor Books, New York, 1974

Wollheim, R., and Hopkins, J. (eds), *Philosophical Essays on Freud*, Cambridge University Press, Cambridge, 1982

Young Bruehl, E., *Anna Freud: A Biography*, Yale University Press, New Haven, CT, 2006

Other Works

Adams, L., letters relating to Freud in City of Manchester Library Archives, 1952–5

Aichhorn, A., *Wayward Youth*, Northwestern University Press, Evanston, IL, 1953

Auerbach, E., *Moses*, Wayne State University Press, Detroit, 1975

Authers, J., and Wolffe, R., *The Victim's Fortune: Inside the Epic Battle over the Debts of the Holocaust*, HarperCollins, New York, 2002

Bell, S., 'A Preliminary Study of the Emotion of Love between the Sexes',

American Journal of Psychology, 40, 1902

Berdach, R., *The Emperor, the Sages and Death*, T. Yoseloff, New York, 1962

Bibring, G. (ed.), Report on the 17th International Psychoanalytical Congress, *International Journal of Psychoanalysis*, 33, 1951, 249–51

Blüher, H., *Secessio Judaica*, Der Weisse Verlag, Berlin, 1922

Boehm, F., *Schriften zur Psychoanalyse*, Ölschläger, Munich, 1978

Brecht, K., Friedrich, V., Hermanns, L., Kaminer, I., and Juelich, D. (eds), 'Here Life Goes On in a Most Peculiar Way': Psychoanalysis before and after 1933, Kellner Verlag, Hamburg, and Goethe Institut, London, 1985

Brook-Shepherd, G., *The Austrians: A Thousand-year Odyssey*, HarperCollins, London, 1996

Burt, C., obituary of Freud, *Nature*, October 1939

Chrzanowski, G., 'Psychoanalysis: Ideology and Practitioners', *Contemporary Psychoanalysis*, 11, 1975, 492–9

Churchill, W., *The Gathering Storm*, Penguin Books, London, 2005

Clare, G., *Last Waltz in Vienna*, Pan, London, 2007

Cocks, G., *Psychotherapy in the Third Reich*, Oxford University Press, Oxford, 2nd edn, 1997

— 'The Devil and the Details', *Psychoanalytic Review*, 88, 2001, 225–44

Danto, E.A., 'Death of a "Jewish Science": Psychoanalysis in the Third Reich', *Journal of Interdisciplinary History*, 34 (1), 2003, 90–91

Díaz de Chumaceiro, C.L., 'Richard Wagner's Life and Music: What Freud Knew', in S. Feder, R.L. Karmel and G.H. Pollock (eds), *Psychoanalytic Explorations in Music*, International Universities Press, Madison, CT, 1993

Diller, J., *Freud's Jewish Identity: A Case Study in the Impact of Ethnicity*, Associated University Presses, London, 1991

Eastman, M., *Heroes I Have Known*, Simon and Schuster, New York, 1926

Eder, M.D., *The Psycho-neuroses in War Shock and Their Treatment*, Blakiston, Philadelphia, 1917

Eickhoff, F., 'The Formation of the German Psychoanalytical Association (DPV): Regaining the Psychoanalytical Orientation Lost in the Third Reich', *International Journal of Psycho-Analysis*, 76, 1995, 945–56

Engelman, E., *Berggasse Nineteen, Sigmund Freud's Home and Offices*, Universe Publishing, New York, 1998

Fenichel, O., *119 Rundbriefe: Hg. Johannes Reichmayr und Elke Mühlleitner*, 2 vols, Stroemfeld, Frankfurt, 1998

Garscha, W.R., and Kuretsidis-Haider, C., 'Justice and Nazi-crimes in Austria 1945–1955 between Self-purge and Allied Control', in '1945: Consequences and Sequels of the Second World War', *Bulletin du Comité international d'histoire de la Deuxième Guerre mondiale*, 27/28, Paris, 1995, 245–55

Goering, M. (ed.), *Sonderheft der Deutschen Institut für Psychologische Forschung und Psychotherapie*, S. Hirzel, Leipzig, 1940

Goggin, J.E., and Goggin, E.B., *Death of a 'Jewish Science': Psychoanalysis in the Third Reich*, Purdue University Press, West Lafayette, IN, 2001

Grosskurth, P., 'The Shrink Princess', *New York Review of Books*, 6 December 1982

Heine, H., *Almansor*, in *Collected Works of Heinrich Heine*, Adamant Media Corporation, Boston, 2001

Hitler, A., *Mein Kampf*, Jaico Publishing House, Mumbai, 2007

Holpfer, E., Loitfellner, S., and Uslu-Pauer, S., 'Wiener Urteile wegen NS-Verbrechen. Abschluss der Erfassung des hauptverhandlungsregisters des Volksgerichts Wien (1945–1955)', *Justiz und Erinnerung*, 7, February 2003, 29–30

Jacoby, R., *Social Amnesia*, Harvester Press, Brighton, 1975

— *The Repression of Psychoanalysis*, Basic Books, New York, 1983

James, W., *The Varieties of Religious Experience*, Penguin Books, London, 1983

Jones, E.R., *The Elements of Figure Skating*, George Allen and Unwin, London, 1931

Keneally, T., *Schindler's Ark*, Hodder and Stoughton, London, 1982

Klein, D., *Jewish Origins of the Psychoanalytic Movement*, Chicago University Press, Chicago, 1985

Knight, R., *'Ich bin dafür, die Sache in die Länge zu ziehen'. Die Wortprotokolle der österreichischen Bundesregierung von 1945–1952 über die Entschädigung der Juden*, 2nd edn, Böhlau Verlag, Vienna, 2000

Krüll, M., *Freud und sein Vater. Die Entstehung der Psychoanalyse und Freuds ungelöste Vaterbindung*, C.H. Beck, Munich, 1979

— *Freud and His Father*, translated by Arnold J. Pomerans, W.W. Norton, New York, 1986

Langer, W., and Gifford, S., 'An American Analyst in Vienna during the Anschluss, 1936–1938', *Journal of the History of the Behavioural Sciences*, 10, 2006, 37–54

Langer, W., Murray, H., Kris, E., and Lewin, B., *A Psychological Analysis of Adolf Hitler: His Life and Legend*, Office of Strategic Services, Washington, 1943

Lawrence, D.H., *Psychoanalysis and the Unconscious* and *Fantasia of the Unconscious*, in *The Works of D.H. Lawrence*, Cambridge University Press, Cambridge, 2004

Léon, M., 'The Case of Dr Carl Gustav Jung: Pseudo-scientist, Nazi Auxiliary', Report to US Department of State and Nuremberg Tribunal, 1946

Leupold-Löewenthal, H., 'Die Vertreibung der Familie Freud 1938', *Psyche-Zeitschrift für Psychoanalyse und ihre Anwendungen*, 43 (10), 1989, 908–28

Lewis, D., *The Man Who Invented Hitler*, Headline, London, 2003

Lockot, R., *Erinnern und Durcharbeiten. Zur Geschichte der Psychoanalyse und Psychotherapie im Nationalsozialismus*, S. Fischer Verlag, Frankfurt am Main, 1985

— *Die Reinigung der Psychoanalyse. Die deutsche psychoanalytische Gesellschaft im Spiegel von Dokumenten und Zeitzeugen (1933–1951)*, Diskord, Tübingen, 1994

Loitfellner, S., 'Aryanisation 1938/39 in Vienna and the People's Court Trials after 1945', in G. Bischof, A. Pelinka and M. Gehler (eds), *Austria and the European Union*, Contemporary Austrian Studies, Vol. 10, Transaction, Somerset, NJ, and London, 2002

Maddox, B., *Freud's Wizard: The Enigma of Ernest Jones*, John Murray, London, 2006

Mahony, P.J., '"The Moses of Michelangelo": A Matter of Solutions', *Canadian Journal of Psychoanalysis*, Vol. 14, 11–43, 1 April 2006

Morton, F., *The Rothschilds*, Secker and Warburg, London, 1963

Moses, R., and Hrushovski-Moses, R., 'A Form of Group Denial at the Hamburg Congress', *International Review of Psycho-Analysis*, 13, 1986, 175–80

Müller-Braunschweig, C., 'Psychoanalyse und Weltanschauung', *Reichswart*, 22 October 1933

— *Streifzüge durch die Psychoanalyse (Welche Position vertritt der Psychoanalytiker heute)*, Reinbeck, Hamburg, 1948

— 'Zur Menschlichen Grundhaltung, Psychologie und Technik der Psychoanalytischen Therapie', *Psychologische Beiträge*, 2, 1955, 56–69

Nitzschke, B., 'Psychoanalysis during National Socialism: Present-day Consequences of a Historical Controversy in the "Case" of Wilhelm Reich', *Psychoanalytic Review*, 86, 1999, 349–66

Oberhummer, W., *Herzig, Josef*, Neue Deutsche Biographie, Vol. 8, Duncker & Humblot, Berlin, 1969, 735

Odens, R., *Hitler the Pawn*, Victor Gollancz, London, 1936

Pollak, J., 'Josef Herzig zum siebzigsten Geburtstag', *Österreichische Chemiker-Zeitung*, 26, 1923, 139f.

— 'Josef Herzig', *Berichte der Deutschen Chemischen Gesellschaft*, 59, 1925, A55–75

Reich, W., *The Mass Psychology of Fascism*, Farrar, Straus and Giroux, New York, 1980

Roazen, P., *Brother Animal: The Story of Tausk and Freud*, Penguin Books, Harmondsworth, 1973

— *On the Freud Watch*, Free Association Books, London, 2003

Roback, A.A., *The Story of Yiddish Literature*, Yiddish Scientific Institute, New York, 1940

Rosenberg. A., *Der Sumpf* [*The Swamp*], Demokratie Zentral-verlag der NSDAP, Munich, 1939

Rückerl, A., *Die Strafverfolgung von NS-Verbrechern 1945–1978. Eine Dokumentation*, C.F. Müller Juristischer Verlag, Heidelberg and Karlsruhe, 1979, 125.

Rüter, C.F., and de Mildt, D.W., *Die westdeutschen Strafverfahren wegen nationalsozialistischer Tötungsverbrechen 1945–1997. Eine systematische Verfahrensbeschreibung mit Karten und Registern*, Holland University Press, Amsterdam, and K.G. Saur Verlag, Munich, 1998

Sauerwald, A., and Muller, A., 'Neue Synthese des 1, 6-Dibrom-*n*-hexans und seine Einwirkung auf*p*-Toluolsulfamid', *Monatshefte für Chemie*, 48 (7), July 1927

— 'Neue Synthese und Reindarstellung des Hexamethylenimins', *Monatshefte für Chemie*, 48 (9–10), September 1927

— 'Über das Verhalten des Aluminiumtriäthyls am Nickelkatalysator bei hoherer Temperatur', *Monatshefte für Chemie*, 48 (9–10), September 1927

— 'Über das Verhalten des Aluminiumtriäthyls am Nickelkatalysator bei hoherer Temperatur', *Monatshefte für Chemie*, 48 (9–10), September 1927

Schur, M., *Freud: Living and Dying*, Chatto and Windus, London, 1972

Skellett, A.-M., Millington, G., and Levell, N.J., 'Sudden Whitening of the Hair: An Historical Fiction?', *Journal of the Royal Society of Medicine*, 101, 2008, 574–6

Steffek, A., and Uslu-Pauer, S., 'Die Kartei der Wiener Volksgerichtsprozesse 1945–1955. Die EDV-Erfassung und wissenschaftliche Auswertung der Kartei der am Volksgericht Wien zwischen 1945–1955 geführten gerichtlichen Voruntersuchungen', *Justiz und Erinnerung*, 3, October 2000, 3–6

Steiner, R., *'It is a New Kind of Diaspora': Explorations in the Sociopolitical and Cultural Context of Psychoanalysis*, Karnac, London, 2000

Thurber, J., *Let Your Mind Alone*, Readers Union, London, 1939

Thurber, J., and White, E.B., *Is Sex Necessary?*, Hamish Hamilton, London, 1952

Uhl, H., *Transformations of Austrian Memory: Politics of History and Monument Culture in the Second Republic*, in *Austrian History Yearbook*, Center for Austrian Studies, 32, Minneapolis, 2001, 149–67

Vasari, G., *Life of Michelangelo Buonarroti*, Folio Society, London, 1971

Wegscheider, R., 'Josef Herzig', *Almanach der Akademie der Wissenschaften*, 75, 1925, 194–8

Wiesenthal, S., speech on the occasion of the AGM of the Documentation Centre of Austrian Resistance (DÖW) in the Old City Hall, Vienna, 11 March 1991, in *Dokumentationsarchivs des österreichischen Widerstandes, Jahrbuch 1992*, Vienna, 1992, 10

Wyllie, J., *The Warlord and the Renegade: The Story of Hermann and Albert Goering*, History Press, Stroud, 2006

Yerushalmi, Y., *Freud's Moses*, Yale University Press, New Haven, CT, 1991

Index